# THE MORAL VISION OF IRIS MURDOCH

*For my grandad, John*

# The Moral Vision of Iris Murdoch

HEATHER WIDDOWS
*University of Birmingham, UK*

Routledge
Taylor & Francis Group
LONDON AND NEW YORK

First published 2005 by Ashgate Publishing

Published 2016 by Routledge
2 Park Square, Milton Park, Abingdon, Oxon OX14 4RN
711 Third Avenue, New York, NY 10017, USA

*Routledge is an imprint of the Taylor & Francis Group, an informa business*

Copyright © Heather Widdows 2005

Heather Widdows has asserted her moral right under the Copyright, Designs and Patents Act, 1988, to be identified as the author of this work.

All rights reserved. No part of this book may be reprinted or reproduced or utilised in any form or by any electronic, mechanical, or other means, now known or hereafter invented, including photocopying and recording, or in any information storage or retrieval system, without permission in writing from the publishers.

Notice:
Product or corporate names may be trademarks or registered trademarks, and are used only for identification and explanation without intent to infringe.

**British Library Cataloguing in Publication Data**
Widdows, Heather
  The moral vision of Iris Murdoch
  1. Murdoch, Iris – Philosophy
  I. Title
  823.9'14

**Library of Congress Cataloging-in-Publication Data**
Widdows, Heather, 1972-
    The moral vision of Iris Murdoch / Heather Widdows.
      p. cm.
    Includes index.
  1. Murdoch, Iris – Ethics. I. Title.

    BJ604.M873W53 2004
    170'.92–dc22

2004019231

ISBN 13: 978-0-7546-3625-0 (hbk)

# Contents

| | | |
|---|---|---|
| *Acknowledgments* | | *vii* |
| 1 | The Breadth of Iris Murdoch's Vision | 1 |
| 2 | The 'Inner Life' of the Individual | 21 |
| 3 | Experiencing Morality | 45 |
| 4 | The Good | 71 |
| 5 | Living the Moral Life | 89 |
| 6 | Art and the Moral Life | 117 |
| 7 | Religion and the Moral Life | 139 |
| 8 | The Future of Iris Murdoch's Moral Vision | 159 |
| *Bibliography* | | *173* |
| *Index* | | *181* |

# Acknowledgments

My thanks must first go to James P. Mackey, who introduced me to Iris Murdoch during my student days and who has continued to be an inspiration in the years since. Special thanks must go to Richard Ashcroft and James Francis, for their advice and criticism. At the University of Birmingham, I would like to thank Christien van den Anker and Sirkku Hellsten and particular thanks must go to Donna Dickenson. I would also like to thank my friends and family, particularly my father, Kit Widdows. In addition, Gillian Widdows, John Widdows, Trevor Anderson, Jo Mowatt and Fiona MacCallum all deserve mention. My final thanks must go to my partner, Matthew Hilton, for his professional and personal support in the completing of this project.

H.W.

# Chapter 1

# The Breadth of Iris Murdoch's Vision

Iris Murdoch has been a significant figure of post-war British life, she is a recognizable 'name' and her career is 'familiar to educated persons, like national folklore' (Conradi, 2001, p. 570).[1] She is perhaps best known as a novelist, publishing 26 novels between her first, *Under the Net*, in 1954, and her last, *Jackson's Dilemma*, in 1995. As a novelist she has been critically acclaimed and her 1978 novel, *The Sea, the Sea*, won the Booker Prize. Without a doubt Murdoch is one of the most celebrated novelists of the second half of the twentieth century, and her novels are complex and challenging and, arguably, 'of all the post-war English novelists she has the greatest intellectual range, the deepest rigour' (ibid., p. 595).[2] However, currently Murdoch is best known, not for her writing, but for the film about her life, simply titled, *Iris*, in which Kate Winslet played the 'young Iris' and Judy Dench the old. The film told the story of Murdoch's life and notably of her death from Alzheimer's and is based on her husband's, John Bayley's, portrayal of her life, *Iris: A Memoir of Iris Murdoch*, which became a best-seller in its own right.[3]

This book is of a different kind, neither about Murdoch's life nor about her novels, but about her moral philosophy, the area of her work that has been least commented upon. It is hoped that this work will provide some small adjustment to this, from an ethicist's point of view, sad imbalance in her legacy.

To have such an impact Murdoch was undoubtedly a significant figure: to have a Hollywood film commemorating one's life is no mean feat. Clearly Murdoch is remembered for her writing, without which there would have been no interest in either Bayley's moving account of her life or in the film. However, whether she will be most remembered for her art or her life is yet to be seen. Murdoch's life is of interest to those who are intrigued by Murdoch's writing, whether her novels or her philosophy, because so much of her work is informed by her own experiences. In particular she draws on her experiences of love and friendship which shaped her own conduct and fed into her writing – literature and philosophy – and also on her experience of the war and its aftermath. She never lost 'the ability either to think about, or to fear, the contemporary world' (Conradi, 2001, p. 561).

Since her death there have been a number of books published on Murdoch's life in addition to Bayley's account: they include a sympathetic and detailed biography by Peter Conradi, *Iris Murdoch: A Life*, which is not only revealing of Murdoch's loves and friendships, particularly pre-1960, but also offers insight into the ideas which shaped her work and her life; and the controversial

2                    *The Moral Vision of Iris Murdoch*

latest addition to the mounting literature by A.N. Wilson, *Iris Murdoch as I Knew Her*, which is a personal account of his relationship with Iris and not a biography.

The present book is not of course a biography in any form, yet it may be of interest, before moving on to her philosophy, to draw a brief sketch of Murdoch's life and person.


**About Iris Murdoch**

Murdoch was born in 1919 in Dublin into a Scots–Irish protestant family, and, though she spent no more than a year in Ireland, her Anglo-Irish heritage remained an important part of her identity. Murdoch described herself as Anglo-Irish and when this was questioned she responded, 'But of course I'm Irish. I'm profoundly Irish and I've been conscious of this all my life, and in a mode of being Irish which has produced a lot of very distinguished thinkers and writers' (Conradi, 2001, p. 27). Ireland continued to play a large part in her imaginative landscape and two of her novels are overtly set in Ireland, *The Unicorn* and, famously, *The Red and The Green*, which recalled the week leading up to the 1916 uprising. Murdoch's Irishness mattered deeply to her, so much so that a comment from a friend questioning 'why Miss Murdoch chose to set *The Unicorn* in Ireland when she so plainly is not at home there' (ibid., p. 460) caused a temporary breach in the friendship.[4]

Murdoch's parents settled in London and, according to all accounts, Murdoch had an unusually happy childhood and good relationships with both her parents. London remained an important city for Murdoch, to which she returned after her undergraduate degree, and later in life she taught at the Royal College of Art, staying in London two nights a week. Murdoch set many of her novels in London and clearly loved the city. It was not Oxford, her home for most of her life, but London which was the 'city her fictional world is in love with: no earlier novelists apart from Dickens and Virginia Woolf loved London so well, or celebrated it as memorably as she' (ibid., p. 585).

Murdoch arrived at Somerville College, Oxford in 1938, initially to read English, although this soon changed to Classics followed by Philosophy, at a time when women in academia were still something of a rarity.[5] Apart from living in London, working at the Treasury during the war years, and a spell working for UNRRA (United Nations Relief and Rehabilitation Administration), followed by a year at Newnham College, Cambridge (1947–8), she had her home in Oxford. Her work for UNRRA brought Murdoch into contact with the desperate plight of displaced persons seeking to be rehomed after the war. Her experience of the relocation camps had a profound effect on Murdoch, both in her political views and also in her affinity with refugees. Her friendships with émigrés are a feature of her personal life, and they often appear in her novels. These experiences also influenced her wish to protect and revere the uniqueness of every individual, both in how she lived her life and in her philosophy. After her stint with UNRRA and a year in Cambridge she returned to St Anne's College, Oxford to tutor and to begin her life as a professional philosopher, which she continued until 1963, when she returned to London for two nights a week to teach at the RCA.[6]

Murdoch's interest in politics began at Oxford in her undergraduate years, and it was at this time in her life that she was particularly politically active; later she became less so, noting that 'politics were . . . "not in her blood"' (ibid., p. 499). However, as an undergraduate, she was dedicated to politics and was a committed and vocal member of the Communist Party. She joined the party in her first days at university and her allegiance continued until at least 1942, when she began work at the Treasury and ceased to be on Party lists, although Conradi suggests that her involvement may well have continued longer.[7] Her commitment was clearly robust, and Frank Thompson writes to her as 'Irushka', suggesting the depth of her attraction and dedication to the communist vision.[8] Gradually her views changed, in part because of her commitment to the sovereignty of the individual and her recognition that totalitarian regimes become dehumanizing. She became enraged by the Labour Party's education policy in the 1970s, leading her to vote Conservative in 1983 and 1987, a turn in her thinking that Wilson traces to the influence of her husband, John Bayley.[9] However, she returned to her familiar left-wing stance and voted labour in 1997, although by this point 'she took almost no day-to-day interest in politics' (Wilson, 2003, pp. 100–101). All of which suggests that, although politically motivated and active in her early years, Murdoch was not politically concerned in the ideological sense, and indeed her fear of totalitarian regimes (evident in her philosophy as well as her journals) led her away from the public and towards the private sphere.[10] The centrality of the individual for Murdoch is revealed in her writing of all types and in the way she lived her life, placing great emphasis on her individual loves and friendships. Her focus was not 'the system' but the individual. Accordingly she sought answers to the age-old question of 'How can I be good?' and correspondingly 'How is it that some human beings are morally better than others? What might make a man good . . . even in extreme situations?' (Conradi, 2001, p. 597). To discover the answers to these questions Murdoch looked to individuals, to her own experience and to those around, seeking in her friends and loves insights into these perennial philosophical questions. She believed that philosophy should directly tackle these questions: 'Ethics should not be merely an analysis of ordinary mediocre conduct, it should be a hypothesis about good conduct and about how this can be achieved. How can we make ourselves better? is a question moral philosophers should attempt to answer' (Murdoch, 1970a, p. 78).

Those who have seen the film, *Iris*, will recall vividly Murdoch's promiscuity and, in her early life, according to Conradi's sympathetic telling, Murdoch did fall in love often – something she was 'absolutely amazed' at in her later life when looking over her old diaries (Conradi, 2001, p.580).[11] Love was important for Iris and she clearly relished being in love and being loved and,

4 *The Moral Vision of Iris Murdoch*

in her journal 20 years later, she recalled, '[Leo] loved me, in the days when Frank and Noel Martin loved me too. And indeed I loved them. My God that was a golden time' (ibid., p. 97). Friendship was just as important to Murdoch as her affairs (although Murdoch had affairs with both sexes and appears to have regarded physical love as a part of the love of friendship). Her friendships and loves informed her work and 'novel after Iris novel depends upon the convention that a court of characters have been friends since college days' (ibid., p. 85). Maintaining her friendships was an essential part of her being (in her later years spending hours a day replying to letters) and she suffered when friendships ended: 'Iris mislaid few friends notably or dramatically, and when losses did happen she brooded over them and counted them significant' (ibid.). Many of Murdoch's friendships and loves were begun at Oxford and through the turbulent war years and these relationships were to last for the rest of her life and be paramount to her self-understanding and to her work.[12] Included in the long list of lasting friendships formed during her undergraduate days are Mary Scrutton (later Midgely), Philippa Bosanquet (later Foot), Mary Warnock, Frank Thompson, Michael R.D. Foot, Hal Lidderdale, Noel Martin, Leo Pliatzky and David Hicks, all of whose 'names resonate through the nearly sixty years of her journals' (ibid.). Murdoch continued to make firm friends and form intimate relationships throughout her life (documented not only in the biographies, but also in the many testimonies from those she befriended). Friendship was of fundamental importance to Murdoch, so much so that Conradi comments that 'the joke about the socialite with "a hundred close friends" was no joke in Iris's case. Unlike the socialite she knew each of them' (Conradi, 2001, p. 568).

Murdoch had many loves; most notable during the early period of her life is her love for Frank Thompson, who did ask her to marry him before he went into active service, a proposal that Murdoch declined (although later she insisted that they were engaged) (ibid., p. 538). This was a significant relationship which began with Murdoch convincing Frank to join the Communist Party. Murdoch was, to Frank, 'muse, sole-mate, keeper of his conscience, and she was often capable of the "passionate intensity" Yeats feared' (ibid., p. 111). Frank was one of the enduring loves of Murdoch's life, and one which continued to be important to her throughout her life and long after his torture and death in Bulgaria in 1944. The growth of this love and its impact on Murdoch is beautifully documented by Conradi, and it is clear that Murdoch was indeed in love with Frank, who, though 'never her lover, preoccupied her all her life' (ibid., p. 157). Throughout this time Murdoch continued to have lovers, including Michael Foot, who later married Philippa, which, at times, caused some distance between the best friends.[13] Despite this obstacle Philippa, from first to last, was an almost necessary friend to Murdoch, one whom she valued perhaps above all others throughout her life. In addition to befriending her peers, Murdoch also formed relationships with academics who became mentors and remained important to her, although the friendships did not always survive her own growth as an intellectual and as a person. Most notable are her undergraduate tutors Eduard Fraenkel and Donald MacKinnon, both of whose influence is evident in her later work, both as providing inspiration for characters in her novels and in shaping her intellectual interests.[14]

Many of Murdoch's affairs affected her work. Her platonic love affair with Frank was the first of a number of relationships which commentators have regarded as influencing the good or 'saintly' characters in her novels. A later love affair of this order was with Franz Steiner, whom Murdoch met in the early 1950s. Franz was a Jewish émigré, a poet and an anthropologist, whose family had all fallen victim to the Nazis. Indeed Murdoch thought of him as another of Hitler's victims when he died in 1952 of a heart condition: a broken heart, she believed. From their journals we know that Murdoch and Franz affected each other profoundly; in their shared reading and deepening understanding of literature and poetry and in their discussion of religion (one of Murdoch's primary interests). On his death, 'Franz joined Frank in Iris's private pantheon of martyrs. She sanctified both' (ibid., p. 341). Both of these affairs influenced her novels: 'Frank helped to inspire her characterization of virtuous soldiers, Franz helped to inspire her scholar saints' (ibid., p. 342).[15]

Two additional affairs are of interest and have supposedly influenced her 'demonic' characters. The first was with Thomas Balogh, with whom she had an unhappy affair while living with Philippa in London; and the second, much later in life, and overlapping with her relationship with John Bayley, with Elias Canetti.[16] Canetti, (introduced to Murdoch by Franz), was alleged to be a cruel, jealous man who was interested in power. Thus he was something of a puppet-master, manipulating the many women who were enthralled by him in violent and humiliating ways, including Murdoch. From him she hid her religious interests and it is probably on his account that she left the Oxford group of theologians, the Metaphysicals, whose interests she shared. More significantly, given Iris's promiscuity (she was described by Wallace Robson, to whom she was once engaged, as 'monumentally unfaithful') she accepted Canetti's jealous dictate that she should not sleep with Bayley. Her relationship with Bayley 'won' in the end, yet even so the figure of Canetti continued to haunt her. Her underlying fear as she moved towards an almost moral mysticism was that he could perhaps be right and his moral atheism and power-wielding nihilism could be the correct vision of the world: a fear that is represented by characters such as Julius King, in *A Fairly Honourable Defeat*, Charles Arrowby in *The Sea, the Sea* and Mischa Fox in *The Flight from the Enchanter*.[17] The fear that Canetti's vision was correct also haunts her philosophy, in her questioning of her conclusions, a fear which, though real, does nor overcome her, because ultimately she cannot believe the dark picture of the world and the human condition which he presents. Murdoch's relationships with both Balogh and Canetti, Conradi suggests, increased her awareness of evil: 'her friend and co-philosopher Patrick Gardiner intuited that something in Iris's past had introduced her to the idea of evil' (Conradi, 2001, p. 373).[18] This awareness of evil (as well as good) is evident in her philosophy as well as her novels.

6 *The Moral Vision of Iris Murdoch*

The other significant relationship which must be mentioned is that with John Bayley, her husband, whom she married in 1956. However, in the light of Bayley's books and the famous film, to comment on this relationship seems perhaps unnecessary and presumptuous.[19] Although there have been questions about whether Murdoch would have approved of the books and the film, and consequently questions about the marriage, according to the evidence of those who knew the couple it seems that they did have a famously happy marriage.[20] Certainly Murdoch's journal entries, reported in Conradi's biography, show Murdoch's need and appreciation for Bayley and her enjoyment in their companionship: 'this partnership was totally necessary for her and John's memoirs of Iris well evoke its absolute mutual taken-for-grantedness' (ibid., p. 534).[21] At the very least this was a lasting relationship and Bayley supported and nursed Murdoch until her death in 1999.

Murdoch's friendships, relationships and loves, those mentioned here and many other important ones, are detailed intimately and movingly in Conradi's biography of Iris and need not be discussed further here. What is relevant to this work is to note the importance that Murdoch placed on both love and friendship. The high regard in which Murdoch held friendship and love shows in her philosophy, both in her insistence that 'we need a moral philosophy in which the concept of love, so rarely mentioned now by philosophers, can once again be made central' (Murdoch, 1970a, p. 46) and in the emphasis she puts on seeing other people as they are rather than as we wish them to be. Murdoch attempted to live this ideal and to respond to the needs of others; she had great belief in the ability of love to 'cure' people.[22] Conradi tells us that many of those who knew her considered her 'a sage (no saint) who gave all her friends unstinting, patient and non-judgemental support, making them feel loved, blessed, accepted, unique' (Conradi, 2001, p. 552). Perhaps Murdoch achieved something of her vision, attaining at least moral improvement, if not goodness itself; Philippa Foot's obituary of Iris points to this, when she speaks of 'Iris's "magical goodness"' (ibid., p. 597).

**Murdoch's Philosophy**

The focus of this book, however, is not on Murdoch's life, or her novels, but her philosophy. A book which attempts to capture Murdoch's moral vision could perhaps be expected to take into account her vision of people and the world which comes through her novels and which she enacted in her life. However, there are a number of excellent books detailing Murdoch's novels and detailing how many of her key ideas, such as the primacy of the good, are revealed in her novels. For the inquisitive reader who wishes to pursue Murdoch's vision further, reading her novels does add to one's understanding of her moral vision. Her novels, as her philosophy, reveal her perennial preoccupation with goodness and what makes people good and evil, as well as exploring the nature of religion in a secular world. Yet Murdoch declares that she is not a philosophical novelist, in the sense that she does not wish to make a philosophical point, but rather philosophy is revealed in her novels simply because that is her expertise.[23] Thus seeking Murdoch's philosophy in her novels is a perilous activity, the more so because she uses her novels to question and explore some of the ideas in her philosophy. Consequently the vision of life found in her novels is from a different perspective from that of her philosophy. Alasdair MacIntyre comments, 'Iris Murdoch's novels are philosophy but they are philosophy which casts doubt on all philosophy, including her own' (quoted by Tracy, 1986, p. 69). Her novels present a darker picture of human reality, although full of humour, in which seeking the good and living the good life is almost impossible for most of her illusion-ridden, egotistical characters: 'if her philosophy is lofty, her best novels are merciless and grim, as well as comical' (Conradi, 2001, p. 540). In addition there are many books and articles already published on Murdoch's novels, which document well how she uses the key concepts of her philosophy, including Elizabeth Dipple's *Work for the Spirit* and Peter Conradi's *The Saint and the Artist*.[24]

Murdoch's novels at best provide a tangential exploration of her philosophical ideas and although at times they help to provide examples of how Murdoch envisages the good featuring in the reality of individual lives, they also present a very different, even conflicting, picture to that of her philosophy. In the light of this, Murdoch's novels only rarely appear in this work, and are always treated with a certain amount of suspicion in terms of discovering Murdoch's philosophical position. However, despite scepticism regarding the use of Murdoch's novels in reading her philosophy, her status as novelist is not insignificant. Murdoch is far better known as a novelist than as a philosopher, and as a novelist she was prolific, whereas as a philosopher she wrote only four books: *Sartre: Romantic Rationalist, The Sovereignty of Good, The Fire and the Sun: Why Plato Banished the Artists* and *Metaphysics as a Guide to Morals*. A collection of her many essays *Existentialists and Mystics: Writings on Philosophy and Literature* was published in 1997, although the essays it contains are from much earlier in her career. One further work which could perhaps be added to her philosophical canon is *Acastos: Two Platonic Dialogues*. These dialogues, on the subjects of art and religion, stand between her philosophy and her literature. *Acastos* is only rarely cited in this work and then only when a point seemed so pertinent that it ought to be included. Given the difficulty arising in all dialogue formats of attributing the view of a certain character directly to the author, the information has been included rather circumspectly and it is always noted that the source is *Acastos*, so that the reader can be aware of the problematic antecedence of the ideas. The relationship of 'Murdoch the novelist' and 'Murdoch the philosopher' will be discussed in detail in Chapter 6.

The aim of the present book is to provide an outline of Murdoch's moral philosophy. Murdoch was influential in moral philosophy in the second half of the twentieth century, particularly in the impact she had on a number of key

8 *The Moral Vision of Iris Murdoch*

thinkers in both moral philosophy and theology. Key thinkers that cite her moral philosophy as influential on their own work include Alasdair MacIntyre, Charles Taylor, John MacDowell and Stanley Hauerwas.[25] Accordingly, Murdoch has been important in at least two major revivals in contemporary moral philosophy. The first is 'moral realism', the position which holds that moral values are discovered rather than made, which was revived in the second half of the twentieth century and upon which Murdoch had 'decisive influence' (Kerr, 1997, p. 70).[26] The second is 'virtue ethics', which is a revival of a pre-Enlightenment view of morality which focuses more broadly on good living and human flourishing, rather than on theories of right action.[27]

Murdoch's philosophy is very different from the philosophy of the majority of her contemporaries, and indeed she opposes almost all the trends of the philosophies of her time. Her continual criticism is that modern philosophy has become reductionist, and so produced an unrealistic picture of the human being which can no longer account for the varied experiences which constitute the reality of human life. Murdoch judges that this reduction is part of the temper of the time which has encouraged philosophy to move towards scientific models; thus she believes that too often 'difficult concepts which cannot easily be explained in simple terms are classified as "emotive" or dismissed as meaningless' (Murdoch, 1992, p. 236). Murdoch traces this in part to the decline of religion and the philosophical uncertainty of those aspects of human life which cannot be judged to be 'facts' in a scientific verificationist model. Murdoch regards this trend towards science as misguided and claims that philosophy has neglected its true work, which is to present an accurate model of the reality of human existence. Therefore she calls on philosophy to return to its roots, and to attempt to describe the wide gamut of human life, which must include concepts which have become difficult for contemporary philosophy. Moreover, Murdoch denies 'that moral philosophy should aim at being neutral' (Murdoch, 1970a, p. 52); rather it should prescribe a way of life. Therefore Murdoch does not move towards science but rather embraces religion and art, considering that any true account of human being must include the artistic imagination and spirituality, both of which she judges to be basic human capacities. How Murdoch accounts for these characteristics will be unfolded during the course of this book. For now it is enough to note that Murdoch's intention is to broaden the modern philosophical framework so that again it includes non-scientific concepts. Such a philosophy, she contends, will re-establish the individual and 'check the increasing power of science' (ibid., p. 76). Murdoch's wish is that philosophy should once again present a picture of the whole of human life and provide succour and insight to all. She suggests that 'ethical theory has affected society, and has reached as far as to the ordinary man, in the past, and there is no good reason to think that it cannot do so in the future' (ibid.). She believes that, in the erosion of religion and the elevation of science, something essentially human has been 'lost'; a phrase we will encounter often as we discuss her moral vision.[28]

*The Breadth of Iris Murdoch's Vision*   9

This wish for a broad philosophy led Murdoch to Plato: a very unusual philosophical commitment in the world of philosophy she inhabited, where 'to "come out" then as a Platonist in morals seemed as bizarre as declaring oneself a Jacobite in politics' (Conradi, 2001, p. 492). Murdoch's interest in Plato places her distinctly outside the mainstream of moral philosophy. Murdoch disliked Plato intensely when she first encountered him as an undergraduate: 'Iris despised Plato, thinking him reactionary, dishonest, full of cheap dialectical tricks. Reading the *Republic* left her feeling aggressive, and she opposed Plato, in letters to a friend, directly to Marx' (ibid., p. 87). However, she gradually began to see Plato as *the* philosopher relevant to the modern age, owing to the similarity of the periods, both being times of 'critical breakdown' (ibid., p. 561).[29] Both periods she regards as times when traditional sources of moral authority have broken down and new sources not yet been found.[30] Therefore, for her, 'Plato is the philosopher – the religious thinker . . . – to whom we must turn' (Kerr, 1997, p. 68). As Tracy comments, 'there is something both strange and courageous in Iris Murdoch's decision to develop a form of Platonism in the late twentieth century' (Tracy, 1996, p. 54). Yet, having considered the available possibilities she found in her contemporaries, eventually Murdoch concluded that only in Plato could she find the varied picture of human being which she sought. Thus she describes Plato as 'not only the father of our philosophy, he is our best philosopher' (Murdoch, 1997 [1978], p. 6). Plato's influence on Murdoch cannot be overestimated, from her 1970s work, *Sovereignty of Good*, to her last great work, *Metaphysics as a Guide to Morals*. Like Plato, she is a moral realist with the good at the centre of her philosophical world, and the myth of the Cave, taken from Plato's *Republic*, provides the metaphor by which the human condition and the moral life can be understood. At times it has been questioned whether Murdoch's reading of Plato is accurate, and she did make Plato 'her own': 'Iris and Plato's voices increasingly become a single indistinguishable composite intellect' (Conradi, 2001, p. 547). Certainly Murdoch is familiar and 'at home' with Plato in a remarkable way, yet she recognizes this and states that 'I am aware of the danger of inventing my own Plato and extracting a particular pattern from his many-patterned text to reassure myself that, as I see it, good really is good and real is really real' (Murdoch, 1992, pp. 510–11). At the very least Murdoch's use of Plato is selective; she is interested in his moral philosophy alone. Yet, whatever else, she is undoubtedly a Platonist, affected by Plato's vision, and any criticism concerning her interpretation of Plato derives from her almost complete identification with his vision as she tries to reinterpret it for the twentieth century. Whatever her failings, she has communicated a vision, and certainly a Platonic vision, as Taylor comments: 'there are old tracks; they appear on maps which have been handed down to us. But when you get in there, it is hard to find them. So we need people to make new trails. That is, in effect, what Iris Murdoch has done' (Taylor, 1996, p. 18).

## Murdoch's Philosophical Style

Yet, despite her major influence which inspired others (now extremely influential thinkers in their own right), Murdoch's own philosophy is too little known. For example, although thinkers she inspired, such as MacIntyre and Taylor, appear on almost every undergraduate moral philosophy reading list, one rarely finds Murdoch at postgraduate, still less undergraduate, level. There are a number of reasons that help to explain this absence. First, Murdoch was very much outside the mainstream of the philosophies of her contemporaries and, second, her philosophy is not always the easiest to read and interpret. Murdoch's focus on the good life and her interest in religion and art marked her out as very different from the analytical philosophers which dominated not only Oxford, but philosophy in general at that time. The individual, the self and the inner life are all concepts which are fundamental to Murdoch's philosophy, but which are regarded with suspicion in the philosophy of Murdoch's contemporaries. This in itself separates Murdoch's philosophy from that of her contemporaries. However, when one considers that Murdoch's interests broaden from this somewhat dubious starting-point into issues from which post-Enlightenment philosophy has shied away and even denied to be part of philosophy (such as the good life, the concept of the good and religion) it is easy to see why Murdoch has so often been disregarded. She was so frustrated with the narrowness of contemporary philosophy that she was described as being 'at war with the desiccation, the detailed casuistry, of contemporary philosophy' (Conradi, 2001, p. 304).[31] The unusual topics of Murdoch's philosophy, which many would regard as not 'proper' philosophy at all, but moving into areas of theology and even psychology, have meant that she has been less studied than she would have been if she had focused upon more usual philosophical issues.

In addition, her eclectic style of argument presents problems, as Murdoch's arguments range over such vast literary and philosophical arenas. She expects the reader to know the works and arguments of philosophers from the pre-Socratics to Derrida, and to be familiar with the canon of Western literature, from Dante to the existentialist novels of her contemporaries, as well as to have some awareness of theology, art and world religions. Moreover, not only does she expect the reader to have a knowledge of these diverse thinkers, books and perspectives, but she also moves between genres and examples, swiftly and without explanation. It is not an exaggeration to say that Murdoch is quite capable of moving from Plato, to Kant, to Wittgenstein, with references to Tolstoy, Shakespeare and Virginia Woolf in the space of a few paragraphs. All of which makes Murdoch a difficult philosopher to read.

The problems caused by the breadth of the topic area are compounded by Murdoch's style, which does not make for easy philosophical reading. As John Kleinig points out in a review of *The Sovereignty of Good*, Murdoch's 'essays are singularly lacking in tightness of argument and clarity of expression' (Kleinig, 1971, p. 112). It is hard to disagree with this judgment; Murdoch

## The Breadth of Iris Murdoch's Vision

does not present systematic, clear arguments, but rather talks around the issue.[32] She begins with one subject and then leaves it in order to discuss a tangentially related topic, returning to the primary subject later, leaving the reader somewhat mystified. This lack of clear argument is a constant criticism made of Murdoch's philosophy; a criticism made not only of *The Sovereignty of Good*, but also of *The Fire and the Sun*: Martha Nussbaum commenting on the 'disappointing absence both of sustained argument and of close examination of particular texts' (Nussbaum, 1978, p. 126) and R.W. Hepburn suggesting that 'more examples would have made for easier understanding and might have clarified just which of the arts her points apply to most convincingly' (Hepburn, 1978, p. 270). This type of criticism reached its zenith in comments about her last and longest philosophical work *Metaphysics as a Guide to Morals*, which was praised by critics for the topics and her ability to link diverse concepts, but which almost caused despair among the philosophical reviewers. For example Gregory Jones felt that 'one cannot help but have the impression that Murdoch spent less time crafting the argument of this book than she does in crafting the story line and characters of her novels' (Jones, 1993, p. 687).[33] Murdoch's earlier works are more tightly argued, and both her first book, *Sartre: Romantic Rationalist* and her later collection of three essays contained in *Sovereignty of Good* are clearer than her last work, *Metaphysics as a Guide to Morals*.[34]

Furthermore, Murdoch often uses arguments that work by analogy and by appeals to experience rather than by analysis of the more usual philosophical type. This is particularly true in her use of historical arguments, where she is tracing the thinkers that have contributed to a philosophical position which she is opposing. She uses this form of argument especially when she is attacking two presumptions in contemporary philosophies, namely, the decline of the 'self' and the elevation of the 'fact/value divide'.[35] In both of these Murdoch tends to use historical arguments, showing how the current situation has arisen incrementally, and thus asserting that current philosophical assumptions are historically conditioned rather than established, or argued for, premises.[36] Although this type of argument succeeds in revealing the historicity of the current positions, and thus their contingency, it fails to address the current positions in their own terms.

Murdoch's unusual style could be regarded as a benefit as it is a result of her breadth of vision and her willingness to attempt to reintroduce into philosophy concepts which have been 'analysed away' and so present a fuller picture of human being. For her, modern philosophy is continually narrow and reductionist, and it is this that 'put her at odds with "dried-up" orthodox philosophy' (Conradi, 2001, p. 268) as she was 'simply interested, as philosophers once in the golden age all were, in everything on earth' (ibid.). However, for others, this lack of the familiar type of philosophical argument is to say the least frustrating, in that it fails to offer analytical arguments of the usual type and so, from this perspective, she does not adequately engage with her contemporaries.

Whatever one feels about the validity of Murdoch's style and approach – either praising it as a welcome humanizing of over-dry analytical philosophy, or regarding it as unclear and not 'proper' philosophy – to read Murdoch one must accept this type of discourse. One will be disappointed if one wishes to find simple, clear definitions along the typical analytical lines, but that does not mean that Murdoch, while arguing in an unusual style, has nothing to offer to the debate. Moreover, given her wish to reintroduce into philosophy concepts which are no longer present in modern philosophy one could argue that she was forced to step outside the usual styles as these forms of argument were structurally unable, owing to their limited language and models of reality, to address the concepts Murdoch discusses. Her aim is not to question the details of the philosophy of her contemporaries, but to change the outlook of philosophy significantly and in its entirety: 'to open up a way of conceiving ourselves as finite beings, who are nevertheless capable of a certain self-transcendence which fulfils and does not negate our humanity' (Kerr, 1997, p. 68). Murdoch herself seems to recognize the limitation of her argumentation and suggests that she is aware she is presenting, if 'not a comprehensive analysis, at least a rival soul-picture which covers a greater or different territory . . . [which] . . . should make new places for philosophical reflection' (Murdoch, 1970a, p. 2). Indeed she continues that she is presenting 'a sketch of a metaphysical theory, a kind of inconclusive non-dogmatic naturalism, which has the circularity of definition characteristic of such theories' (ibid., p. 44).[37]

In this sense perhaps Murdoch is better described as a moral visionary than as a strict moral philosopher (although this is as much a comment on the narrowness of modern philosophy as on Murdoch's work). Even those who have criticized her for a lack of sustained argument have welcomed her work and hailed her as important. In this vein Kleinig, while criticizing her lack of clarity, declares her to be 'a visionary and her endeavour is to "get us to see" an alternative' (Kleinig, 1971, p. 112). Likewise H.O. Mounce, in a review of *The Sovereignty of Good*, criticizes her for being difficult and obscure, but praises her for her freshness, stating that she 'wishes to persuade us that the picture should be changed' (Mounce, 1972, p. 170). This type of response to Murdoch seems ubiquitous – her vision 'lacks enough detail to be clear, but it offers an imaginative picture, largely old yet very refreshing' (Wallace, 1970, p. 726) – therefore it is as a visionary that we should consider her, rather than as a typical analytical philosopher.

Murdoch's assertion that 'man is a creature who makes pictures of himself and then comes to resemble the picture' (Murdoch, 1997 [1957], p. 75) shows why Murdoch is so committed to presenting an alternative picture of human being rather than critiquing in the more usual philosophical manner.[38] It is this type of broad picture which attracted and inspired Charles Taylor, who pictorially states that 'we were trapped in the corral of morality. Murdoch led us out not only to the broad fields of ethics but also beyond that again to the almost untracked forests of the unconditional' (Taylor, 1996, p. 5).[39]

Murdoch does present a moral vision, a vision which she regards as a truer picture of human being, one which is Platonist, individual and undeniably personal. This is not surprising as she writes in her journal that 'for me philosophical problems are the problems of my own life' (Conradi, 2001, p. 269).

**Chapter Outline**

The intention of this book is to present Murdoch's philosophy in a thematic and systematic way in the hope that this type of presentation will provide the reader with far easier access to her ideas. This book is neither a critical analysis of her philosophy nor an attempt to remove from her work the features which make her work disquieting for contemporary philosophers. Rather it is an outline of Murdoch's moral philosophy which accurately presents her views in an ordered and clarified way. The hope is that this retelling of Murdoch's moral vision may allow her key insights, which have inspired so many, to come to the fore and be understood more easily. In light of this aim, this book presents Murdoch's philosophical insights, drawn together from the work of her whole career, in as straightforward a manner as possible. There is a certain amount of discussion throughout the book about her ideas and comments on her work taken from other sources. However, in order to provide a correct representation of her moral philosophy, criticism has largely been reserved for the last chapter, which discusses the implication of Murdoch's ethics in the current context.

Murdoch's moral vision will be outlined over the course of seven further chapters. Chapter 2, 'The Inner Life of the Individual', describes the importance of the individual and the concepts of 'the self', 'consciousness' and the 'inner life' to Murdoch's philosophy. Murdoch wishes to find a philosophy which can accommodate 'inner experience': that which is not observably verifiable but nonetheless real. The individual's personal experience is fundamental in Murdoch's account of the way moral value is recognized and in the individual's capacity to be good. True morality is not, for Murdoch, about right action, but about becoming good. Such a concept of morality necessitates a concept of the inner life which recognizes different qualities of consciousness, as right action derives from a good quality of consciousness. In her attempt to reassert the concept of the self, Murdoch comes into direct conflict with the philosophies of her contemporaries from existentialism and empiricism (in the earliest years of her philosophical career) to Derrida's structuralism (more usually termed 'deconstruction' or 'post-structuralism') in her last philosophical work, *Metaphysics as a Guide to Morals*. This chapter discusses Murdoch's opposition to and criticisms of the philosophies of her contemporaries and her own concept of the individual and the inner life.

Chapter 3 outlines moral experience. Murdoch takes experience as the starting-point of her moral philosophy and criticizes other philosophies in the

14        *The Moral Vision of Iris Murdoch*

light of how well they fit her concept of moral experience. It is in one's experience of the world that Murdoch believes that moral values are recognized. In order to assert this realist conception, in which moral knowledge is derived directly from the experience of moral value, Murdoch again has to counter prevalent presumptions of modern philosophy, notably the fact/value divide. This chapter will explore Murdoch's arguments for rejecting the fact/value dichotomy: in particular, her criticisms of those who maintain the dichotomy from its origins in Hume and Kant, through Wittgenstein's philosophy to its endpoint in Derrida's structuralism. Having discussed Murdoch's refutation of the fact/value divide, this chapter then goes on to explore her concept of moral experience and the type of moral philosophy which she believes derives from the recognition of the reality of moral values.

Having described the nature of moral experience, in Chapter 4 we come to the heart of Murdoch's philosophy, to the moral value of the good. The reality of the good we recognize in our own experience and it is this primary value of the good which inspires the moral life. In this chapter Murdoch's arguments for the good – arguments from perfection and her version of the ontological argument – will be expounded and critiqued.

In Chapter 5 we move away from the construction of Murdoch's realism described in the first half of the book, in which the inner life, moral values and the good are established, and towards her picture of the moral life: a life lived in response to good. The moral life for Murdoch is a quest from illusion to reality, in which the human being progresses from the natural state of egoistic illusion towards a clearer vision of reality and towards the good. This chapter will outline Murdoch's understanding of moral living, the nature of moral change, and tools which enable this change, especially her concept of attention and her inspirations for the quest: learning, art and love.

Chapter 6 brings us to a key feature of Murdoch's philosophy, the place of art in the moral life. Murdoch divides 'good' and 'great' from 'bad' or 'mediocre' art; she then defends good art from Plato's criticisms of art as illusion. Good art is presented as an aid to the moral life because it is truth-telling and reveals reality as well as, in a secular age, providing access to transcendence. This chapter explores the dual nature of art (it can both delude and also reveal the real) and its place in the moral life, and finishes with a discussion of Murdoch's own artistry and the relation between her art and her philosophy.

Chapter 7 presents the final key theme of Murdoch's philosophy, that of religion. Murdoch argues that the decline of religion is the most significant feature of the modern age, which has had far-reaching implications for all the concepts which Murdoch is keen to defend: the individual, the inner life, moral experience and spirituality. She discusses the decline of religion and the impact that this has had on these aspects of human life, and then goes on to discuss how religious imagery and tools can aid the moral life. Because of the help that religion can give to the moral life, Murdoch claims that religious imagery should be reclaimed, as should spirituality, by the secular world. In this vein

## The Breadth of Iris Murdoch's Vision

she advocates demythologizing Christianity to produce a godless religion, which preserves the individual and values without illusory, supernatural beliefs. The chapter outlines Murdoch's view of religion, from its decline to her picture of a godless religion and the creation of a mystical Christ which can aid the moral life.

The final chapter of the book brings together all the threads of Murdoch's philosophy which have been outlined in previous chapters: the individual's inner life, moral experience, the good, the moral life, art and religion. Murdoch's moral vision will be discussed and critiqued in its totality. In light of this discussion, the implications of Murdoch's ethics for the current ethical debate will be explored and Murdoch's legacy will be assessed.

## Notes

1   The assertion of Murdoch's familiarity Conradi supports with examples, such as an advert for British Rail which 'showed a contented passenger reading *Henry and Cato*' (Conradi, 2001, p. 570).

2   In this work Iris Murdoch is referred to simply as 'Murdoch', despite A.N. Wilson's assertion that this convention is a 'modern brutality which refers to her by surname alone' (Wilson, 2003, p. 10). When others refer to Murdoch their terminology is maintained; therefore 'Iris', 'Iris Murdoch', 'IM' and 'Dame Iris' will all appear in this work.

3   Questions about whether he should have written the memoir and what it would have meant to Iris abound. Peter Conradi, a friend to both Iris and John for many years and author of her biography, *Iris Murdoch: A Life*, seems to approve of John Bayley's work, stating that 'those closest understood that this helped him, hurting no one' (Conradi, 2001, p. 591): a defensive comment in itself.

4   Murdoch's Irishness is detailed well in Conradi's biography, *Iris Murdoch: A Life*, in a chapter entitled 'You ask how Irish she is?' which records that even as she became more confused towards the end of her life in the winter of 1997–98 she soothed herself by asserting that she was Irish. Conradi describes that even at this point her Irishness, that was 'visible in every decade of her life, was then, as it had always been, a source of reassurance, a reference-point, a credential, somewhere to start out from and return to' (ibid., p. 29). A.N. Wilson also has a chapter in his book, *Iris Murdoch as I knew Her*, called 'Considers herself Irish'.

5   She was informed by the Dean on her arrival that 'you must seriously realise that you have to be careful how you behave. It isn't a joking matter, the women are still very much on probation at this university' (ibid., p. 82).

6   Both Conradi and Wilson state that Murdoch left her Oxford post because of a threatened scandal caused by an obsessional affair that Murdoch had with a fellow female don.

7   Conradi notes that Murdoch's apparent leaving of the Party may well have been done on the orders of the Party in order for her to begin work at the Treasury, and he cites information which suggests that she continued to be a committed communist (ibid., pp. 128, 144). However, she became increasingly disenchanted with communism and in July 1943 wrote to Frank that she found unbearable the 'suppression of the individual most Eastern philosophies have at their heart' (ibid., p. 174); 'Eastern' here refers to 'Eastern Europe'. At this time her interest in religion is growing, not that she becomes uncritical of it, but it does signify a distinct departure from the communist creed.

16 *The Moral Vision of Iris Murdoch*

8 Frank was the brother of E.P. Thompson, famous British historian of the twentieth century, with whom Murdoch had a passionate if platonic affair, from her undergraduate days until his death in 1944.

9 Wilson describes Murdoch as having 'absorbed John's Right-of-Genghis-Khan views on most subjects' (Wilson, 2003, p. 43).

10 Wilson suggested that Murdoch joined the Communist Party for religious reasons (Conradi, 2001, p. 172). Therefore, it is perhaps no surprise that her interest in religion, and her refusal to separate religion and philosophy, began in 1945 at the time of her disillusionment with the Communist Party. Indeed it is in 1946 that she first began reading theology (including Buber, who was still to influence her in her last philosophical work), and in 1946 she went on her first retreat to Malling Abbey. This conclusion seems to be further borne out by a journal entry of 1947 which suggests that she regarded communism and religion as similar, stating that, 'It occurs to me that I entertain the idea: "One day I shall return to the party", and the idea "One day I shall join the Roman Church"' (ibid., p. 274).

11 Philippa Foot recalled an incident of herself and Iris listing the men that had proposed to them: 'Philippa's "list" was soon done. As Iris's went on and on Philippa asked her crossly whether it might not save time if Iris listed the men who had *not* yet asked her to marry them' (ibid., p. 167).

12 The importance of friendship characterized something about Murdoch's character and she suffered when she lost a friend as if she had mislaid them; she 'believed that university friendships lasted for life. Hers were to' (ibid., p. 85). Wilson also comments on this, stating that 'IM had a big heart, and a tremendous desire to remain friends with ex-lovers, ex-mentors and even, a more taxing thing than this, ex-friends' (Wilson, 2003, p. 174).

13 Conradi suggests that, in this affair, Murdoch may have been attempting to find a substitute for the absent Frank; 'in becoming his lover Iris was arguably getting as close to Frank himself as she could manage. She was not able to conceal this from Michael, who perceived himself as a "stand-in"' (Conradi, 2001, p. 176).

14 MacKinnon's interest in theology and religion is evident in both Murdoch's novels and philosophy. Moreover, MacKinnon's view that 'philosophy and theology are somehow to be brought back together again' (ibid., p. 126) is one that Murdoch put into practice, particularly in her last philosophical work, *Metaphysics as a Guide to Morals*. Murdoch's friendship with MacKinnon ended because of what he saw as portrayals of himself and his marriage in Murdoch's novels (ibid., pp. 275–58, 439–41). The friendship deteriorated to the point that he denounced her at a dinner, saying that 'there was real evil there' (ibid., p. 440).

15 Conradi suggests that Murdoch is referring to Frank when her '*alter ego* says in *The Black Prince* that she reveres no one except great artists and "those who say No to tyrants"; or, at the end of *The Red and the Green*, Frances thinks of the "inconceivably brave" Irish dead of Easter 1916, "made young and perfect forever"' (ibid., p. 195). Franz Steiner inspiring those 'good' characters of Peter Saward in *The Flight from the Enchanter*, Willy Kost in *The Nice and the Good* and Tallis Browne in *A Fairly Honourable Defeat* (ibid., p. 442). However, when questioned, Murdoch insisted that the only good characters in her novels were Stuart in *The Good Apprentice* and Tallis in *A Fairly Honourable Defeat* (ibid., p. 479).

16 Canetti's most famous novel, *Auto da Fé*, published in English in 1946, won the Nobel Prize for Literature in 1981.

17 Although, as Conradi notes, Murdoch denies putting either Franz or Canetti into her work (Conradi, 2001, p. 390). In fact she 'stoutly maintained that she never drew her characters from life, a practice she held morally abhorrent – "bad form" – which would inhibit her.

## The Breadth of Iris Murdoch's Vision

When friends saw themselves in her books, she said, this was generally "vanity" on their part' (ibid., p. 439).

18  Despite Murdoch's strange relationship with Canetti and his cruelty, which aroused 'strong emotions of admiration, subservience, fear and dislike' (ibid., p. 349) their friendship continued until his death.

19  In fact, making a sketch of Murdoch's life, with no personal relationship and knowledge is presumptuous. However, given the interest in Murdoch as a person it would be remiss not to mention her famous life at all. Being aware of this inadequacy it would be best for interested readers to refer to the biographies which have been used to draw this sketch.

20  Although Wilson refuses to believe that it was Bayley's intention to diminish Murdoch, as he believes the memoirs and the subsequent film did, he describes Bayley as 'passionately and unreasonably jealous' (Wilson, 2003, p. 57). Wilson believes that Murdoch, as an intensely private person, would have hated the type of publicity that the film and memoir have brought, and declares that Bayley lost control when he wrote the book, and feels that the book shows 'resentments, envy, poisonously strong misogyny and outright hatred of his wife' (ibid., p. 9). Wilson thinks that this is borne out by Bayley's revelation to him that, after *The Bell*, he didn't read Murdoch's novels (Wilson, 1973, 2003). Accordingly he suggests that 'JOB's preservation of his version of IM's memory could now be viewed as a kind of revenge' (Wilson, 2003, p. 260).

21  Wilson likewise reports their commitment to marriage, stating that 'clearly it had been part of the deal between IM and JOB that, however unfaithful she was, they would never, ever separate . . . JOB and IM were as firmly married as anyone in England. Divorce was unthinkable, and they always spoke of it as the ultimate folly' (ibid., p. 56).

22  In response to the suicide of a friend and former pupil, Murdoch blamed herself and wrote in her journal 'she cd [*sic*] have been saved by love, a great deal of love, whatever the psychiatrists could or couldn't manage – I feel sick and stifled with misery about this' (Conradi, 2001, p. 453).

23  The relationship between Murdoch's philosophy and her novels is discussed further in Chapter 6.

24  Other books include, *Iris Murdoch*, by Frank Baldanza, *Iris Murdoch*, by Deborah Johnson and *Iris Murdoch*, by Hilda D. Spear.

25  Stanley Hauerwas generously states that 'I sometimes wonder if I have ever said anything of importance that was not stolen from Iris Murdoch' (Hauerwas, 1996, p. 190). Charles Taylor, although he doesn't always agree with her, praises her as a trail-blazer and teacher, a compliment that Murdoch returns, describing his book, *Sources of the Self*, as 'wise and learned' (Murdoch, 1992, p. 166). In addition, 'John MacDowell would read and re-read *The Sovereignty of Good* and declare himself positively influenced' (Conradi, 2001, p. 303).

26  Moral realism asserts that moral values are real and that properties 'exist' in the world 'out there' and are independent of human desires and wishes. Succinctly put, moral realism 'is the metaphysical (or ontological view) that there exist moral facts' (Smith, 1991, p. 402). Murdoch is certainly a realist in that the nature of moral value is not created by human wishes and desires, but for her the moral reality is the human reality: she is not concerned with what exists 'outside' the world of human perception. Therefore she differs from many realists in their wish to equate moral facts with scientific facts and, as we shall see, Murdoch denies the fact/value dichotomy, and holds a less pseudoscientific view. Although she herself never applied this term to her philosophy, yet she has had great influence on contemporary realist thinkers and, most prominently, on John MacDowell.

27  Virtue ethics turns away from legal concepts, such as obligations, and focuses on right action. Morality is set in the context of living a 'good life' and being a good person,

18 *The Moral Vision of Iris Murdoch*

focusing on virtues and the whole of life rather than primarily on correct acts and moral rules. This ancient view of morality declined with Enlightenment thinking, and has been revived in the last few decades, a revival which is in part due to the influence of Murdoch.

28 The feeling that something has been 'lost', that 'there is a certain moral void' (Murdoch, 1997 [1962], p. 171) echoes some of the contemporary worries about a 'moral crisis' and 'process of demoralisation' which will be discussed in more detail in the final chapter.

29 In this vein Murdoch argues that Plato continues to be relevant for us today, asserting that 'the methods of philosophy change, but we have not left Plato behind, which is also to say that philosophy does not make progress in the way science does' (Murdoch, 1997 [1978], p. 6).

30 Many of Murdoch's preoccupations are the same as Plato's, and she holds that Plato's primary concern, like hers, is to present a picture of human being: 'Never has a philosopher more clearly indicated that salvation concerns the whole soul: the soul must be saved entire by the redirection of its energy away from selfish fantasy toward reality' (Murdoch, 1997 [1976], p. 419). In addition both are concerned with 'the moral reform of religious concept and religious practice' (ibid., p. 440) and Murdoch regards this quest for workable religious concepts as similar, stating that 'traditional city state religion was now undergoing a crisis of "demythologisation" not totally unlike that of present-day Christianity' (ibid.).

31 Iris moved so far from the analytical philosophy of Oxford that her paper in honour of Philippa Foot on the Ontological Argument for the existence of good was declined as being too theological (Conradi, 2001, pp. 586–7).

32 Indeed, in *Metaphysics as a Guide to Morals*, she admits that 'I hope in what follows to "talk around" some of these questions. Such "talking" may constitute and indicate answers' (Murdoch, 1992, p. 237), suggesting that Murdoch was aware that she does not provide convincing arguments of the usual philosophical type.

33 This criticism is echoed by Diogenes Allen who states that 'Murdoch's presentation of her views calls to mind a person going into various shops, looking over the merchandise and making comments to a friend about the merits, demerits, and usefulness of the items on display' (Allen, 1993, p. 24). This criticism is perhaps also true of her teaching, which while inspiring and life-changing for some students, is described by others as merely 'unfocused' (Conradi, 2001, p. 293). Likewise Wilson comments that, 'while she once might have been a good philosophy tutor, she never in the quarter-century I knew her expressed ideas clearly' (Wilson, 2003, p. 149).

34 A book which, while vastly varied, at times contains some of Murdoch's greatest philosophy, as Wilson also suggests, stating that in 'this too-long, troubled book there are occasional passages of greater insight and precision than anything else she ever wrote' (ibid., p. 241).

35 These issues will be discussed respectively in Chapters 2 and 3.

36 In an interview Murdoch commented that 'often philosophy fails because of what might be called imaginative or obsessive conceptual errors, false assumptions or starting-points which send the whole investigation wrong' (Murdoch, 1997 [1978], p. 12). Given this, it seems that Murdoch's style of argument is deliberate and one which Murdoch believes can be successful.

37 Murdoch does not consider this lack of clarity to be a problem, and declares the pseudoscientific view of her contemporaries which she is opposing as 'similarly circular' (Murdoch, 1970, p. 44) and goes on to say that their argument is unconvincing.

38 Murdoch does not use inclusive language, as one would perhaps expect, or hope, given her place as one of the first group of women to break through in academia. Whether and to what extent Murdoch was a feminist is open to question. Conradi reports both her fear of

## The Breadth of Iris Murdoch's Vision

a separation between the sexes which she saw in 'women's lib' (Conradi, 2001, p. 279), and of acts which are 'symptomatic of her regard for the freedom of women' (ibid., p. 178).

39  As Conradi notes, 'her urge to find an alternative and more accurate description of our condition . . . has long driven both her fiction and her philosophy' (Conradi, 1997, p. xxii).

Chapter 2

# The 'Inner Life' of the Individual

Underlying Murdoch's moral philosophy is a concept of the individual as the 'owner' of their 'inner life' and of inner activity as morally significant. It is upon this belief in the individual's consciousness and personal (moral) experience that Murdoch's moral philosophy is built. It is also here, in her assertion of the self and the 'inner life', that Murdoch finds herself in stark conflict with the philosophies of her contemporaries, philosophies which have at best doubted, and at worst totally disregarded, the self.

The concept of self which Murdoch is trying to assert is not the 'unified self' of Descartes' philosophy, of a solitary 'knower' whose ideas are clearly identifiable and which reveal true reality. Rather she is claiming that, however disunited the self is (both historically as the individual changes over time and in the mixed experience of the 'stream of consciousness' which contains much indistinct and various material), it is nonetheless a necessary concept which philosophy must retain. Her insistence on the priority of the self is an assertion that the individual's consciousness and experience, however difficult to define, is an important source of moral experience. Hence Murdoch wishes to reclaim a concept of a valid 'inner life' which 'belongs' to the individual; by the 'inner life' Murdoch means one's inner monologue, emotions and responses to the world, indeed all that happens 'inside' the individual. To deny the self, consciousness and the inner life is, for Murdoch, to deny the reality of the individual and to ignore an important source of knowledge, particularly moral knowledge.

Murdoch's moral philosophy is premised on the reality of the individual self, so much so that she states that 'the central concept of morality is "the individual"' (Murdoch, 1970a, p. 30). So committed is she to reviving a philosophically valid picture of the self and establishing the validity of inner experience that Antonaccio describes Murdoch's preoccupation with reintroducing viable concepts of the self as 'a central interest of Murdoch's thought for forty years, and . . . perhaps the greatest source of her influence on ethical inquiry' (Antonaccio, 2000, p. 86).[1] The concept of the self is the starting-point for Murdoch's broader philosophical vision, which depends on the capacity of the individual to have meaningful inner experience and to recognize and experience different levels of consciousness. What Murdoch wishes to establish, the necessary concept around which her philosophy is constructed, is a robust understanding of the self, which includes an active inner life and a substantive conception of consciousness. As Genevieve Lloyd rightly notes, she 'wants to get the "inner" back into the scene of morality; to

21

22                    *The Moral Vision of Iris Murdoch*

emphasise the moral importance of perception, as distinct from the outer, publicly observable effect of the will' (Lloyd, 1982, p. 63). For Murdoch, this picture of the self as an individual with active inner life is fundamental for any moral philosophy and, for her, 'moral philosophy should begin with an accurate picture of man and yet allow, or show how, man may improve morally' (Dunbar, 1978, p. 516). She wishes to find a way for us to speak meaningfully about the self and also to present the self as the place of moral happening; she seeks 'a radical affirmation of the existence of others . . . as separate, unique beings' (Antonaccio, 2000, p. 103).

   In our exploration of Murdoch's concept of the self we will begin by discussing the pictures of the self which Murdoch finds in the philosophy of her contemporaries and also her criticisms of these philosophies. Her own picture of the self is written in this context, in response and opposition to the prevalent philosophical positions of the self; from existentialism at the beginning of her career to structuralism in her later work. In consequence her arguments for the self and the inner life are very much 'against the philosophers of her own generation' (Kerr, 1997, p. 70) and their presentations of the self.

## The Destruction of the Self

Murdoch traces the decline of philosophically workable concepts of the self to ideological changes which have occurred post-Enlightenment and, in particular, to the decline of a religious worldview.[2] She argues that 'the theological idea of the soul has been a support to the concept of the self in philosophy' (Murdoch, 1992, p. 166), although, 'as theology and religion lose their authority the picture of the soul fades and the idea of the self loses its power' (ibid.). As a result of the decline of religion, and the accompanying philosophical ideology, we not only have lost belief in God – a change which Murdoch welcomes – but have also lost our concept of self and concluded that 'the "individual" with his boasted "inner life" is really some kind of illusion' (ibid., p. 151). Included in this loss are, for Murdoch, not only those religious concepts which she praises Enlightenment and post-Enlightenment philosophies for removing, but also essential concepts such as the individual, consciousness and experience. Murdoch argues that this philosophical shift is profound, and indeed she describes it as an 'apocalyptic change in human consciousness, involving vast social changes and the disappearance of old local ideas of individuals and virtues' (ibid., p. 210). As a result Murdoch holds that 'twentieth-century man . . . . finds his religious and metaphysical background so impoverished that he is in some danger of being left with nothing of inherent value except will-power itself' (Murdoch, 1997 [1970], p.224).

   Murdoch regards the erosion of the concept of the individual as a change which has happened in a piecemeal fashion, and one of which we (as philosophers and lay persons) have not been fully aware. Murdoch argues that this is because 'the charm and power of technology and the authority of a

The 'Inner Life' of the Individual 23

"scientific outlook" conceal the speed with which the idea of the responsible moral spiritual individual is being diminished' (Murdoch, 1992, p. 426). The consequences of this shift now beset philosophical and lay thinking and the concept of the self is discredited or neglected (ibid., p. 78). As a result, both in academia and in modern society, we experience a 'haunting sense of loss' (Murdoch, 1997 [1953], p. 43).

For Murdoch, filling this void is central; we must reject the current denial of the inner and establish a working concept of self. Murdoch does not advocate returning to the united self and she welcomes the criticisms that have been made of the self by post-Enlightenment philosophy. Therefore she does not wish to reclaim unreconstructed the traditional concept of the unified self or the theological soul; rather she argues that a new concept should be developed which takes account of the criticisms and insights of post-Enlightenment philosophy. For Murdoch morality is grounded in the individual and therefore the need to rehabilitate the self is absolutely necessary and the proper task of moral philosophy. She suggests that post-Enlightenment philosophy has expertly critiqued previous positions, but has failed in the task of using these insights to create a new vision: philosophy 'has been busy dismantling the old substantial picture of the "self", and ethics has not proved able to rethink this concept for moral purposes' (Murdoch, 1970a, p. 47).

## Rejecting the Self: Hume and Kant

Murdoch traces the philosophical rejection of the self to the rejection of the Cartesian worldview, and finds the roots of the disunited self in the combined legacy of Hume and Kant. The views of her contemporaries that she opposes (particularly those of the existentialists and the empiricists) she regards as direct successors of this tradition, so much so that she states, 'we are still living in the age of the Kantian man, or Kantian man God' (Murdoch, 1970a, p. 80). Kantian man she defines as 'free, independent, lonely, powerful, responsible, brave, the hero of so many novels and books of moral philosophy' (ibid.). Murdoch regards this as an 'attractive but misleading' (ibid.) picture of the human person which dominates twentieth-century philosophy, not least because she deems this picture of man to be 'the ideal citizen of the liberal state' (ibid.).[3] This neo-Kantian man we shall discuss in detail shortly in the existentialist and empirical embodiments to which Murdoch most vehemently objected. First, however, we will briefly consider Murdoch's description of the way the once-central concept of the self became at best peripheral to mainstream philosophy.

The initial rejection of the self was part of the shift from a religious worldview, which Murdoch believes rightly brought criticisms and clarity to many concepts which had been unjustifiably accepted without proper analysis. Murdoch includes in this the unquestioned acceptance of an individual soul, self or mind; a presumption of unity which reached its zenith in Descartes'

24 *The Moral Vision of Iris Murdoch*

assertion of the 'the solitary knower, with his purified access to clear and distinct private data' (Murdoch, 1992, p. 150). The dismissal of this picture Murdoch regards as correct, and she praises the post-Cartesian thinkers for their proper recognition that 'thinking is not a mental composition repeated aloud verbatim, spoken words do not have to have mental equivalents, recognition and remembrance do not depend on comparison with inner pictures, words are not names of things' (ibid., p. 152). However, rejecting the over-confident Cartesian picture of a unified self within which there are clear and identifiable mental data which can be fully known, Murdoch argues, should not lead to a full rejection of the self. This has been the trend in post-Cartesian philosophies, which have 'usually been concerned with "immediate awareness", perceptions for instance, as bearers of knowledge rather than of value, and have in this interest reduced the ordinary concept of "inner" activity' (ibid., p. 172). Murdoch's assertion is that there is no need to move from a correct scepticism and criticism to the complete negation of the self. Here she states that it is

> one thing to present sound anti-Cartesian critical arguments about sense data, momentary inner certainties, or the role of memory images in remembering; it is quite another to sweep aside as irrelevant a whole area of our private reflections, which we may regard as the very substance of our soul and being as somehow unreal, otiose, without relevant *quality* or *value*. (ibid., p. 157)

Murdoch's claim is that, while philosophy was right to deny previous Cartesian pictures of the self, this should not result, as she argues it has tended to, in the conclusion that 'all private inner refection was in some sense incoherent, inaccessible and vague' (ibid., p. 150) and thus to elimination of all theories of the self (ibid.).

Murdoch sees the erosion of the self as being formalized initially in the work of Hume, who 'held that the self was a sort of "illusion" . . . fragmentary experiences held together by strong habits of imagination' (Murdoch, 1992, p. 164). Murdoch accepts much of Hume's criticisms of the concept of the self and even goes as far as to state that, 'as for consciousness and its weirdness there does seem to be a *décalage*, a slipped connection, between the moment-to-moment flow and the procedure, however continuous, of the inner monologue or inner life' (ibid., pp. 258–9). Certainly she recognizes the truth of Hume's assertion in her own experience (and experience, as we shall see, is fundamental to Murdoch's constructive moral vision) accepting that 'possibly, Hume's ramshackle and unsatisfactory idea of consciousness as a continuum of units, fused by association and habit and containing certain morally tinged items such as feelings of approval, most resembles a childish picture of what we feel like!' (ibid., p. 221). Thus Murdoch does not simply deny Hume's criticisms of the self and, like him, she recognizes that the self is not, on reflection, a collection of distinct mental objects of the Cartesian order. However, neither does she conclude that because inner experience is opaque

The 'Inner Life' of the Individual    25

there is no possible concept of the self. Indeed she points out that Hume himself did not adopt the conclusions his hypothesis implied as, although Hume 'attacked the idea of the unified self . . . [he] . . . admitted that as soon as he left his study and his philosophical work, all his old illusions, his strong, natural beliefs resumed their force' (Murdoch, 1997 [1972], p. 253). Thus although Hume, rightly according to Murdoch, noted the lack of unity in consciousness and the self and criticized the false conception of the soul/self, this did not affect his ability to live, outside his study, as if the self existed: because of his cheerfulness, habit and common sense.[4]

Having traced the first important stage of the erosion of the self, Murdoch turns to Kant, whom she considers to be the second pillar, along with Hume, of the view she finds in her contemporaries of the insubstantial self. Murdoch describes Kant as unhappy with Hume's view, as 'he was not prepared to rest scientific knowledge upon a psychology of association of ideas' (Murdoch, 1992, p. 221). Kant's picture was based, not on the stream of fragmented experience, but on reason which 'allowed no sense to the idea of discrete units of experience' (ibid.). For Kant, consciousness is 'strictly the correlate of formulated true or false factual judgements about states of affairs' (ibid., p. 223). Thus, Murdoch argues, for Kant 'there is no such thing as "moral experience", or moral consciousness as a "morally coloured" awareness' (ibid., p. 222). What Kant describes as consciousness is not an active, individual experiential (moral) resource, but rather 'an empty consciousness, a structure of intuition, understanding, reason, which is the same in every rational creature' (Murdoch, 1997 [1952], p. 134).

The inner life of the distinct individual and an inner experience which is particular to the agent is wholly rejected by Kant, because to allow it would be dangerous to the concept of the rational agent who discovers moral value in the universal faculty of reason. As a result, inner and emotional experience is dismissed, as the 'entire world of our emotions and desires is irrelevant to morality' (Murdoch, 1997 [1959b], p. 262) and therefore moves from this 'messy and ambiguous region of the emotions to the undoubted clarity of the choice and the act' (ibid.). In sum, for Kant, moral action relies on reason and hence he turns 'away from the chaos of empirical inwardness to the clarity of overt action' (ibid., p. 268).

This picture of human being for Murdoch is the one that is embedded in post-Kantian philosophy, and its two 'most profound influences have been Hume and Kant' (Murdoch, 1997 [1961], p. 287).[5] Murdoch's contention is that Hume's conception of the 'elusive and fragmentary nature of our introspectible awareness' (Murdoch, 1992, p. 256) has combined with the Kantian assertion of universal reason and away from the inner life, leading succeeding philosophers to construct their moral pictures around the 'will and imperatives' (ibid.). The picture of the moral individual which results from this view is one which retains the idea of the individual moral 'agent as a privileged centre of the will . . . but since the old-fashioned "self" no longer clothes him he appears as an isolated will' (Murdoch, 1970a, p. 49).

26     *The Moral Vision of Iris Murdoch*

Fundamental to this picture of the moral individual is the elevation of the will over and above any other aspect of the inner life, to the extent that only the solitary will can be counted as real. Murdoch's claim is that 'much modern philosophy (existentialist and analytical) follows Kant here: since value has clearly no place in the empirical (scientific) world it must be given another kind of importance by being attached directly to the operation of the human will' (Murdoch, 1997 [1966], p. 195). Indeed Murdoch would seem to class all forms of post-Kantian philosophies as deriving their pictures of the self from this point of view, from existentialism or voluntarism – which 'emphasises and values will-power, is of course an offspring of the thought of Immanuel Kant' (Murdoch, 1997 [1970], p. 224) – to her final contemporary opponent Derrida's structuralism.[6] In this vein she argues that 'the younger Sartre, and many British moral philosophers, represent this last dry distillment of Kant's views of the world. The study of motivation is surrendered to empirical science: will takes the place of the complex of motives and also of the complex of virtues' (Murdoch, 1970a, p. 48).[7] It is to these, as Murdoch constructs the history, later examples of this view, in particular, those of existentialism and empiricism, that we will now turn.

### Rejecting the Self: Murdoch's Contemporaries

The picture of human being Murdoch finds in the philosophies of her contemporaries she describes as 'a sort of Newspeak which makes certain values non-expressible, the reasons for this are to be sought in current philosophy of mind and in the fascinating power of a certain picture of the soul' (Murdoch, 1970a, p. 2). For Murdoch, as Scott Dunbar notes, none of these philosophies presents 'a realistic description of what the human condition is like' (Dunbar, 1978, p. 515). The soul/self picture presented, and the picture of the human being it implies, is one which Murdoch outlines in various forms throughout her work: views which, though they may have different characteristics in different schools of thought, she often equates when it comes to their treatment of the self. In 1970, in her book *Sovereignty of the Good*, Murdoch outlines a 'picture of "the man" of modern moral philosophy' (ibid., p. 4), which she derived from the work of Stuart Hampshire, which she saw as 'fairly central and typical, and it has the great merit that it states and elaborates what in many modern moral philosophies is simply taken for granted' (ibid.).[8] (Murdoch began her philosophical career looking to Sartre's existentialism, which she hoped would provide a means to rescue consciousness.[9] However, by this point in her work, she had concluded that, despite appearances, Sartre's view of the inner life was in fact similar to those of her other contemporaries.) Therefore we will begin this part of the discussion by presenting one of Murdoch's descriptions of the 'modern philosophical man' or 'totally rational man' which characterizes the views of her contemporaries.

The 'Inner Life' of the Individual 27

In this picture of 'modern philosophical man', 'action' is reduced to that which brings about observable change in the world, and accordingly the 'inner or mental world is inevitably parasitic upon the outer world' (ibid., p. 5). Therefore it is only as far as the inner effects the outer, evidenced by changes in the observable world through acts of will, that the inner has any significance. Thus the will is the primary attribute of the inner life, as this is the point where it connects with the outer, observable world: 'I identify myself with my will' (ibid.). The picture of 'ideally rational man', who identifies himself with his will, is characterized by 'clarity of intention' (ibid., p. 7), we 'aim at total knowledge of our situation and a clear conceptualisation of all our possibilities' (ibid.). Thought is only aimed at direct actions, the 'mental life is . . . a shadow of life in public' (ibid.), 'what is "inward", what lies between overt actions, is either impersonal thought, or "shadows" of acts, or else substanceless dream' (ibid.). What is real is the outer not the inner; nothing of significance can happen in consciousness, there is no inner individual experience, for '"reality" is potentially open to different observers' (ibid.). In this construction of the self, the 'personal being is the movement of our overtly choosing will' (ibid., p. 8) and, as in the Kantain picture of the self, of which this picture is the successor, the will is isolated, 'isolated from belief, from reason, from feeling, and yet is the essential centre of the self' (ibid.). The consequences of this view of personhood, Murdoch contends, leads to a reductionist picture of morality, one in which the agent surveys the facts and, in a 'condition of totally responsible freedom' (ibid.), makes a choice and then, via a corresponding act of will, produces an action which can be observed.

This picture of 'modern philosophical man' Murdoch suggests unifies the behavourist, existentialist and utilitarian views:

> it is behaviourist in its connection of the meaning and being of action with the publicly observable, it is existentialist in its elimination of the substantial self and its emphasis on the solitary omnipotent will, and it is utilitarian in its assumption that morality is and can only be concerned with public acts. (Ibid., p. 9)[10]

Murdoch tends to equate all the views of her contemporaries which neglect the inner with the 'existentialist view', and indeed she defines Hampshire's view in this way, as it too asserts 'the primary value of freedom itself and there are the secondary values which consist of the things chosen' (Murdoch, 1997 [1966], p. 197).

Having initially been impressed with Sartre (her first book being *Sartre: Romantic Rationalist*) she later rejected his position.[11] In her early essays on the 'inner life' she praises Sartre's existentialism, and believes it has 'immediate appeal to many people' (Murdoch, 1997 [1950a], p. 104) as he succeeded in giving 'a philosophical form to something which, piecemeal, most of us can recognise in the crises of our own lives' (ibid.). Murdoch's interest in Sartre seems to have been born precisely from her wish to assert the concept of self and the inner life. Consequently, she turned to Sartre because of what Conradi defines as her 'deep dissatisfaction with Anglo-Saxon philosophy, which had in her view largely abandoned fruitful discussion of either "consciousness" or "moral value"' (Conradi, 1997, p. xxii). Murdoch takes Sartre seriously because Sartre takes consciousness seriously, and although he 'attacks the idea of the unified self. . . [and] explores the viscous insubstantial nature of consciousness' (Murdoch, 1997 [1972], p. 250), he still locates the individual in the reality of consciousness. In this vein Murdoch speaks of Sartre as attempting to 'display the general structure of human consciousness . . . Sartre is seeking in the consciousness for the *a priori* basis of objective reality' (Murdoch, 1997 [1952], p. 133). Murdoch was clearly very impressed with this approach, and his attempt to describe the nature of human consciousness and she states that 'it is here, in this sort of semi-psychological description and analysis, that existentialist writings are at their most brilliant and illuminating' (ibid.).

However, despite her initial infatuation with existentialism, Murdoch ultimately found existentialism unsatisfying in its attempt to preserve the individual consciousness, and Murdoch's work exhibited 'a growing scepticism and hostility towards existentialism' (Conradi, 1997, p. xxviii). Sartre's recognition of consciousness as the core of human existence and his assertion of the importance of emotion in this regard – 'emotion is primarily consciousness of the world as qualified in a certain way' (Murdoch, 1997 [1950b], p. 117) – Murdoch suggests 'has at first glance a certain daring and illuminating attractiveness' (ibid.). This attractiveness derives not least from the existentialist 'void' which Murdoch believes does 'account for a peculiar feature of moral choice, which is that strange emptiness which often occurs at the moment of choosing' (Murdoch, 1997 [1951], p. 35). However, although initially Murdoch is attracted by this concept and recognizes Sartre's descriptions in her own experience, we shall see that, as her philosophy developed, she was dissatisfied with the existentialist explanation and sought other explanations for the feeling of void. Thus, while Murdoch praises Sartre's defence of consciousness, she considers the picture he presents of consciousness as ultimately unrealistic as, although 'Sartre concludes that an outsider cannot know better than I the meaning of my state of mind; but he does not consider what is, for me, the meaning of my state of mind. He seems to treat meaning as a given constituent of the transparent cogitatio' (Murdoch, 1997 [1950b], p. 119). Murdoch objects to this transparency, and condemns it as an 'unrealistic and overoptimistic doctrine' (Murdoch, 1970a, pp. 46–7). Her main criticism is that Sartre's picture of consciousness is reductionist, by reducing morality simply to the free choice of the will, for 'on the one hand there is the mass of psychological desires and social habits and prejudices, on the other hand there is the will' (Murdoch, 1997 [1961], p. 289). The emphasis on the freedom of the will, for Murdoch, makes 'meaning egocentric' (Murdoch, 1997 [1952], p. 139), as 'freedom, considered as negation and project, is the main character of human consciousness' (ibid., p. 137). Indeed Murdoch might be tempted to say the freedom of the will is the only aspect of the inner life which survives in Sartre's existentialism, because 'it is the

The 'Inner Life' of the Individual      29

individual choice which founds freedom and value, giving to my actions a meaning which otherwise they would not have . . . I am free as long as I am conscious' (ibid., p. 138). For Sartre, then, the individual is outside the world,

> by attributing to the individual an empty lonely freedom, a freedom, if he wishes, to 'fly in the face of the facts'. What it pictures is indeed the fearful solitude of the individual marooned upon a tiny island in the middle of a sea of scientific facts, and morality escaping from science only by a wild leap of the will. (Murdoch, 1970a, p. 27)

The existentialist will becomes the loci of all moral personality, and this 'solitary will' is considered to be totally free and consequently 'the world it moves in must be devoid of normative characteristics, so that morality can reside entirely in the pointer of pure choice' (Murdoch, 1970a, p. 42). Thus Murdoch concludes that Sartre's picture of self-knowledge is 'negative and destructive' (Murdoch, 1997 [1957b], p. 149) and inaccurate.[12] The elevation of the individual consciousness denies both the reality of the world, the reality of other people and the complex nature of the inner self: 'truth somehow depends on him. There is no human nature, Sartre tells us, there is only the human condition' (Murdoch, 1997 [1952], p. 134). For Murdoch, as we shall see more clearly in the next chapter, this separation of consciousness and the rest of reality is misguided, and she states that 'it becomes clear that it is a mistake to demand a single clear essence for a vague concept, that the question of objectivity or truth cannot be excluded at any point from an analysis of our consciousness of the world' (Murdoch, 1997 [1950b], p. 120).

    Thus, although she recognizes that 'Sartre begins by rejecting the more or less behaviouristic theories' (ibid., p. 116), she eventually comes to the conclusion that the picture of the individual he espouses is little different from the behaviourist model he opposes. Hence she speaks of the 'existentialist–behaviourist type of moral psychology' (Murdoch, 1970a, pp. 10, 20; 1992, p. 50). As Conradi notes, by the time Murdoch wrote *Sovereignty of the Good* 'existentialism' stands for both 'Anglo-Saxon and Continental European philosophies' (Conradi, 1997, p. xxvi); in short, for all the philosophies of her contemporaries. At this point she has come to classify 'together as existentialist both philosophers such as Sartre who claim the title, and philosophers such as Hampshire, Hare, Ayer, who do not' (Murdoch, 1970a, p. 35). Murdoch argues that 'existentialism and empiricism . . . share a number of motives and doctrines . . . both philosophies are against traditional metaphysics, attack substantial theories of the mind, have a touch of Puritanism, construe virtue in terms of will rather than in terms of knowledge . . . are neo-Kantian' (Murdoch, 1997 [1959b], p. 267).

    Murdoch's concept of empirical man, which she attributes to British empiricism and linguistic analysis, derives in part, according to Murdoch, from the work of Wittgenstein. 'Linguistic analytical man', whom she finds in Hampshire, Hare, Ryle and Ayer, she believes finds echos and inspiration

30 *The Moral Vision of Iris Murdoch*

in the work of Wittgenstein. In this picture Murdoch considers the inner life to be like the existentialist picture, in that it is the outer effect of action (following the inner act of will) which is fundamental. Although existentialism appears at first glance to offer a robust description of consciousness, we have seen that, according to Murdoch, this collapses into the will, which ultimately leads to the reduction of the inner, and the predominance of the outer. Both philosophies distrust the inner: Sartre's existentialist man 'mistrusts his inner life and finds it insubstantial: to attribute substance to it is to fall into insincerity' (ibid., p. 269); and empirical/linguistic man likewise denies the reality of the inner life. Here Murdoch looks to Wittgenstein. Murdoch contends that Wittgenstein's denial of the inner life – I cannot know what I am thinking, but only what another is, as verification can only be outward and empirical (Murdoch, 1992, p. 160) – has had a profound effect on empirical philosophy. Thus she argues that post-Wittgensteinian philosophy has 'tended to remove ideas of "consciousness" and of "presence" from the philosophical scene' (ibid., p. 220). Murdoch attributes these Wittgensteinian tendencies to the philosophies of 'Hampshire, Hare, Ayer, Ryle and others' (Murdoch, 1970a, p. 12).

Wittgenstein's reliance on outward criteria for certain knowledge results in the denial of the inner in its entirety: 'Wittgenstein seems to have banished . . . the whole multifarious mixed-up business of our inner reflections, thought-being, experience, consciousness' (Murdoch, 1992, p. 297). To illustrate this conclusion Murdoch uses the example of Wittgenstein's argument concerning how concepts are known. 'Red' like any other concept can only be known by its public structure, established in shared situations. Murdoch responds that, if knowledge of 'red' can only be known in the public sphere, then how much more does this theory of knowledge bear down upon the 'very much more shadowy inner entities which might be supposed to be the "objects" of which mental concepts are names' (Murdoch, 1970a, p. 11). More importantly, Murdoch, with her preoccupation with moral activity, wishes to deny Wittgenstein's assertion that concepts such as decision are public concepts. From Wittgenstein's analysis the concept of 'decision' is learnt by 'watching someone who says "I have decided" and who then acts' (ibid., p. 13): '"decision" is not a mental act – the concept depends on (is verified by) public outward action' (Murdoch, 1992, p. 152). The concept 'decision' from this perspective has no inner element, decision can only be known by outward action. Murdoch protests vehemently at this assertion and wishes to assert that 'inner' decisions do indeed have meaning, and she states that 'Wittgenstein's image of "outer criteria" seems, in his use of it, unbearably narrow' (ibid., p. 275). Murdoch believes that Wittgenstein was 'embarrassed' by the concept of experience and hence the 'inner' and thus she asks, concerning his suspicion of the inner, 'can there not be too fierce a removal of entities deemed to be unnecessary and unknowable?' (ibid., p. 270). Murdoch believes that what began in the post-Cartesian era as valid criticisms of unquestioned concepts has gone too far, away from a reasonable and necessary critique 'toward a more thorough denial of the "inner life"' (ibid., p. 152).

*The 'Inner Life' of the Individual* 31

When the Wittgensteinian (linguistic/empirical view), which asserts that 'there is no inner life, and moral concepts too must have meaning through definite external criteria' (Murdoch, 1997 [1956], p. 79) is combined with the existentialist view that 'morality is choice' (ibid.), the result is 'modern philosophical man'. This picture then is a 'fusion of two dominant strands in recent philosophy – the Wittgensteinian repudiation of the "inner life", which construes inner states of self as shadows, as it were, cast by public observable behaviour; and the Kantian location of moral worth in the will' (Lloyd, 1982, p. 63). For such a man the moral life becomes one of 'sets of external choices backed up by arguments which appeal to facts' (Murdoch, 1997 [1956], p. 80). This picture combines 'linguistic analytical man' (who has the characteristics of 'freedom (in the sense of detachment, rationality), responsibility, self awareness, sincerity, and a lot of utilitarian common sense' (Murdoch, 1970a, p. 49)) and Sartre's existentialist man (who likewise has similar characteristics of freedom, responsibility, self-awareness and of course the primary existentialist value, of sincerity). Murdoch makes the parallels clearer in her paper 'The sublime and beautiful revisited' in which she contrasts 'Ordinary language man' (from 'linguistic empiricism', Murdoch, 1997 [1959b], p. 270) and 'Totalitarian man' (from Sartre's form of existentialism) which, though different in detail, she regards as similar in a number of ways:

> existentialism shares with empiricism a terror of anything which encloses the agent or threatens his supremacy as a centre of significance. In this sense both philosophies tend toward solipsism. Neither pictures virtue as concerned with anything real outside ourselves. Neither provides us with a standpoint for considering real human beings in their variety, and neither presents us with any technique for exploring and controlling our own spiritual energy. (Ibid., p. 269)

All of these pictures identify 'the true person with the empty choosing will' (Murdoch, 1970a, p. 35). Moreover, by reducing the inner life to the act of will, 'I' becomes nothing more than 'a foot-loose, solitary, substanceless will. Personality dwindles to pure will' (ibid., p. 16). Therefore, according to Murdoch, these philosophies ultimately collapse into 'solipsism, moral relativism, and the unreal and romantic oscillation between behaviourism and free will' (Conradi, 1997, pp. xxvi–xxvii).

The final picture of the individual she considers is that of Derrida's structuralism, with whom she is most concerned in her later work (as we shall see more clearly in the following chapter). The reason for this is that the existentialist picture she first admired, but then was so keen to discredit, became less predominant by the time of her later writing, and Conradi suggests that this was in part due to Murdoch's criticisms of the position: 'It is hard to escape the conclusion that by the late 1970s Iris Murdoch had helped to render existentialism out of date' (ibid., p. xxix).[13] Indeed this seems to be borne out by Murdoch's assertion that 'structuralism has replaced existentialism as a popular "philosophy of our time"' (Murdoch, 1992, p. 157). Murdoch is highly

32　　　　　　　　*The Moral Vision of Iris Murdoch*

critical of structuralism, as she sees it as a determinist philosophy which threatens, not only the individual, but all concepts of experience and truth. We shall focus on Murdoch's criticisms of structuralism in detail in the next chapter; for now, however, it is simply worth noting that Murdoch believes that structuralism threatens the individual and produces a philosophy in which 'consciousness vanishes' (ibid., p. 374). Because, for Derrida, knowledge and meaning are language dependent, there 'can, really, be no knower, only a network of meanings (the infinitely great net of language itself) under which there is nothing' (ibid., p. 187). Therefore no knower, no consciousness, no concept of an individual self; 'the concept of the individual which we have inherited from centuries of thinkers cannot any longer be taken for granted' (ibid., p. 202). Murdoch praises this removal of certainty regarding the falsely assumed unity of the self, and indeed praises structuralism (along with Wittgenstein) for removing errors and false assumptions. However, Murdoch wishes to defend the self (not the unquestioned unitary self of Descartes, but the reality of a complex inner life), thus she asserts that 'the implications of structuralism with its threat to accepted conceptions of truth, value, individual, impels us (felicitously) to argue in new ways for what we take to be fundamental and have perhaps too much, both as philosophers and laymen, taken for granted' (ibid., p. 215), which of course is what Murdoch is attempting to do.

Although structuralism raises new issues for Murdoch, her criticisms that the individual inner has been reduced away remains the cause of her attack on structuralism no less than on her previous opponents in the debate (existentialism and empiricism, to categorize crudely). Her wish to stop this reductionism becomes the source of her constructive philosophy to defend the individual self and a complex structure of the inner life. Indeed, as Conradi notes, despite the differences in these philosophies, Murdoch clearly conceived of them as constituting a similar threat to the inner and thus being related, as 'both tend towards and encourage moral relativism and solipsism. Both arrogantly divide the world between determinism and free will' (Conradi, 1997, p. xxix). Murdoch rejects all of these positions and continues to defend the concept of the self against them; as Antonaccio notes, 'throughout her diverse philosophical, political and literary writings over a half-century, she protested against reductionist accounts of the human individual bequeathed by modern philosophy and modern science' (Antonaccio, 2000, p. 76).

## Murdoch's Response

For all these philosophies which Murdoch is writing in opposition to – existentialism, behaviourism, empiricism, linguistic analysis and structuralism – 'there is nothing "in" the mind except otiose imagery, daydreams, viscous stuff, (etc.), then morality must *consist* of *de facto* conduct or acts of will' (Murdoch, 1992, p. 50). Murdoch completely rejects these pictures and argues that they are 'not, and cannot by tinkering be made, the philosophy we

# The 'Inner Life' of the Individual

need' (Murdoch, 1970a, p. 46). These philosophies for Murdoch present false pictures of the human condition and she states that 'our picture of ourselves has become too grand, we have isolated, and identified ourselves with, an unrealistic conception of will, we have lost the vision of a reality separate from ourselves' (ibid., p. 47).

In Murdoch's view the world is not morally inert, therefore the total freedom of the existentialist will cannot be accurate, nor can the inner life be reduced to the action of a solitary, rational will, leaving morality as nothing but choice and action. In the next chapter we will consider the moral features of the world which constrain individual freedom. For the second half of the present chapter we will consider Murdoch's alternative vision of the inner life upon which her concept of moral experience, so central to her moral realism, which presents 'the self not merely as a choosing agent but also as a being with mysterious inward depths who finds itself encompassed by a moral world' (Antonaccio, 2000, p. 45) is based.

Murdoch rejects all the pictures of the self presented by her contemporaries and she argues that we must 'resist tendencies which give value and effective function only to the outer (thought of as "moral acts" or as linguistic activity), or regard the "inner life" as fantasy and dream, lacking identity and definition, even as a fake illusory concept' (Murdoch, 1992, p. 348). Positions which regard the inner in this light lead, according to Murdoch, to 'a behaviourist moral philosophy, or toward an existentialist or structuralist reduction . . . [or] . . . utilitarian moral thinking' (ibid.), all of which Murdoch regards as misguided. Murdoch accuses philosophy of lacking the 'energy to defend or re-examine the old idea of the self, the truth-seeking individual person, as a moral and spiritual centre' (ibid., p. 161). As we have seen, Murdoch values the post-Cartesian critique of the self, and praises these philosophies (including structuralism which, as we shall see in the next chapter, she is highly critical of) for 'removing old Cartesian errors' (ibid., p. 153). Moreover, she continues that 'it is a merit of structuralism to indicate to us, with so much energy and so much learning, that the concept of individual which we have inherited from centuries of thinkers cannot any longer be taken for granted but must be defended' (ibid., p. 202). Yet, although recognizing the validity of these attacks in removing false assumptions about the self, they have rendered problematic 'the common-sense conception of the individual self as a moral centre or substance' (ibid., p. 153). It is for this ordinary sense of self that Murdoch wishes to find some philosophically acceptable place; a place for 'the *present*, the moment-to-moment consciousness which philosophers tend to be embarrassed by, to neglect, to analyse away' (ibid., p. 219). Murdoch argues that

> the concept of experience or consciousness has been passed over because philosophical styles have not offered a suitable mode of description and because philosophers have lacked the motives to attempt description, for instance in cases where a Kantian positive conception of the moral will, separate from and interrupting the stream of experience, deprives ordinary awareness and 'mere feelings' of value, interest, and function. (Ibid.)

34 *The Moral Vision of Iris Murdoch*

For Murdoch this reaction, while understandable, is extreme and indeed leads to a false picture of the human being in which the self has been lost: 'how does all this leave us, the individuals, where does it leave our thought-stream, our private reflections, where does it leave *truth*, if our foundations are so shaky and our judgements so shadowy?' (ibid., p. 272). While Murdoch accepts as valid the removal of a unified concept of the self, she does not believe that the self should be removed from philosophy altogether. She argues (as indeed Hume did when outside his study), that we 'believe with complete undoubting confidence in the real existence of the things (the "external world") round about us; and (it may seem) with similar confidence in our own existence, the authority of our own mind, the indubitable immediacy and continuity of our conscious self' (ibid., p. 160). Murdoch argues that philosophy, in recognizing the difficulty of adequately accounting for the self, has responded simply by ignoring the concept – a mistake which she wishes to rectify.

Murdoch believes that this neglect of the self must be addressed and philosophy must seek to analyse the new disunited self, arguing that

> phenomena such as 'thoughts' and 'symbolic experiences' must find their place too in any philosophical description of the mind. It is such happenings, heavily weighted as they so often are with a content which seems to go beyond consciousness, that give to the idea of 'immediate experience' that inexhaustible richness. (Murdoch, 1953, p. 58)[14]

The re-establishment of a viable concept of the self Murdoch regards as fundamental to producing an accurate model of human personhood. Without a concept of the self, Murdoch fears that the notion of experience will be lost; 'the detailed mobility of consciousness, its polymorphous complexity and the inherence of its constant evaluation, is lost' (Murdoch, 1992, p. 237). Murdoch here is defiant; she asks, 'what about morality and responsibility and individuals? And what about ordinary consciousness and experience . . . Something is lost, the existing incarnate individual with his real particular life of thought perceptions and moral living' (ibid., p. 202). In a similar vein, at a different point Murdoch repeats her criticism, stating that 'we feel we have lost something: our dense familiar inner stuff, private and personal, with a quality and a value of its own, something which we can scrutinise and control' (ibid., p. 153). This conviction, that 'something is lost', functions as a starting-point for her own positive conception of the self. Murdoch recognizes that her wish to defend the self is, in part, an emotional reaction and accepts that 'this naïve reaction needs to be philosophically justified' (ibid., p. 202) and it is her attempt to do this – to reinstate the inner life and the self – which we will now explore.

## Reclaiming the Self

Murdoch's aim is philosophically to find a way of reclaiming the self, a means of describing the realm of the inner, to fill the 'void in present-day moral

The 'Inner Life' of the Individual 35

philosophy' (Murdoch, 1970a, p. 46), to find 'a working philosophical psychology ... which can at least attempt to connect modern psychological terminology with terminology concerned with virtue' (ibid.). Murdoch believes that finding a way to describe the self philosophically should be a central task of moral philosophy. She holds that we should seek to escape the implications of present-day philosophy and to overcome the difficulty in describing the self which besets the current situation; a situation described by Murdoch as 'one of those exasperating moments in philosophy when one seems to be being relentlessly prevented from saying something which one is irresistibly impelled to say' (ibid., p. 21). As Conradi states, Murdoch's aim is to find a means by which 'moral philosophy can discuss and reclaim "consciousness", "experience" or "introspectabilia"' (Conradi, 1997, p. xxv). While Murdoch accepts the criticisms of a unitary self of which she is an heir, she objects to the neglect of the self in light of these criticisms, and regards philosophy as having failed to create an alternative vision of the self which takes these criticisms into account: 'where the central problem of human consciousness is concerned the alleged "disappearance" of the self has not led to any new philosophical enlightenment, or clear indication concerning how we are to discuss in a more realistic way a demythologised and (apparently) disunited self' (Murdoch, 1992, p. 162).

Murdoch recognizes the philosophical difficulties of the 'old unified self' and even asks whether we should even attempt philosophically to recognize the concepts of 'self', 'experience' and 'consciousness', as she does accept that these concepts do seem to imply 'the name of something, soul, ego, psyche, essential person' (ibid., p. 147); an assumption which she recognizes in light of the post-Cartesian critique would be a naïve position. Yet, despite the difficulty in accommodating the concept of the self, she continues to regard the individual self as a primary concept of human experience (and, as we shall see, particularly human moral experience). She insists that '"self" is a concept which does not trouble us as ordinary people. We get along with being the self without difficulty' (ibid.). The recognition that the self is an intuitive concept in ordinary life is, for Murdoch, a starting-point and a recurring theme throughout her work, and she asserts that 'the layman lives at peace with "consciousness", with all its obscure implications of "ownership" and "presence". It is what is most his own, he is responsible for it, even though it may seem to include so much that is not momentary or personal or private or clearly visible' (ibid., p. 173). It is this ordinary recognition of the self, including its fragmentary nature, that Murdoch wishes to defend philosophically, and she argues that 'the "person" we wish to defend here, endorsed by common-sense, is not so easily magicked away. Our present moment, our experiences, our flow of consciousness, our indelible moral sense, are not all these essentially linked together and do they not *imply* the individual?' (ibid., p. 153). For Murdoch they clearly do, and upon the concept of the individual and individual experience her moral philosophy depends, for the self is necessary if we are to conceive of '*perception*, and awareness of detail ... as the property of the individual' (ibid., p. 378) and the seat of moral experience.

36 *The Moral Vision of Iris Murdoch*

Murdoch asserts the concept of the individual self, with an inner life, whose inner experience is fundamental; for her, this seems to be an almost self-evident starting-point; 'we must believe in causality, in persons and objects and in the substantial continuity of our own being. What would it be not to?' (ibid., p. 164). Despite the fragmentary nature of the self, Murdoch asserts that 'what we call "the stream of consciousness" – surely . . . is something fundamental' (ibid., pp. 172–3); indeed so much so that Murdoch contends that 'so far from raising doubts about morality, it seems to me that morality is "proved" by its indelible inherence to the secret mind' (ibid., p. 259); this is because the 'moment-to-moment reality of consciousness . . . is, after all, where we live' (ibid., p. 257).

## Describing the Inner

Murdoch intends to show that the inner life can indeed be at least to some extent described, explained and communicated, and that the inner as well as the outer has validity. Indeed, Murdoch argues that a picture of human being and human reasoning which lacks a concept of the inner life is a false picture, as without the inner 'something vital is missing' (Murdoch, 1970a, p. 9). Indeed, as early as 1951 in her paper, 'Thinking and Language', Murdoch argues that thought and the inner life can be metaphorically described and that this 'technique' we use 'naturally, as part of our ordinary living, and that there seems no philosophical reason for abandoning it. One should rather attempt to investigate it and make it if possible more accurate' (Murdoch, 1997 [1951], p. 39): something which Murdoch proceeded to spend the next 40 years trying to do. Murdoch considers that the correct response to the difficulties of the self, so strenuously pointed out by her contemporaries, 'should not be to denounce an illusion and suggest that the inner *is nothing*, or is at best shadowy and nameless. One should attempt a new description' (ibid., p. 38). Murdoch defends the inner and declares, in contrast to her contemporaries, that 'surely there are *private* decisions? Surely there are lots and lots of objects, more or less easily identified, in orbit as it were in inner space? It is not . . . silent and dark within' (Murdoch, 1970a, p. 13).

Murdoch contends that, simply because the inner is hard to describe and certainly fragmentary, there is no reason to believe it does not exist. She states that inner happenings

> are hard to 'pin down' or describe precisely. They elude close observation (although so do many physical sensations), they are difficult to sum up (so is the smile of the Mona Lisa), their movement is hard to characterise (so is that of the waves), they have to be defined in terms of their intention (so would a sketchy drawing) and described as part of a total process (so would a movement made as part of a game). (Murdoch, 1997 [1953], pp. 48–9)

Yet despite this difficulty for Murdoch the inner life is indubitably 'there', it exists and moreover is fundamental to the establishment of the individual.

## The 'Inner Life' of the Individual

Hence Murdoch talks of the 'shyness and elusiveness of the mental event' (ibid., p. 48), a description which is accurate, but in no way belies the reality of the event. Murdoch argues that all we have to do to establish the reality of the inner is to examine our own experience, saying that 'we know what it is like to try to recall a state of mind – it is *as if* there is something there the exact character of which we cannot yet quite descry' (Murdoch, 1997 [1951], p. 41). In her last philosophical work, *Metaphysics as a Guide to Morals*, she continues to assert this conviction:

> We can examine our own states of mind and test them, we see 'into' them, we need not accept them at their face value (do I really intend this act, do I really love this person?), nor are we bound to dismiss them as mere dreamy fancies or drifting rubble. (Murdoch, 1992, p. 265)

Therefore, for Murdoch, 'our "innerness" may be elusive or hard to describe but it is not unimportant' (ibid.). When the inner life is permitted we recognize that 'the intense lively privacy of the individual "inner life" presents itself as something not to be analysed away' (ibid., p. 278). Consciousness then becomes a concept which is 'unique, essential, and difficult to talk about, yet what is closer and (in a sense) what else is there?' (ibid., p. 328). Inner experiences Murdoch claims 'are not unusual experiences or ones especially connected with aesthetic or philosophical reflections . . . these marvels are happening all the time' (ibid., p. 266). Moreover, it is inner experience which forms the fundamental mode of our human being. Experience – '*experience is consciousness*' (ibid., p. 279) – 'is deep and complex, it has density, thoughts and perceptions and feelings are combined in the swift movement of our mode of existence' (ibid.).

For support for her argument Murdoch turns to literature, and particularly to novels, where she says that, despite the difficulty in describing philosophically an inner event when we read literature, we have no difficulty in understanding the inner events of characters in novels, just as we can understand other people's descriptions of their inner lives: 'not that we necessarily offer each other the same descriptions . . . and that yet we can understand each other and even come to influence what the other experiences' (Murdoch, 1997 [1951], p. 37). Given the difficulty in present-day philosophy in describing the reality of consciousness, Murdoch suggests that 'the boundaries of what may be called "conscious awareness" or "consciousness" are hazy, and some of these outer areas are more easily suggested by novelists and poets than analytically described by philosophers' (Murdoch, 1992, p. 196). Murdoch asserts that 'we have no difficulty in understanding novelists, and it is natural here to speak of awareness, perceiving, experiences, consciousness, and to speak of someone's world' (ibid., p. 264). For example, inner monologues are of supreme importance in novels and Murdoch cites *Daniel Deronda*, stating that, 'when Gwendolen hesitates to throw the lifebelt to her detested husband, who subsequently drowns, it matters very much to her to

38                    *The Moral Vision of Iris Murdoch*

know whether or not at the moment she intended his death' (Murdoch, 1997 [1951], p. 36). Accordingly, in novels, 'we follow, in context, these descriptions of states of consciousness with no difficulty' (Murdoch, 1992, p. 171). Moreover, Murdoch argues that 'streams of consciousness in fiction are usually moral indicators' (ibid., p. 258) and show us changes in consciousness; 'we understand what a bad texture of consciousness is like, equally we understand what a good one is like, and what sort of changes lead from one to the other' (ibid., p. 261). Murdoch cites examples of such changes, 'such well-known phenomena' (ibid.), from literature: 'Anna Karenina's consciousness of Kitty's family before she falls in love with Vronsky is quite different from what it is afterwards . . . Pierre sees a different world after he realises that his marriage to Helen was a *moral* mistake' (ibid.).

**Inner Activity**

It is this moral change, moral activity, which occurs in the privacy of the inner life which Murdoch is so keen to assert. Indeed, as we shall see more clearly in the course of the next few chapters, it is personal experience which provides us with our awareness of moral value, around which the whole of Murdoch's moral philosophy is constructed. Having asserted the importance of inner activity and its moral importance, Murdoch goes on to describe the nature of the inner life and inner moral change using the example of a mother-in-law's moral deliberation and consequent change which happens entirely in the inner realm:

> A mother, whom I shall call M, feels hostility to her daughter-in-law, whom I shall call D. M finds D quite a good-hearted girl, but while not exactly common yet certainly unpolished and lacking in dignity and refinement, D is inclined to be pert and familiar, insufficiently ceremonious, brusque, sometimes positively rude, always tiresomely juvenile. M does not like D's accent or the way D dresses. M feels that her son has married beneath him. Let us assume for purpose of the example that the mother, who is a very 'correct' person, behaves beautifully to the girl throughout, not allowing her real opinion to appear in any way. We might underline this aspect of the example by supposing that the young couple have emigrated or that D is now dead: the point being to ensure that whatever is in question as *happening* happens entirely in M's mind . . . M tells herself: 'I am old-fashioned and conventional. I may be prejudiced and narrow-minded. I may be snobbish. I am certainly jealous. Let me look again.' Here I assume that M observes D or at least reflects deliberately about D, until gradually her vision of D alters. If we take D to be now absent or dead this can make it clear that the change is not in D's behaviour but in M's mind. D is discovered to be not vulgar but refreshingly simple, not undignified but spontaneous, not noisy but gay, not tiresomely juvenile but delightfully youthful, and so on. (Murdoch, 1970a, pp. 17–18)

Murdoch wishes to argue that, in this example, nothing has happened in the outer realm; the mother-in-law's 'outward behaviour, beautiful from the start, in no way alters' (ibid., p. 18). Murdoch recognizes that there are different readings of the mother-in-law's behaviour and that various motives could be attached to her, for example, that she deludes herself, or indeed it could be concluded that 'M decided to behave well to D and did so; and M's private thoughts will be unimportant and morally irrelevant' (ibid., p. 18). Yet Murdoch does not wish to take this essentially 'outer' view, rather she wishes to assert that 'there is at least something introspective which has occurred, however hazy this may be' (ibid., p. 19). Moreover, Murdoch wishes to say that what has occurred has been inner activity of a moral kind: 'that M has been *doing* something, something which we approve of, something which is somehow worth doing in itself. M has been morally active' (ibid., pp. 19–20). This for Murdoch is something that 'we want to say and to be philosophically permitted to say' (ibid., p. 20). In addition, Murdoch wishes to say that this inner moral activity is connected to the particular individual: that 'M's activity is peculiarly *her own*. Its details are the details of *this* personality; and partly for this reason it may well be activity which can only be performed privately' (ibid., p. 23). Murdoch asserts that this sense of inner activity and especially this type of moral change which involves internal struggle, while excluded from philosophical discourse, 'far from being something very odd and hazy, is something which we find exceedingly familiar' (ibid., p. 22).

Murdoch's conception of inner activity is that it is both private and moral and that it is the seat of moral decision making. The stream of consciousness, however fragmentary and 'lost' this stream may be, is a 'place where we are at home, which we *seem* to leave and then return to, which is the fundamental seat of our freedom, has moral colour, moral sensibility' (Murdoch, 1992, p. 260). Thus Murdoch is claiming 'consciousness or self-being as the fundamental mode or form of moral being' (ibid., p. 171). At one level this is the assertion that one can feel 'morally responsible for having had a particular thought' (Murdoch, 1997 [1953], p. 46) but at a more fundamental level Murdoch is arguing that moral evaluation, choice and action reside in the inner life, not that action is not a necessary part of morality, but that it is not separable from the inner: 'the inner needs the outer and the outer needs the inner' (Murdoch, 1992, p. 348).[15]

## Morality and the Inner Life

Murdoch claims that her picture of morality as residing in the inner life (connected to actions) of the agent, is a familiar picture to the ordinary person.[16] Murdoch supports this claim by considering how we perceive other people and their actions. She suggests that when we consider what a person is like only part of our evaluation is based on what they do, how they act; in addition, 'we consider something more elusive which may be called their total vision of life . . . the texture of a man's being or nature of his personal vision' (Murdoch, 1997 [1956], pp. 80–81). In other words we are interested in how

40 *The Moral Vision of Iris Murdoch*

they think and feel about the world and other people; we need to know their inner life before we can make a judgment. It is these signifiers of the inner which we seek in order to know a 'person's "moral nature" or "moral being"' (ibid., p. 81). If we wish to describe a person as good 'we are led also to reflect on his states of consciousness, his capacity for recollection, for reflection, for *attention*, for the deep intuitive syntheses of moral vision' (Murdoch, 1992, p. 378). The nature of the good life we will explore in detail later; however, for the moment, from Murdoch's example of the mother-in-law, we can see something of what she intends to convey by different qualities in states of consciousness, her conviction that there is a '(morally) higher and lower self evidenced by higher and lower thoughts and actions' (ibid., pp. 147–8). In the example of the mother-in-law we saw that it is a change towards a more moral perception of the daughter-in-law which Murdoch wishes to praise as a moral activity. Murdoch goes as far as to hold that 'morality, as the ability or attempt to be good, rests upon deep areas of sensibility and creative imagination, upon removal from one state of mind to another' (ibid., p. 337). In our one example (at present) of the mother-in-law we can see this philosophy in action. For Murdoch moral activity is found in the change of the mother-in-law's quality of consciousness or state of mind; hence, for her schema to work, 'the concept of consciousness and the concept of value "must" be internally linked' (ibid., p. 256).

## Conclusion

In Murdoch's picture, moral evaluation and decision making is conceived very differently from the way it is in the pictures of the self we considered in the first half of this chapter. The concept of 'choice' is dramatically reduced. The moral self is not connected to choice, to acts of will, rather moral activity lies in the background which has prepared us for choices, in the inner life, which 'goes on continually, not something that is switched off in between the occurrence of explicit moral choices' (Murdoch, 1970a, p. 37). It is not the moment of choice which is important, but 'what happens between such choices is indeed what is crucial' (ibid.), and the 'between' is the action of the inner life. The experience of moral value and the nature of the moral life in Murdoch's moral vision will be discussed in more detail in the following chapters, yet for now we must recognize the importance of the self to Murdoch's philosophy. The inner life must be regarded as real and important – 'the experiential stream as a cognitive background to activity' (Murdoch, 1992, p. 267) – as it is in the inner life 'in the tissue of life that the secrets of good and evil are found' (Murdoch, 1970a, p. 54). Moral activity according to this view is constantly occurring and is connected to the whole of one's being (again a concept we will return to) and as a consequence 'moral tasks are characteristically endless' (ibid., p. 28), as our 'concept of consciousness, the stream of consciousness, is *animated* by indicating a moral dimension' (Murdoch, 1992, p. 260). The inner life is then essential as it is the individual who is the moral agent and

## The 'Inner Life' of the Individual 41

recognizes moral values, has moral knowledge and strives to be good. For now the importance of individual selves who have inner lives and perform moral activity is all we need to recognize, as from here Murdoch will go on to assert that 'we need the concept of consciousness to understand how morality is cognitive; how there is no ubiquitous gulf fixed between fact and value, intellect and will' (ibid., p. 265). The use to which Murdoch puts the concept of the self in her moral philosophy we will explore in the following chapters as we build a full picture of her moral vision. Clearly, Murdoch's view of the self is controversial and runs contrary to almost the whole of twentieth-century philosophy. Yet, despite the controversy, if one is to consider her philosophy at all, one must accept the possibility of inner experience and the self. Arguably, Murdoch has not presented arguments for her concept of the inner; rather she has asserted that the current pictures of human being are inadequate because in her opinion, human beings are simply not like that. However, even if one is not convinced by Murdoch's arguments, one may still feel that her assertion that 'something is lost' points to reductionism in current philosophical pictures of the self and morality. This recognition is enough to make Murdoch's comments on the inner life valuable and Murdoch will have succeeded in her attempt at least to get us to imagine, 'to "get us to see" an alternative' (Kleinig, 1971, p. 112) picture of the self.

## Notes

1 This is evident from her first paper, 'Thinking and Language', published in 1951, which is concerned with describing inner events, to her final philosophical work, *Metaphysics as a Guide to Morals*. Indeed so important did Antonaccio judge the importance of rehabilitating the inner life and consciousness to Murdoch that she titled her book on the subject *Picturing the Human: The Moral Thought of Iris Murdoch*.

2 The decline of religion and the effect of this are another central preoccupation of Murdoch's that is evident throughout her work, and will be explored incrementally when the topic arises and in detail in Chapter 7, on religion.

3 Murdoch observes at many points that this view of personality, deriving, according to her, most notably from the combined thinking of Hume and Kant, is 'the liberal theory of personality' (Murdoch, 1997 [1959b], p. 262): the 'natural mode of being of the capitalist era' (Murdoch, 1997 [1970], p. 224), and 'the heir of nineteenth-century Luciferian pride in the individual and in the achievements of science' (ibid., p. 226). It is one which 'suggests individualism, self-reliance, private conscience and what we ordinarily think of as political freedom, in that important sense where freedom means not doing what is right but doing what is desired' (ibid., p. 224). In the liberal view of man 'we picture the individual as able to attain by reflection to complete consciousness of his situation. He is entirely free to choose and responsible for his choice. His morality is exhibited by his choice' (Murdoch, 1997 [1957a], p. 70).

4 Indeed Murdoch seems to praise Hume in this regard, commenting that 'Hume's remedy lies here nearest to common-sense: habit and custom conceal the lack of any genuine foundation' (Murdoch, 1992, p. 258). A comment she repeats, 'Hume overcame his scepticism by cheerfulness and common sense' (ibid., p. 272)

42 *The Moral Vision of Iris Murdoch*

5   The origins of her contemporaries' picture of the self being found in the conjunction of the philosophies of Hume and Kant is a point which Murdoch returns to on many occasions; it 'combines the philosophical insight of Hume (we live in a world of disconnected facts) with that of Kant (morality is rational and seeks universally valid reasons)' (Murdoch, 1997 [1956], p. 79). One side of the picture is derived from the 'Humian and post-Humian side. On the other side, we derive from Kant' (Murdoch, 1997 [1961], p. 288); 'the remote ancestors of this view are Hume, Kant, and Mill' (Murdoch, 1997 [1956], p. 77). Murdoch does not dwell on the contribution of Mill, although she does suggest that this view 'more surreptitiously . . . embodies the morality of Mill ("a creed learnt by heart is paganism")' (Murdoch, 1997 [1956], p. 78).

6   Murdoch uses 'structuralism' or 'Derrida's structuralism' somewhat confusingly to denote what would usually be termed 'deconstruction'. Given the prevalence of this term in her work, the text follows her (albeit unusual) terminology. However, as we shall discover, her major criticisms of post-structuralism are concerned not with the picture of the self, but with the fact/value divide and their location of meaning in language.

7   Although Murdoch traces this view primarily to Hume and Kant, at times she seems to attribute it in a general form to all post-Kantian thinkers. As already noted, she reads the view in Mill and utilitarianism, calls it the liberal view, as well as attributing it to other thinkers. For example, at one point she describes it, not as a combination of the Humean and Kantian visions, but as deriving from Kant, Wittgenstein and Freud: 'this position represents . . . a happy and fruitful marriage of Kantian liberalism with Wittgensteinian logic solemnised by Freud' (Murdoch, 1970a, p. 9).

8   Hampshire's view is mostly taken from his book *Thought and Action* (1959), although he and Murdoch did know each other well and were friends as well as intellectual opponents (Conradi, 2001).

9   Murdoch described her meeting with Sartre in 1945 in a letter, stating that 'I am busily reading everything of his I can lay my hands on. The excitement – I remember nothing like it since the days of discovering Keats & Shelley & Coleridge when I was very young' (Conradi, 2001, p. 215).

10   Again here Murdoch adds that this view is 'also incidentally what may be called a democratic view, in that it suggests that morality is not an esoteric achievement but a natural function of any normal man' (Murdoch, 1970a, p. 9).

11   In her early work Murdoch was clearly enamoured by Sartre and she 'shared a deep sympathy with Sartre's underlying liberal assumption about the value of the individual freedom, even though she believed his philosophy failed adequately to support these values' (Antonaccio, 2000, p. 73). Yet Murdoch, unlike Sartre, does not isolate the self by equating it with the will, but rather 'grounds the self in a larger ontology of value' (ibid., p. 74).

12   However it is not clear where Murdoch draws the line between Sartre's novels and his philosophy, as clearly she is, especially in her early work, very impressed with the appeal of his philosophy, yet she states that, 'as a philosopher he attacks the idea of the unified self, explores the viscous, insubstantial nature of consciousness, and as a writer he describes his consciousness' (Murdoch, 1997 [1972], p. 250). Perhaps she prefers his literary accounts. However, as we shall see in Chapter 6, she is highly critical of the philosophical novelist and of Sartre in particular.

13   As Peter Conradi notes, in her 1978 interview for the BBC with Bryan Magee, Murdoch failed to mention existentialism at all, suggesting that by this point in time her interests had moved on (Conradi, 1997, p. xxix).

14   It is Murdoch's aim, as we will see more clearly in the next chapter, to establish that it is (moral) experience that makes the establishment of the inner so fundamental to her realism.

*The 'Inner Life' of the Individual* 43

15  She is emphatic in her insistence that she does not deny the importance of actions and the outer in morality: 'I would not be understood, either, as suggesting that insight or pureness of heart are more important than action . . . overt actions are perfectly obviously important in themselves, and important too because they are the indispensable pivot and spur of the inner scene. The inner, in *this* sense, cannot do without the outer' (Murdoch, 1970a, p. 43).

16  Indeed she argues that her own picture of the inner (moral) activity is one which 'would, to the ordinary person, be a very much more familiar image than the existentialist one' (Murdoch, 1970a, p. 30), and also, one would presume, this applies to the other alternative pictures of morality and the individual, including the structuralist perspective of which she is so critical in her later work, discussion of which we will encounter in more detail in the following chapter.

# Chapter 3

# Experiencing Morality

In the last chapter we explored Murdoch's critiques of the prevailing philosophies of her contemporaries and her dissatisfaction with their pictures of the self, regarding them as reductionist. In opposition to such schemas Murdoch asserts the importance of the 'inner life' and celebrates the capacity of individuals to have knowledge about themselves and the world. For her, ordinary human experience is a vital source of knowledge, particularly moral knowledge. It is from experience that we know that moral values are real, and in light of such experience that we order our thoughts and feelings, and according to which we act.

Having established the place of the inner life in Murdoch's philosophy in this chapter, we will consider the manner in which values are known. The conviction that moral values can be known, and are fundamental in the way we picture (and consequently act in) the world leads Murdoch to reject any division between fact and value, again in opposition to prevalent assumptions. Values are of a different order to facts; however, they are no less real. As Antonaccio notes, Murdoch is writing explicitly against 'the view that moral judgements lack truth status, she insists that human beliefs and judgements of value (aesthetic, moral, religious or otherwise) are not merely "opinions" or subjective exclamations, but fundamental modes of knowledge and explanation which refer meaningfully to the world' (Antonaccio, 2000, p. 50). Kerr sums up Murdoch's position well, stating that she 'is totally opposed to all those theories in ethics and aesthetics which may be classified as non-realist, anti-realist or projectivist' (Kerr, 1997, p. 84).

In this chapter we will begin by considering Murdoch's assertion of the continuity between fact and value and her critique of alternative positions. We will then go on to examine her realist conception of values known through ordinary experience and fundamental to all evaluation and decision making. Therefore, in the course of this chapter, as well as further exploring Murdoch's critiques of alternative philosophies, we will begin to see her substantive moral vision emerge.

## Confronting the Fact/Value Divide

Crucial to Murdoch's realism is the conviction that knowledge of value is rooted in experience of the world and forms the ground of all knowledge. In order to do this Murdoch must counter the prevalent division between fact

46 *The Moral Vision of Iris Murdoch*

and value which has dominated nineteenth- and twentieth-century Western philosophy, to the point where it tends to be assumed unquestioningly. Murdoch rejects this position and adopts a 'moral language that does not depend on a sharp distinction between fact and value' (Antonaccio, 2000, p. 121). Murdoch presents the fact/value divide as a process which grew out of philosophers' attempts to preserve value from encroaching scientific worldviews. Murdoch regards this approach as misguided, but initially well-meaning, the intention being to protect value, but one which ultimately resulted in the negation of value and, in its final stage – identified by Murdoch with 'Derrida's structuralism' – threatens the concept of truth in all its major forms.[1]

Murdoch traces this philosophical division of fact and value remorselessly through many influential thinkers and their schools of thought, including Hume, Kant, Moore, Marx, Sartre, Heidegger, Wittgenstein and Ayer, and ending with Derrida. Her aim is to show that the division which now dominates modern philosophy was neither envisaged nor intended by many of the thinkers influential in its establishment. Moreover, she hopes that, by her questioning the various stages of the process, the seeming unassailability of the division can be undermined. She regards the fact/value dichotomy as 'the most important argument in modern moral philosophy – indeed it is almost the whole of modern philosophy' (Murdoch, 1997 [1957a], p. 64) and it is this she must counter to assert her own realist vision. Indeed, her wish to overturn this argument is a primary inspiration and motivation for her philosophy as a whole. As Kerr comments, 'her own fear over the years has plainly been the fact/value dichotomy which has dominated philosophy since at least Hume and Kant [and] has had immensely destructive effects throughout our culture in aesthetics and especially in the realm of ethics' (Kerr, 1997, pp. 72–3).[2] Thus, if her own realist perspective is to be established, she must first successfully show the fallacy of the fact/value dichotomy.

## The Beginnings of the Fact/Value Divide: Hume

Murdoch begins with Hume, to whom she traces the beginnings of the fact/ value distinction, suggesting that its roots lie in his assertion that we cannot derive 'ought' from 'is'. Hume's important role in this process was to assert that moral values and judgment are matters of sentiment rather than reason: 'morality is determined by sentiment. It defines virtue to be *whatever mental action or quality gives to a spectator the pleasing sentiment of approbation*; and vice the contrary' (Hume, 1975 [1777], p. 289). Consequently, Hume's assertion means that morality becomes a matter of sentiment, rather than one of knowledge or reasoning. As a result, 'his doctrine means that moral distinctions do not report any objective features at all: moral goodness or rightness is not any quality or any relation to be found in or among objective situations or actions, and no purely intellectual or cognitive procedure can issue in moral judgement' (Mackie, 1980, p. 2). The assertion that morality is concerned with sentiment rather than reason is supported further by his conviction that motivation is also derived from sentiment (or desire, as it has later been equated in belief/desire theories – although for Hume 'sentiment' is broader than 'desire' as it is a capacity shared by all humans and an important tool for moral judgment[3]). For Hume,

> reason being cool and disengaged, is no motive to action, and directs only the impulse received from appetite or inclination, by showing us the means of attaining happiness or avoiding misery: Taste, as it gives pleasure or pain, and thereby constitutes happiness or misery, becomes a motive for action, and is the first spring or impulse to desire and volition. (Hume, 1975 [1777], p. 294)

Murdoch would accept a part of this early distinction, recognizing that values are of a different order from facts, as a valid premise for moral philosophy, since

> a proper separation of fact and value, as a defence of morality, lies in the contention that moral value cannot be *derived* from fact. That is, our activity of moral discrimination cannot be explained merely as one natural instinct among others, our 'good' *identified* with pleasure, or a will to live, or what the government says (etc.). (Murdoch, 1992, p. 26)

However, to accept that morality is sentiment and moreover that moral motivation is unconnected to knowledge and reason and derived from sentiment is a view that she cannot allow, as, particularly in its later forms, non-cognitivism is in danger of leading to subjectivism and relativism, views incompatible with Murdoch's realism.[4] For, once we move to values as non-cognitive and divide fact from value, as Kerr notes, 'it is fatally easy to slide into supposing that what is judged to be right and wrong can never be the facts but must always be nothing more than arbitrary and optional projection of our subjective feelings about the situation' (Kerr, 1997, p. 73). This is a possibility which Murdoch must avoid at all costs.[5] However, the thesis as it stands in Hume does not lead to these conclusions. For Hume, moral values remained universal, in that moral sentiment springs from a common human nature, from which we derive customs, habits and feelings which guide conduct, since morality is based on 'some internal sense or feeling, which nature has made universal for the whole species' (Hume, 1975 [1777], p. 173). Morality then is based on a shared moral sense, which for Hume is shown by the fact that 'the epithets *sociable, good-natured, humane, grateful, friendly, generous, beneficent*, or their equivalents, are known in all languages, and universally express the highest merit' (ibid., p. 176). Therefore morality continues to be regarded as universal and a reality by virtue of a shared human nature and, as Mackie comments, Hume 'leaves open the possibility that there should be objectively prescriptive moral truths or valid principles, some of which are discovered by a moral sense or by a faculty of moral intuition' (Mackie, 1980, p. 63). Thus value remains, in these shared responses to the world, part of the philosophical picture.

48 *The Moral Vision of Iris Murdoch*

Nonetheless, although in Hume the fact/value divide does not lead to relativism and he retains a strong concept of moral value, albeit recognized by the emotions, morality categorized as sentiment marks the beginning of a non-cognitive understanding of moral value. Later, when morality as sentiment is coupled with positivist philosophy, the possibility of moral objectivity is increasingly threatened. Because of such consequences Murdoch attacks Hume's division as false because it places moral value outside the sphere of normal (cognitive) knowledge. As a result, knowledge of value is seen as belonging to a different, and eventually lesser, order than other forms of knowledge. Thus facts become thought of as real and objective and values as on a par with feelings (an extrapolation from Hume's 'sentiment') and therefore subjective and uncertain. Truth therefore at this point becomes connected to fact and no longer to value.[6]

In addition to rejecting the hypothesis that moral value and judgment is a matter of sentiment, not surprisingly Murdoch also counters the secondary and related assertion that motivation is not cognitive.[7] If we placed Murdoch within the contemporary classifications in terms of motivational theory, Murdoch would be a cognitivist internalist.[8] However, to describe her so is to accept categories which Murdoch would deny. Murdoch challenges the divide between belief and desire (parallel to her rejection of the fact/value divide) which so dominates current theories of moral motivation. In her view, like fact and value (as we shall see more clearly as her vision of the moral life unfolds), belief and desire are also connected, as 'vision (as a form of knowledge or belief) itself contains desire that motivates the will to moral action . . . a moral belief automatically compels the will to act' (Antonaccio, 2000, p. 146). This, of course, is a Socratic view, that true knowledge results in right action. Murdoch's position regarding motivation is broadly Socratic. However, for her, attaining true knowledge of reality is a moral task in itself and by no means an easy one. For Murdoch, as we will explore in detail in later chapters, knowledge and action are related: 'not only does vision condition the will, but the will may also influence vision' (ibid.).

## Continuing the Fact/Value Divide: Kant, Post-Kantians and Wittgenstein

Kant, as Murdoch after him, was alarmed by the implications of Hume's non-cognitive conception of value and responded by asserting a cognitive moral picture in which moral value was determined rationally. For Kant moral knowledge is available; we know what is right and wrong by recognition of the moral law. Clearly, Murdoch has sympathy for Kant's conception of morality as ubiquitous and his wish to defend 'the unconditional or categorical nature of morality independently of theism by grounding it transcendentally in consciousness rather than in the command of a divine law giver' (Antonaccio, 1996, p. 225).[9] However, in his attempt to establish value as cognitive and grounded in rationality, Kant widens the fact/value division further, again from the best motives. In asserting the fundamental place of value, he continues to present knowledge of values and the moral law as a different order from knowledge of the contingent world of facts. Because of this, Murdoch rejects Kant's move, commenting that his 'sharp distinction between fact and value tends to make all morality "abstract" in relation to an alien world into which no value has been allowed to seep' (Murdoch, 1992, p. 382). Murdoch argues that this abstraction of value leads, even more so than with Hume's division, to the separation of fact from value. Accordingly she judges Kant and Kantians 'wrong to exclude knowledge from virtue' (Murdoch, 1997 [1959b], p. 284) since 'with the removal of Kant's metaphysical background [the] individual is seen as alone' (Murdoch, 1997 [1961], p. 288).[10] In other words, when removed from the Kantian background of the moral law, value becomes less easy to recognize and further removed from the reality of ordinary experience than before Kant's attempts which were intended to ensure the solidity of moral value.

This division between fact and value, now entrenched, continues in all subsequent moral philosophy, to the extent that Murdoch describes post-Kantian philosophy as being 'largely attempts at different versions of the fact–value distinction' (Murdoch, 1992, p. 40). The dichotomy between fact and value is, in Murdoch's reading, now ingrained into philosophical thought to the extent that it becomes an (unquestioned) premise of moral philosophy, both cognitive and non-cognitive. It is this foundational assumption with which Murdoch takes issue.[11] Murdoch wishes to assert that values are known in a not wholly dissimilar manner from facts. Moreover, she contends that dividing fact from value limits our concept of knowledge to nothing more than knowing facts, and facts conceived of according to the verification model. Such a model of knowing Murdoch deems reductionist, undermining not just our ability to know moral value but also our ability to have knowledge about many aspects of human life. True knowledge, for Murdoch, consists only to a very small extent of knowledge of empirical facts. The aesthetic, spiritual and emotional are also threatened by the ascendancy of 'fact' and no longer considered to be arenas of 'true' knowledge. Like value they become sentiment, preference and opinion.

Murdoch concludes that all divisions between fact and value ultimately reduce the sphere of human knowing and diminish our ability to perceive accurately the human (value-laden) world. For example, she argues that Moore's famous distinction between fact and value 'isolated and diminished his concept of good; as this distinction, in its many guises in moral philosophy, tends to do' (ibid., p. 46). Murdoch makes similar assessments as she traces the fact/value divide through post-Kantian philosophies, for example, Marxism, existentialism, behaviourism and eventually structuralism. In tracking the rise of the fact/value divide she continues to present the process as one which began innocently as an attempt to preserve value from an encroaching scientific worldview, but which inevitably resulted in value (and other essentially human aspects of the world) being negated, eventually to the point of irrelevance and virtual non-existence.

50 *The Moral Vision of Iris Murdoch*

Murdoch goes on to discuss Wittgenstein's contribution to the process of separating fact from value in detail.[12] The lack of explicit discussion of morality in Wittgenstein's philosophy Murdoch suggests stems from a wish (not dissimilar to Kant's) to protect value and keep it pure.[13] His refusal to talk about morality she regards as part of his more general refusal to talk about anything which resists clear and accurate definition. Such a stance Murdoch again attributes to valid motives, those of not wishing to discuss concepts and realities which can easily be misrepresented and misunderstood. Murdoch believes Wittgenstein had (at least in his early work) a strong sense of moral value. Murdoch quotes from his letters to Ludwig Ficker regarding the *Tractatus*, where Wittgenstein states that

> the book's point is an ethical one. I once meant to include in the preface a sentence . . . what I meant to write then was this: My work consists of two parts: the one presented here plus all that I have not written. And it is precisely this second part which is the important one. (Murdoch, 1992, p. 29)

Thus, far from being unaware or unconcerned with ethics, Murdoch argues that Wittgenstein was fundamentally aware of its importance, but he did not want to discuss what could not be fully defined and so risk falsehood. As a result, 'moral judgements were not factual, or truthful, and had no place in the world of the *Tractatus*' (Murdoch, 1970a, p. 48). Murdoch, while understanding his reasons for this policy of silence, condemns such an approach: 'such silence is contrary to respectable human instincts, we must talk, it keeps things going and out of traditions of ordinary talk great geniuses arise who make the impossible possible' (Murdoch, 1992, p. 123). Murdoch contends that absence of value (even if for admirable reasons) in Wittgenstein's philosophy means value is first forgotten and ultimately vanishes. Even if this is not always the case in his own work (as we have seen, Murdoch attributes to Wittgenstein a strong value awareness) it is without a doubt the position adopted by his followers. Murdoch suggests that even Wittgenstein, in his later philosophical period, was guilty of removing value completely (forgetting value rather than wishing to protect it). Accordingly, she accuses him of thrusting 'ethics almost out of philosophy' (Murdoch, 1970a, p. 48) and comments that, in *Philosophical Investigations*, one is left with a 'sense of loss' as the 'philosophical dichotomies and formulations often communicate this "reductive" feeling, the sense that something essential is now missing' (Murdoch, 1992, p. 49). That which is essential is of course, for Murdoch, value. The absence of value from Wittgenstein's philosophy is, for Murdoch, a typical example of the consequences of dividing fact from value, by now a philosophical orthodoxy. The ignoring of value in Wittgenstein is further justified by the verification model of facts. Murdoch comments that 'the verificationist view of meaning, entering philosophy from the side of natural science, made a violent impact on ethics' (Murdoch, 1997 [1957a], p. 60). Strengthening the divide and further isolating the supposedly true category of

*Experiencing Morality* 51

facts: 'ethical propositions were clearly and firmly separated from other types of proposition and have remained so ever since' (ibid.).

In Murdoch's understanding the beginnings of the division are misguided, but well motivated, and she argues that this 'misleading though attractive distinction . . . (as it is used by Kant and Wittgenstein for instance) is to *segregate* value in order to keep it pure and untainted, not derived from or mixed with empirical facts' (Murdoch, 1992, p. 25). Value was intended to benefit from the division by retaining a demarcated area, which would not be encroached upon by the increasingly dominant scientific paradigm enamoured of empirical fact. Unfortunately, this attempt produced the opposite effect: a 'diminished, even perfunctory, account of morality, leading (with the increasing prestige of science) to a marginalisation of "the ethical"' (ibid.). As a consequence, values became irrelevant and facts regarded as the only 'real' features of the world. Accordingly,

'Value' becomes difficult to discuss. The area of fact becomes more extensive and more present to us . . . Scientific views and methods spread from their proper place in science into peripheral areas. All sorts of theorists (including some philosophers) begin to feel that they must eschew value preferences and discussions of value, and offer themselves as neutral scientific workers. (Murdoch, 1992, pp. 50–51)

In this manner not only is the ethical marginalized but moral philosophy is also changed. Philosophy emerges from this metamorphis as a pseudo-scientific explanatory system, with little (and in some cases almost no) grounding in ordinary experience and reality.

## The Final Stage of the Fact/Value Divide: Structuralism

The final stage of the philosophical process which divided fact from value and so resulted in the marginalization of morality Murdoch identifies with structuralism, a philosophy which she regards as dangerous and pernicious in its absolute subjugation of the ethical. Murdoch argues that structuralism is the end-point of the division of fact and value, at which point truth is severed from meaning – the very consequence Kant feared would result from non-cognitive understandings of moral value. Structuralists complete the process of dividing fact from value by making an additional move to Wittgenstein's (and for different motives) in their claim that meaning is 'entirely enclosed in the self-referential system of language' (Murdoch, 1992, p. 193). The location of meaning within the language system, rather than in the real 'out there', or at least experienced, world is, for Murdoch,

the crucial move which, in structuralist theory, separates meaning from truth, outlaws the idea that truth rests on some kind of relation with a non-linguistic reality, and in effect denies the very possibility of truth. The removal from language of any reference except to other parts of language sweeps away not only the correspondence

52 *The Moral Vision of Iris Murdoch*

theory, but any theory, of truth. Meaning, then, is an internally self-related movement or *play* of language. (Ibid.)

Thus Murdoch declares that 'value, morality is removed by the structuralist picture if taken seriously' (ibid., p. 190).[14] The structuralist location of meaning in language Murdoch believes runs contrary to everything we know about the world from our ordinary, and for her correct, experience. Structuralism's critique of ordinary language gives 'the impression that our ordinary language is being, as it were, prised off the world, and is thus withering away' (ibid., p. 209), so destroying the individual's ability to grasp, order and act in their world. This is in direct contrast to her own view in which 'moral language . . . is an instrument of the individual's knowledge of herself and the world rather than determined by a public context on which all agents can agree' (Antonaccio, 2000, p. 90). Accordingly, she describes structuralism as 'non-moral, since it erases the idea of truthfulness and the common-sense idea of freedom which goes with it'(Murdoch, 1992, p. 200). Thus structuralism undermines the individual's ability to attain knowledge through experience and so threatens our fundamental conceptions of what it means to be human. In removing meaning from ordinary common-sense experience key concepts such as '"truth" and "reality" are at issue . . . and the sense attached to them . . . in question' (ibid., p. 179). Therefore, in the removal of truthfulness and value from ordinary human experience, structuralism denies the possibility of knowledge as traditionally attained. Such a rejection of ordinary experience, for Murdoch, means that structuralism is simply not true as, in presenting language as a carrier of all meaning, it fails to recognize (or, worse, deliberately obscures) the fact that 'statements are made, propositions are uttered, by individual incarnate persons in particular extra-linguistic situations, and it is in the whole of this larger context that our familiar and essential concepts of *truth* and *truthfulness* live and work. "Truth" is inseparable from individual contextual human *responsibilities*' (ibid., p. 194).[15]

Given the primacy of the individual and the ubiquity of moral value in Murdoch's thought, it is no surprise that language, like everything else, is for her primarily a moral medium. In our uses of language, Murdoch argues that we are 'almost always morally active . . . if we attempted to describe this room our descriptions would naturally carry all sorts of values' (Murdoch, 1997 [1978], p. 27). Thus language must always be connected to individuals: as Antonaccio describes, 'an affirmation of human agency is consistent with an acknowledgement of the constructive nature of language; in fact it is required by it' (Antonaccio, 2000, p. 174). Individuals, then, are not trapped in a 'sea of language' but create and evaluate by using language. For example, 'we naturally create metaphors in the context of certain kinds of attempts to describe . . . this is typical of our use of language to fix in a semi-sensible picture some aspect of our activities – and such fixing is using, or creating, concepts' (Murdoch, 1997 [1951], p. 40).[16] We are not passive in our relation to language but active and creative, as well as influenced and created by language.

*Experiencing Morality* 53

In essence, Murdoch regards structuralism as nothing more than an elaborate con. Given this reading, it is no surprise that Murdoch finds little to recommend Derrida's structuralism. She dismisses it as a theory built on a small (true) insight which has been taken and manipulated to the point that even this initial insight is so removed from its context that it is false. Taken as a whole, the structuralist picture is false and, moreover, sinister as it undermines access to knowledge and reality. It is not that Murdoch sees no truth in structuralism, but rather that she thinks that the insight of the philosophy (that language is crucial in creating meaning) has been exaggerated beyond its scope, because language, though a constituent part, 'does not exhaust the meaning of the real; reality must be understood in an important sense as existing "outside" language' (Antonaccio, 2000, p. 183). Murdoch accepts that:

> Yes of course language is a huge transcendent structure, stretching infinitely far away out of our sight, and yes, when we reflect, we realise that often we cannot say quite what we mean or not quite know what we mean. Common-sense does not usually take the trouble to reflect as far as this, or if it has done so realises that nothing is really being changed and meaning and truth are what they have always seemed. (Murdoch, 1992, pp. 188–9)

By exaggerating this premise – that meaning is language-dependent – and applying it beyond its proper sphere, the truth that structuralism does possess becomes false. For although 'we can see lots of little systems, but we can't see any big general one, and anyway, words surely have definite meanings when we apply them in *particular contexts*. If this were not so we couldn't distinguish between true and false' (ibid., p. 201). Thus, even on its own terms, the structuralist premise has been stretched too far, producing not a philosophy (based on analysis of reality and experience) but rather a magical system. This is an oppressive and mysterious conception of the world. It is a picture which is both false and dangerous in the threat it presents to morality and the individual and thus to the very essence of what it means to be human.

Consequently, Murdoch regards structuralism as a pernicious and destructive doctrine which must be actively defied and denied. It presents a false vision of reality, which denies ordinary forms of knowledge in order to give its proponents a sense of power. The removal of value is for Murdoch an almost impossible task and therefore she argues that it has been done with deliberate intent, for 'value is only with difficulty expelled from language for scientific purposes' (Murdoch, 1997 [1978], p. 27): in this case the pseudo-scientific purposes of the structuralists for the purposes of controlling knowledge. Advocates of structuralism become 'high priests': those with access to the explanatory theory of life and essential interpreters of ordinary experience.[17] The structuralist schema is so out-of-fit with ordinary (and, for Murdoch, correct) understandings of reality that explanation and access have to be provided at length in order for others (that is, ordinary individuals) to accept the structuralist vision. This aspect of structuralism leads Murdoch to classify

54 *The Moral Vision of Iris Murdoch*

it as 'a form of a familiar and enduring style of thought, Gnosticism, knowledge as power. Here the search for truth becomes a search for magic formulae and the seeker desires to become a privileged initiate of a secret cult, a sorcerer or *pharmakeus*' (Murdoch, 1992, p. 208). Murdoch strenuously opposes the structuralist view, arguing that, if it were to become dominant, in ordinary understandings, as well as academic and literary circles, it would be devastating and not only affect our ability to gain knowledge, but correspondingly lessen our drive to attain knowledge of the world. In this vein she argues:

> If all meaning is deferred our ordinary distinctions, for instance between what is clearly true and what is dubious and what is false, are removed and we begin to lose confidence (as structuralists urge us to do) in what is made to seem the simple, old-fashioned, ordinary concept of truth and its *related morality*. If in some 'deep sense', it cannot be finally established whether or not the cat is on the mat, then how can we have the energy to trouble ourselves about the truth or falsity of more obscure and difficult matters? (Ibid., p. 194)

In Murdoch's analysis, then, structuralism destroys human ability to grasp meaning and, in the wake of this, destroys conceptions of moral value and correspondingly destroys possibilities of moral living, including human communication and interaction; in other words, access to all that is true, authentic and meaningful in the creation of ordinary human life. In addition, Murdoch argues that structuralism, with its all-encompassing explanatory framework, devours all non-structuralist forms of thought. As it spreads to other discourses it damages, not just philosophy, but all frameworks of knowledge and meaning, for example anthropology, history and literature, together with their own methodologies and methods of verification. These are methods which, for Murdoch, are different from each other and equally valid. Moreover, it is 'only when the idea of truth as relation to separate reality is removed that they can seem in this odd hallucinatory light to be similar' (ibid., p. 202).

## Rejecting Structuralism and the Pseudoscientific Approach

Clearly for Murdoch, the consequences of embracing structuralism are devastating both academically and for all human communication and knowing. Structuralism then, must be opposed, in part because of its consequences, but more fundamentally because it is simply not true. Structuralism's non-correspondence theory of truth is contradicted for Murdoch by the reality of the world and our experience; she argues that in ordinary life a certain amount of 'truth-seeking . . . is essential for survival' (Murdoch, 1992, p. 195). In truth-seeking – an ordinary activity where we test our knowledge of reality against the world – we attain knowledge. For example, in Murdoch's schema, 'we have to learn the meaning of moral words such as "love" gradually, not only through the given rules of ordinary language but also through our inward

# Experiencing Morality

experience of love, our knowledge of ourselves and others' (Antonaccio, 2000, pp. 92–3).[18] In the process of attaining knowledge

> the (essential) idea of 'correspondence' is in place, not as a rival theory of truth, but as representing the fundamental fact and feel of the constant comparison and contrast of language with a non-linguistic world, with a reality not yet organised for present needs and purposes. Of course we are constantly conceptualising what confronts us, 'making' it into meaning, into language. But what we encounter remains free, ambiguous, endlessly contingent, and *there*. (Murdoch, 1992, pp. 195–6)

For Murdoch language does not create reality, or at least it is not creation *ex nihilo*, but it is creation and interpretation from a reality which is 'out there'. As we have seen, Murdoch maintains that structuralism is a false depiction of reality and ordinary life, yet, despite its fallacy, Murdoch recognizes that it is an attractive (and therefore dangerous) doctrine, particularly in the modern world, and she attributes the attractiveness of structuralism to four main reasons.

First, structuralism is attractive in its aping of science which, in the modern context, makes it appear to offer superior (in the sense of more factually correct and certain) interpretations of the world,[19] although Murdoch, like others in modern moral philosophy and theology, believes that this is not the case, because 'morality on the empiricist or scientific model cannot do justice to what human beings are actually like' (Antonaccio, 2000, p. 93).[20]

Second, and related, the aping of science allows structuralism to pretend to neutrality. Again this is a false position which Murdoch believes covers the moral premise of 'non-morality': that the 'supposedly neutral analysis of morality contains suppressed moral assumptions' (ibid., p. 39). Murdoch argues that, given the all-encompassing nature of morality, morally neutral frameworks are impossible. Therefore, instead of being openly moral and presenting an explicit moral framework, they hide their moral assumptions. In Murdoch's eyes this is what structuralism does. It pretends to be neutral, in an attempt 'not to moralise, and . . . study the logical structure of moral language and have the neutrality of logic' (Murdoch, 1997 [1957a], p. 74). The claim that all philosophies have moral premises (in the case of structuralism an anti-moral premise), Cora Diamond asserts is 'an important part of her [Murdoch's] argument' (Diamond, 1996, p. 82). Specifically, she points out that 'the supposed ethical neutrality of moral philosophy is illusory . . . her argument could be said to show the ideological character of moral philosophy: it works to exclude certain moral conceptions' (ibid., pp. 82–3).

Third, the knowledge structuralism offers requires complete acceptance of the structuralist meta-theory, giving its adherents a superior position vis-à-vis ordinary life and language, creating 'experts' with expert knowledge. Ordinary experience becomes viewed with suspicion and as a dubious source of knowledge which, being outside the structuralist premise and framework, can offer little access to reality. With structuralism in ascendance, Murdoch suggests that 'quasi-scientific technical modes of discourse . . . are treated as ultimate truths,

56 *The Moral Vision of Iris Murdoch*

and *contrasted* with a conceptually vague "ordinary language" composed of conventional assumptions and illusions, and which if solemnly uttered by some non-technical thinker is inevitably in bad faith' (Murdoch, 1992, p. 162).

Fourth, Murdoch argues that structuralism, like all forms of determinism, is attractive in that it precludes the necessity of human striving and responsibility. If meaning and truth are removed from the sphere of the individual they cannot be recognized, thus negating the necessity for human response and action. Like all forms of determinism, structuralism offers the possibility of individual abdication from the daily tasks and judgments entailed by the moral life (and Murdoch would argue from all life). 'The easy life' is always an attractive (and at the same time repellent) vision of the world. In Murdoch's words,

> the charm of determinism haunts the metaphysical concept of Being. It is a place where attractive quasi-scientific theories of ultimate reality can breed. We are tempted to imagine an alien material which we cannot transcend and where morality and personal responsibility, as it were, stop. Here a general theory reinforces our natural sloth, our weariness and covert despair. (Ibid., p. 479)

This determinist worldview, which begins with the fact/value dichotomy and culminates in structuralism, is reductionist and is a vision which misrepresents the reality of human (moral) experience. Murdoch presents her own philosophy – described by Antonaccio as an attempt to 'preserve as irreducible the value of the individual and its freedom from deterministic modes of existence' (Antonaccio, 2000, p. 169) – in direct opposition to it. As we have seen, Murdoch regards the erosion of value as devastating, resulting in the 'feeling that we cannot now justify the reality or identity of our most important thoughts and most precious awareness. We are losing the *detail*' (Murdoch, 1992, p. 49). Philosophy of this type (and Murdoch would class much of nineteenth- and twentieth-century philosophy in this bracket) fails as it 'attempts to offer a 'neutral' analysis which ignores morality (value) or treats it as a special subject; whereas the inherence of evaluation, of moral atmosphere, pressure, concepts, presuppositions, in consciousness, constitutes the main problem [of philosophy] and its importance' (ibid., p. 237). This move to supposed neutrality and a pseudoscientific stance is, for Murdoch, all wrong, although, as discussed, she recognizes the attractiveness of this view in the modern context. In contrast, Murdoch argues that 'philosophy is not a kind of scientific pursuit, and anyone who resorts to science is falling straight out of philosophy. It is an attempt to tease out in thought our deepest and most general concepts. It is not easy to persuade people to *look* at the level where philosophy operates' (Murdoch, 1997 [1978], p. 8).

## The Task of Philosophy

This move towards a supposedly neutral scientific model which negates moral value and experience Murdoch contends has led philosophy and philosophers

*Experiencing Morality* 57

to fail, and as a result she argues that 'much of present-day moral philosophy misses obvious and essential considerations which cannot simply be "left outside"' (Murdoch, 1992, p. 241). This is not just a failure to meet a need (for Murdoch a very real need; that of analysing and interpreting the everyday value concepts with which we order and structure our lives) but also, by excluding the fundamental moral issues, philosophy fails to present a successful (that is, believable and realistic) framework at any level. For 'it is impossible to describe the mind philosophically without including its moral mobility, the sense in which any situation is individualised by being pierced by moral considerations, by being given a particular moral colour or orientation' (ibid.).

Murdoch argues that philosophy should proclaim the inadequacy of its current methodologies and paradigms, such as structuralism, and reassert the priority of experience as the starting-point of philosophy. From this starting-point alternative (false) pictures can be countered, as done by Murdoch herself in her attack on structuralism, which takes from experience a very different understanding of language from that presented by structuralism. This is a picture derived from the experience of being a language user and which implies 'responsibility and the possibility of truth' (ibid., p. 211). For Murdoch, the need for philosophy to take an alternative stance and champion such positions cannot be overstated. She calls on philosophers to defend frameworks which support the individual and moral value since 'traditional ideas of truth, freedom and personality are at stake, and we must remind ourselves that the frightening future is not yet with us and can be resisted' (ibid., p. 208). Murdoch contends that, despite the prevalence of scientific frameworks, traditional conceptions have not been eroded; such erosion would indeed be difficult if we accept Murdoch's premise that human beings are fundamentally moral, as it would require radical dehumanization. In such a vein she argues that 'prophesies about moral-less value-less societies of the future belong to science fiction, or would if science fiction writers could imagine them. We know the difference between a hypothetical and a categorical imperative' (ibid., p. 473). Murdoch believes the reality of moral value is revealed in every aspect of human life, not only in our experience and relationships but also in our use of language. Language she contends is 'full of *values*, we rely daily upon intuitions and distinctions, life passes on, we have to trust our memories, we have to trust the truthfulness of other people' (ibid., p. 281). Language is not just about written words (the structuralists' position), but also about tones and gestures and communication between (moral) human beings and importantly relates to the reality of the thoughts, feelings of human beings.

Murdoch's reliance on experience and her invoking of 'common-sense' is easily dismissed by structuralists as a naïve position, which misunderstands the nature of language. However, while this criticism works for those who have adopted the structural premise, it does not work if one does not accept the premise and adopt the structuralist ideology. Indeed the ability of structuralists to dismiss common-sense as a valid philosophical premise and indeed any form of argument which does not adopt the structural premise is

58                    *The Moral Vision of Iris Murdoch*

for Murdoch proof that the structuralist ideology is a form of gnosticism, a faith system which is fully explanatory for those who 'believe' in the core tenants and from which starting-point any alternative position can be dismissed. Murdoch would then regard such criticisms as based on an enclosed belief system and therefore unable to communicate with other systems or take account of what for her are key sources of knowledge, such as experience. Murdoch insists that any accurate moral philosophy must incorporate the individual and the moral and the aesthetic – however unscientific (in that they defy simple clarification and verification) they may be. It must embrace them as key sources of knowledge and repositories of human truth: 'Philosophy, if it is to give much-needed help to the human race, indeed if it is to *survive*, must stay with its austere traditional modes of truth-telling' (ibid., p. 268). Philosophy has been horribly misled by the division of value from fact; as Kerr notes, Murdoch traces all subsequent reductionism back to 'the imposition of a false philosophy, the grid of the fact/value dichotomy' (Kerr, 1997, p. 80), a false framework which philosophy must now reject wholesale.

Murdoch is well aware that relativist, reductionist and deterministic philosophies are gaining ascendancy and are difficult to counter. In this manner she questions her position asking, 'are there "deep structures" in the mind, or the soul? How is one to deny the claim, in the sense in which Thrasymachus for instance meant it, that there is nothing deep? Should philosophical approaches to the problem recognise the omnipresence of a moral sense in thinking and knowing?' (Murdoch, 1992, pp. 238–9). Again, for Murdoch the answer is 'Yes', morality must be central and the starting-point of all serious philosophy. Moreover, relativistic positions, such as those held by Thrasymachus (once again winning adherents in the modern world) must be countered. Furthermore, Murdoch knows that asserting traditional sources of human knowledge derived from experience is not a simple task and she fears (as we shall discuss in more detail in later chapters[21]) that deep (for example, moral and aesthetic) sources of knowledge are in part illusory, in the sense that these sources are illusory in the unity they promise. So much is she troubled by such fears that she asks, 'well, *is* there, discoverable by *philosophy*, deep structure, and if we assume (as of course we may not) that (somehow) there is or *must be*, what mode of philosophical speech can deal with it?' (ibid., p. 237). For Murdoch, experience reveals that there are deep aspects of life (even though they may lack unity) and it is these which moral philosophy should be attempting to articulate.[22] 'Depth' is one of Murdoch's central concepts which she employs to represent the profound moral, aesthetic and spiritual conceptions through which human beings create meaning and identity. She describes depth thus:

> The metaphor of depth, generally understood, is difficult to explain in other terms . . . there is something about the human spirit which seems to some thinkers to *demand* a search for 'deep foundations'. Herein, it is often felt, there is something *essential*; and this essential thing must be built into the explanation at the start, or

*Experiencing Morality* 59

else it tends to fly away and become problematic and remote and extremely difficult to integrate. (Ibid., p. 55)

She asserts, therefore, that philosophers must 'attempt to make models of the *deep* aspects of human life' (ibid.) and should not be ashamed of taking a broad view of truth. Philosophy must return to attempting to clarify and analyse the traditional (and eternal) questions of moral philosophy and again embrace its essential 'positive task of finding a simple open mode of discourse concerning ordinary evident (for instance moral) aspects of human life' (ibid., p. 212). Murdoch proposes that there are 'deep' questions about the reality of human (moral) experience which the philosopher ought to address in order to do the philosophical job properly. To this end she suggests that 'moral philosophers should be frankly and realistically high-minded in the sense of recognising the unique and profound presence and importance of a moral sense. They should be liberal-minded, not cynics, reductionists, relativists, but able to scan a wide vista of human life' (ibid., p. 297). She accepts that this view of philosophy is out of step with present-day views of philosophy, particularly among those who have adopted the fact/value dichotomy unquestioningly.

This picture of philosophy and its task, as we have seen in the course of this chapter, runs contrary to most modern philosophy, from which questions of value have been almost entirely excluded. Philosophy should not be, as it has so often become, a descriptive pseudoscientific endeavour which aims for clarity in a reductionist sense, but rather it should engage with all aspects of human experience, including those that resist simple definition and clarification. Therefore, in order to 'do' moral philosophy properly, we need a wider vista as 'moral concepts do not move about *within* a hard world set up on science and logic. They set up, for different purposes, a different world' (Murdoch, 1970a, p. 28).

Philosophical reflection must be based on the assumption that 'deep', non-scientific, essentially human sources of knowledge are real and accordingly philosophy must, despite the difficulty, attempt to account for these aspects of human experience, however out of fit with current modes of discourse such approaches might appear. Only this type of approach, which makes human experience central, can hope to provide an accurate and full representation of human life. We must strive in our moral reflection for points 'at which reflection, however beset, must stand firm and be prepared to go on circling round an essential point which remains obscure. As in the working of a ratchet, one must hold anything which seems like an advance, while seeking a method of producing the next movement.' (Murdoch, 1992, pp. 238–9). In this manner the discipline of philosophy should (re)orient itself and focus on experience and 'deep' questions of human meaning and resist the urge to be pseudoscientific or present itself as a simple form of discourse, since 'philosophy is "abstract"; a term not easy to define or explain. It is delicately managed conversation that moves between degrees of generality in order to promote understanding of very general features of our lives' (ibid., p. 212). If

60 *The Moral Vision of Iris Murdoch*

carried out in this way philosophy will again be able to perform essential work for humanity and will even succeed in rescuing a holistic sense of human being and value.

## Experiencing Value

Having criticized the philosophies of her contemporaries – a critique which has been described as 'a wholesale reinterpretation of the notion of "moral fact"' (Antonaccio, 2000, p. 37) – Murdoch turns to constructing her own philosophy. Her starting-point is experience, and questions of value and truth are considered in a broad framework.[23] Truth is a question of what is 'really there', but what is really there is not limited to pseudoscientific factual frameworks. Truth is more than asserting that 'the cat is on the mat', it is a 'larger idea which can contain, turning toward the individual, ideas of "truthfulness" and "wisdom"' (Murdoch, 1992, p. 183). Facts on their own, understood as discrete pieces of data, do not constitute a neutral truth which is capable of conveying some sense of meaning or saying anything essential about the world. For Murdoch, facts are not inert but connected to value by individual (moral) judgment, an unavoidable and continual mode of evaluation and knowledge. Incredulous at the fact/value divide and philosophy's aspiration to science and rejection of experience as its starting-point, Murdoch asks, 'do we really think there are specifiable sets of neutral facts which in the light of reason give a moral direction? Is it not rather that the prime situation is already to a considerable extent "read" (or worked upon) when the problem arises?' (ibid., p. 384).[24] Value cannot be divided from fact, just as it cannot be divided from any aspect of human judgment and living, but rather 'value goes right down to the bottom of the cognitive situation' (ibid.). If we ignore this background, Murdoch argues, we lose value conceptions and thus erode our self-understanding, our ability to comprehend our own and others' behaviour, for a 'separation of meaning from truth not only "removes" morally responsible truth-seeking speech in particular situations, it also leaves our ordinary conduct inexplicable' (ibid., p. 211). Such a conclusion she regards as self-evident, proved simply by looking at experience, as 'the world which we confront is not just a world of "facts" but a world upon which our imagination has, at any given moment already worked' (Murdoch, 1997 [1966], p. 199). It is this self-evident truth about human beings that she believes philosophy should be articulating and defending. Thus, she argues:

> Any moral philosopher must (should) appeal to our general knowledge of human nature. Morality is and ought to be connected with the whole of our being ... The moral life is not intermittent, or specialised, it is not a peculiar separate area of our existence. It is into ourselves that we must look: advice which may now be felt, in and out of philosophy, to be out of date. The proof that every little thing matters is to be found there. Life is made up of details. (Murdoch, 1992, p. 495)

*Experiencing Morality* 61

Murdoch suggests that we perceive the world as 'morally coloured', arguing that we cannot 'really imagine morality without an intimate relation with consciousness as perceptions, feelings, streams of reflection' (ibid., p. 222). All facts then are viewed in a value-ridden way; in other words, the world is always perceived morally. She criticizes philosophers who deny this as ignoring what she regards as obviously and self-evidently true. She retorts:

> If we feel loss, what kind of mistake do we think has been made? Is there then no 'moral knowledge' or 'moralised fact', such as common-sense seems to demand? Does not value *colour* almost all our apprehensions of the world, and is this colour something which must be withdrawn in order to purify the will? We struggle here with imagery. Are our ordinary personal (and precious) 'value perceptions' to be made either impossible or ineffable? (Ibid., p. 52)

Murdoch does not deny that facts are 'real' but rather she denies that facts are the only, or even the primary, reality. Indeed, facts are a form of knowledge and reality which cannot be separated from value and our other ways of knowing. For

> we relate to facts through truth and truthfulness, and come to discover that there are different modes and levels of insight and understanding. In many familiar ways *various* values pervade and *colour* what we take to be the reality of our world; wherein we constantly evaluate our own value and those of others, and judge and determine forms of consciousness and modes of being. (Ibid., p. 26)

Such a position by no means denies the importance of facts as, of course, 'everyday moral decisions normally involve consideration of details' (ibid., p. 349). However, facts are always known and interpreted in the context of a value framework for 'value inheres in consciousness, morality colours an outlook, light penetrates a darkness . . . After all do I not wish to connect morality with knowledge? With truth, *ergo* with knowledge' (ibid., p. 238). Thus every decision is made within a value framework and facts are known, organized and ultimately understood only within that value context; in Murdoch's terminology the world is morally coloured. It is wrong therefore to assume that Murdoch presumes there is 'an objective world of facts apart from the activity of an individual thinking consciousness . . . the moral world is always already constituted by the individual mind that is internally structured in relation to a background of value' (Antonaccio, 2000, p. 94). 'Moral colour', then, conveys the complex reality of decision making in which facts, values, individual experience, relationships and so on are all factors which frame and affect the (value) judgments of everyday life. Moreover, to deny this broad conception is to curtail artificially moral thinking and action and leads to 'moral error . . . a "lack of realism" (lack of a suitably wide and reflective attitude to facts) and would be judged as such in light of a rival moral attitude concerning what was morally relevant' (Murdoch, 1997 [1956], p. 94). To deny this link between fact and value is to undermine human knowing, 'to be a human being

62                           *The Moral Vision of Iris Murdoch*

is to know more than one can prove, to conceive a reality which goes "beyond the facts" in . . . familiar and natural ways' (Murdoch, 1997 [1966], p. 199). Morality is 'not the response of an autonomous and isolated will to a set of scientifically conceived "facts", but a matter of seeing things justly' (Kleinig, 1971, p. 113).

If we reject the fact/value dichotomy and instead assert a broad conception of truth, in which the experience of value is part of reality, even though it fits uneasily into literal, factual models of knowledge which predominate, we can begin to see Murdoch's realist conception. To suggest that facts, and facts alone, can constitute 'reality' (because they are empirically verifiable), for Murdoch, is simply nonsense and shown to be false by brief reflection on experience. For Murdoch (just as for Plato and largely for Kant), morality is central, fundamental and unavoidable (Murdoch, 1992, p. 63), since 'value judgements are everywhere in human self-expression' (ibid., p. 94). Everything is coloured by value. Recognition of value is not complex but part of everyday cognition: 'outside the laboratory, or untroubled by philosophy, our perceptions, which so largely constitute our experienced-being, are intensely individual and polymorphous. Seeing, thinking and "interpreting" are mixed. And, for instance, instinctive value judgement and intuitions are involved' (ibid., p. 278). She argues that 'fact and value merge in quite a innocuous way' (Murdoch, 1997 [1956], p. 95) for when we conceive of '"moral facts" in the sense of moral interpretations of situations where the moral concept in question determines what the situation is, and if the concept is withdrawn we are not left with the same situation or the same facts' (ibid.). Therefore making moral judgments is no more complex than making judgments about facts. As Antonaccio recognizes, for Murdoch, 'we do not impose value on a morally neutral world of facts . . . the world is already constituted as moral world through our perception' (Antonaccio, 2000, p. 96). Moral judgments are simply part of human experience and knowledge:

> We are mixed into the world around us which we touch and assimilate largely through a vast medium of metaphor, and achieve, fundamental to human life, truth, out of which in turn we are able to set up and 'place' the necessary systems of the strictly factual. How we can *do* these things may seem, if we pause and stare at it, a mystery. But out in life we perform all these feats without difficulty. (Murdoch, 1992, p. 459)

Murdoch's assertion of the fundamental place of value in our lives and the importance of value for ordering, structuring and comprehending our world is painted vividly in a description of the way human beings would experience an alien culture:

> The human scene is one of moral failure combined with the remarkable continued return to an idea of goodness as unique and absolute. What can be compared to this? If space visitors tell us that there is no value on their planet, this is not like saying there are no material objects. We would ceaselessly *look* for value in their

*Experiencing Morality* 63

society, wondering if they were lying, had different values, had misunderstood. (Murdoch, 1992, p. 427)

## The Primacy of Morality

Human beings, then, are by their nature primarily moral agents, in the sense that making value judgments is the means by which we interpret and order the world (and the facts which constitute the world) and so determine our place in it. Moral judgment is a continual process, 'not a matter of specialised isolated moments of moral choice, appearing in a continuum of non-moral activity. These movements and responses are occurring all the time. The reality of the moral requirement is proved by the world' (Murdoch, 1992, p. 297). We are all in every aspect of life moral agents for 'morality is ubiquitous and we expect a primary recognition of it' (ibid., p. 333). Morality for Murdoch is the fundamental background which makes the distinctively 'human elements' of life possible. It is necessary and essential and cannot be removed from the human picture without removing the essence of human being and the possibility of human knowledge. For 'there is something about moral value which goes *jusqu'au bout*. It must go all the way, to the base, to the top, it must be everywhere, and is in this respect unlike other things . . . It adheres essentially to the conception of being human, and cannot be detached' (ibid., p. 426).[25] Thus we recognize and know values in our continual recognition of the world around us just as we do, although less fundamentally, facts.

The unavoidable nature of morality is crucial for Murdoch's philosophy and establishing her version of moral realism. As Antonaccio notes, Murdoch's realism insists that 'morality cannot be reduced to subjective terms, but is connected to objective conditions, such as truth, perfection and reality' (Antonaccio, 2000, p. 168). Moral awareness and judgment are essentially what make us human, as 'the possession of a moral sense is uniquely human; morality is, in the human world, something unique, special, *sui generis*, "as if it came to us from elsewhere". It is an intimation of "something higher". The demand that we be virtuous. It is "inescapable and fundamental"' (Murdoch, 1992, p. 26). Moral judgment is our method of self-expression and self-understanding for it is

> as moral agents we have to try to understand the world and thereby to construct 'our world'. Since morality is compulsory (we cannot avoid moral choices) some form of moral *cognition* is compulsory and we have to set up at least the forms of a distinction between what is real and what is not. (Ibid., p. 385)

Murdoch's view, then, is undeniably realist and described as 'cognitivist in that it assumes that morality is a matter of knowledge undertaken by a thinking consciousness that judges values according to an objective norm of truth and falsity' (Antonaccio, 2000, p. 113).[26] Morality cannot be anything but real – it is evident in all areas of our daily life:

64     *The Moral Vision of Iris Murdoch*

all learning, all cognition, all truth-finding and testing of verification, in perception, in mathematics and (I add) in art, in craft, in love, indicate the connection of the good and the real. Serious reflection is *ipso facto* moral effort and involves a heightened sense of value and a vision of perfection. (Murdoch, 1992, p. 437)

Thus morality and 'the moral good is certainly established as cognitive, the unconditional is seen to belong to the structure of human reality, the evidence is everywhere in our experience' (ibid., p. 439). It is experience which reveals to us the reality of moral value and its absolute nature (by which Murdoch means its fundamental place in human living). Murdoch is not invoking any external source for moral value (as we shall discuss further in later chapters), the human reality is enough, for, even in a largely secular world, 'we continue to recognise moral absolutes just as we continue to use moral language. Kant was right to take our recognition of duty as something fundamental. We manage it' (ibid., p. 473). Morality as absolute is, for Murdoch, the only possible conclusion if we take our experience seriously, for 'we feel, it *must* live, morality must be *fundamental* in human life' (ibid., p. 467).

Against this moral background we recognize moral values and moral requirements (although this task is difficult and involves lifelong striving, as we shall discuss fully in later chapters). Values are discovered by examining our uniquely human experience of the world as morality lies at the heart of that experience. Murdoch's primary moral value is the good which provides the background moral colour to life, in light of which other moral values are known. The value of the good is connected to truthfulness and knowledge which are in turn connected to all our everyday value concepts, such as generosity and kindness. As we have shown, experience is the source of all real knowledge for Murdoch, for what other source of knowledge do individuals have? It is through experience that we know of the reality of moral values, most forcefully of the moral reality of goodness: 'People know about the difference between good and evil, it takes quite a lot of theorising to persuade them to say or imagine they do not' (ibid., p. 497). Murdoch argues that this is not a mystical assertion or conception of the world (although we shall see that mysticism is indeed important for Murdoch), but ordinary everyday experience of that which is real:

> Non-philosophical people do not think that they invent good. They may invent their own activities, but good is somewhere else as an independent judge of these. Good is also something clearly seen and indubitably discovered in our ordinary unmysterious experience of transcendence (the progressive illuminating and inspiring discovery of *other*) the positive *experience* of truth, which comes to us all the time in a weak form and comes to most of us sometime in a strong from (in art or love or work or looking at nature) and which remains with us as a standard or vision, an *orientation*, a *proof* of what is possible and a vista of what might be. (Ibid., p. 508)

The place of the good as the central concept in Murdoch's philosophy will be discussed in full in the next chapter. What is crucial here is the fundamental reality of moral value as revealed by experience. However, although we all have, by virtue of our humanity, knowledge of the reality of moral values, how we perceive (or how clearly we perceive) moral values differs. Clearly perceiving moral values is the task of the moral life and involves striving and effort to rid ourselves of false pictures of reality: as Kaalikoski comments, 'truthfulness (realism) is a moral achievement, a virtue' (Kaalikoski, 1997, p. 147). In this sense, for Murdoch, the moral life is a quest – like the Platonic quest – from illusion to reality, reality being value.[27] Yet, despite these differences, we all recognize value through our daily experience and determine our lives accordingly, for 'knowledge (language) is essentially related to morality by the idea of truth . . . there is an orientation towards goodness in the fundamental texture of human nature' (Murdoch, 1992, p. 474). Even though we perceive reality differently (more or less accurately depending on our personal pilgrimage) our moral knowledge derives from the same source: from moral experience and, ultimately, the good. For Murdoch, 'we are moving through a continuum within which we are aware of truth and falsehood, illusion and reality, good and evil. We are continuously striving and learning, discovering and discarding images' (ibid., p. 250). Thus, for her, morality is the unavoidable touchstone of human life: 'the idea of absolute, as truth and certainty is contained in ordinary exercises of cognition, it is already inherent in the knowledge which suggests our duty, it is *in* our sense of truth; however feeble or "specialised" our response may be' (ibid., p. 304).

Value impinges upon all aspects of our lives – our work, our relationships and our conception of the world – 'all awareness includes value *as* the (versatile) agility to distinguish true from false' (ibid., p. 221). Value is known intuitively and instinctively, a normal part of experience, informing activities of 'scholarship, science, art, everyday life' which all 'involve searching for coherence ("making sense of things") and dealing suitably with the innumerable contingent elements which impede, divert, or inspire the search. This is an abstract description of what we are doing all the time' (ibid., p. 195). However, although morality is unavoidable and moral values are known and experienced by all human beings – 'morality is not just what we happen to think' (Kerr, 1997, p. 76) – the quality of the experience varies, for morality has to be *worked* at and reflected upon (again this will be returned to in the following chapters). All moral values are therefore connected, although not in a strict hierarchy, as Murdoch is suspicious of structured systems which strive for unity. Following Plato, she links the good to truth, reality and knowledge and it is in light of this that other values must be (morally) judged and assessed. For example, Murdoch argues that 'truth is very close to good, closer than, for instance, generosity. "Generosity" may be a form of egoism, which needs to be purified by a patient use of intelligence and a sense of justice. Humility requires realism and humour. Often we must forget our dignity but not always' (Murdoch, 1992, p. 325). Goodness and truth are the source (or alternatively the end point) of all moral values, yet all values are connected and recognized in the course of ordinary experience.

66 *The Moral Vision of Iris Murdoch*

Moral value, then, is a given, known and influential in all human judgments and action. It is 'there' and it is our task as moral agents to perceive it accurately. As Kerr reads her, 'we live in a world that makes claims on us, morally, ethically – claims we can ignore, claims to which we may be blind, but we are not the ones who invent them or project them – we find them, discover them' (Kerr, 1997, p. 87). How clearly one perceives values depends on the quality of the individual's consciousness and (moral) vision. How our vision of values differs and how we respond to the reality of moral value will become clearer as we discuss the moral life and the good in subsequent chapters. For now we have seen that, for Murdoch, there is no divide between fact and value. Indeed, value provides the background from which we perceive all facts. Thus the moral world, not the empirical world, is primary. The proof of the moral reality as the background and source of our judgments is found and proved by everyday experience of ourselves and our interaction with the world.

**Conclusion**

This chapter has shown us Murdoch's core convictions upon which her philosophy is built: particularly that moral value is real in the 'out there' world, or at least in the world as perceived by human beings. In order to establish this picture of moral value Murdoch had to counter the fact/value dichotomy and critique the prevailing philosophies, particularly structuralism, which she saw as the culmination of the fact/value dichotomy. We then explored Murdoch's realist conception of moral values which for her are fundamental to all aspects of human living. This conviction is based on her assumption that human beings are essentially moral beings and morality is ubiquitous in human life, hence her conviction that all situations are morally coloured. Taken together with her commitment to the individual, explained in Chapter 2, we can now see the grounds on which Murdoch rejects much modern moral theory and judges it reductionist. From this basis, that of returning to experience and taking a broad approach to truth and reality (which includes non-empirically viable, but irredeemably human factors), we can see Murdoch's moral vision begin to take shape. Our understanding will grow as we move into the next chapters and consider the key value of her moral universe (the good) and then her holistic vision of the moral life as a way of being.

**Notes**

1  Murdoch uses 'structuralism' or 'Derrida's structuralism' somewhat confusingly to denote what would usually be termed 'deconstruction'. Given the prevalence of this term in her work, the text follows her (albeit unusual) terminology.

2  This comment is in light of Murdoch's comment that it is always significant to ask a philosopher 'what he is afraid of'. Kerr believes that Murdoch fears philosophies which

# Experiencing Morality

adopt the fact/value dichotomy and certainly she is afraid the fact/value dichotomy will be universally accepted and so change our vision of what it means to be human.

3   Contemporary theories of moral motivation are drawn from Hume's assertion that motivation comes from sentiment. They assert that both belief (beliefs are concerned with the facts of the world and are open to rational criticism) and desire (desires are derived from wishes about what the world should be) are necessary for action to take place. Moral judgments express beliefs about the situation, but they will only be acted upon if the agent has the desire (which is non-cognitive and emotional) to do so.

4   While non-congitivism and realist positions do not entirely determine the moral theories and practices a theorist will endorse they are essential indicators. For example, a realist belief is unlikely to result in relativist and subjective understandings of value. Likewise, non-cognitivism is far more likely to lead to relativism and subjectivism, although a non-cognitivist could still endorse some kind of universalism by asserting that human beings have similar enough moral responses to agree on substantive agreed values: for example, Hume's early version based on an assumption of shared human nature or, in more modern terms, shared conceptions of human rights or negotiated values (Parekh, 2000).

5   A position we find in the philosophy of A.J. Ayer, who regards value statements as significant only in so far as 'they are ordinary "scientific statements"; and that in so far as they are not scientific, they are not in the literal sense significant, but are simply expressions of emotion which can be neither true nor false' (Ayer, 1988, p. 27). Values are unverifiable as there is 'no relevant empirical test' (ibid., p. 30) and thus are 'pseudo-concepts' (ibid.) with 'no objective validity whatsoever' (ibid., p. 32). Thus values simply express and arouse emotion and as such have been termed 'Boo–Hurrah' theories (McNaughton, 1988, p. 17).

6   Murdoch would reject Hume's non-cognitivism and present a realist picture in which values are real and recognized and acted upon cognitively.

7   Murdoch denies the belief/desire theory of motivation as a false dichotomy. However, present-day cognitivists are divided into internalists (like Murdoch who believe that motivation is cognitive) and externalists. The externalist asserts there are moral facts, but argues that the non-cognitive emotion (desire) is still necessary for motivation. Such congitivists argue that this assertion does not entirely divide belief from desires as 'the vast majority of people will have at least some desire to comply with what they perceive to be their moral obligations' (Brink, 1989, p. 49). The danger for such cognitivists is that the moral facts of the situation become secondary and, like non-cognitivists, they have difficulty in accounting for moral authority, conflict and demand. Other modern philosophers, particularly virtue ethicists who are influenced by Murdoch, for example Michael Stocker (Stocker, 1997), also reject the divide between belief and desire.

8   Internalists reject the belief/desire theory in its totality. They assert that motivation arises from the recognition of value, claiming that it is 'inconceivable that someone could recognise a moral fact and remain unmoved or fail to have reason to act' (Brink, 1989, p. 43). Thus they argue that there is 'an internal or conceptual connection between moral considerations and action or the sources of action' (ibid., p. 38) and therefore 'moral considerations necessarily motivate or provide reasons for action' (ibid., p. 42).

9   For Murdoch transcendence and immanence are a false dichotomy, and she rejects this as she does other dualistic dichotomies with which she disagrees, such as the fact/value and belief/desire divides. Her conception of the relation between transcendence and immanence will be returned to in detail in Chapter 4.

10   Although modern Kantians would deny this and argue that in fact the individual is not alone, nor is duty, in the Kantian sense, dependent on his transcendental concept of the

68 *The Moral Vision of Iris Murdoch*

moral law. For example, the Kantian Marcia Baron argues that, 'although in many passages Kant does seem to attribute a special value to duty as a primary motive, this is generally an illusion' (Baron, 1995, p. 187). However, the redefinition of Kantianism, or more accurately the broadening of Kantianism, is largely in response to the rise in virtue ethics and Baron admits that 'Kantians can utilize the work of virtue ethicists to enrich Kant's account of virtue' (Baron et al., 1997, p. 48). Murdoch, as one of the inspirations for modern virtue ethics, could perhaps claim some responsibility for the reorientation of the ethical debate and indeed it would be likely that Murdoch would find much to recommend modern Kantian moral philosophy.

11    The debate about moral facts is one of the hottest debates in the current realist/non-cognitive divide. On the one hand, the non-cognitivists continue to argue, like Ayer, that there are no such things as moral facts. Other anti-realists, such as subjectivists and projectivists, argue that moral facts are invented or 'in some very broad sense subjective' (Mackie, 1977, p. 18). Famously, J.L. Mackie argued that, if moral values were objective, then they 'would be entities or qualities or relations of a very strange sort utterly different from anything else in the universe' (ibid., p. 38). On the other side of the debate, realists argue that moral facts are not vastly distinct from other facts, nor are ways of recognizing them. Realists who make these types of arguments are Richard Boyd (1988), David Brink (1989), Gilbert Harman (1989) and Nicholas Sturgeon (1986). John McDowell also famously argues that, although not the same as facts conceived in an absolute conception of the world, values are similar to secondary qualities (such as colour) and therefore, although dependent on human perception, are undoubtedly part of the 'out there' world (McDowell, 1978, 1983).

12    It is important to note that Murdoch, while arriving at Cambridge one year too late to be tutored by Wittgenstein, met him and befriended a number of his students; thus her obsession with his philosophy is well documented (Conradi, 2001, pp. 262–6). Indeed her first novel, *Under the Net* (the 'net of language') explores Wittgenstein's view of language and arguably Wittgenstein appears in the character of Hugo: 'those who see Wittgenstein in Hugo are not wholly misled: both have Central European Origins, a tormented love-life, a care for their boots, give up their fortune, are associated with hospital work, employ the word 'decent' as high commendation' (ibid., p. 381).

13    Kant's intention is to protect value and keep it at the core of human life; Wittgenstein's intention is simply not to discuss that which he felt could not be defined and was therefore easily misunderstood.

14    Murdoch presents this view forcibly, albeit in a different context, as a political tactic to remove individual agency in a fictional form in her Platonic dialogue, *Art and Eros*: 'That's the new tyranny in a nutshell, a programme for Tyrants. A few rules manipulating the language . . . words perish, and nobody can speak of truth' (Murdoch, 1987, p. 38).

15    The nature of language not as an overarching structure is supported by her view of literature, which we will consider in detail in Chapter 6. Her criticism of linguistic analysis in this context is illuminating. She states that, whatever the prevailing theory, 'the writer will make his own choice, and use language as he pleases and as he can, and must not be bullied by a theory into imagining that he cannot tell a plain tale, but must produce self-consciously verbal texts which fight against ordinary modes of intelligibility' (Murdoch, 1997 [1978], p. 24). However, this said, Murdoch does recognize that structuralist linguistic theory has had an impact on contemporary literature and she admits that 'there has been a kind of crisis in our relation to language, we are much more self-conscious about it, and that does affect writers' (ibid., p. 26).

16    Murdoch continues the example 'as when, for instance, we speak of having a bond with someone which remains unbroken through times of emptiness or even hostility. Such a

## Experiencing Morality 69

mode of speech is so natural to us we might be surprised when its metaphorical character is pointed out' (Murdoch, 1997 [1951], p. 40).

17  The structuralist response would of course be that Murdoch can only present her philosophy in language and therefore her criticism is ungrounded. How can Murdoch prove that anything does actually exist outside language? Murdoch would regard this response as further supporting her critique that structuralism is the equivalent of gnosticism, for, like any fundamentalist position, once you accept the premise (in this case that all meaning is contained in language) the argument cannot be countered.

18  This view, in which Murdoch was highly influential, is echoed in the work of some contemporary ethicists who also oppose the pseudoscientific conception of the world. For example, Charles Taylor is critical of the epistemological and empirical paradigm of much current ethics which he thinks has 'wreaked . . . great havoc in ethics theory' (Taylor, 1999 [1982], p. 129). He suggests that this paradigm 'makes us quite incapable of seeing how reason does and can really function in the domain, to the degree that it does not fit the model. We cut and chop the reality of, in this case, ethical thought to fit the Procustean bed of our model of validation. Then, since meta-theories cannot be isolated from one another, the distortive conception begins to shape our ethical thought itself' (ibid.). Taylor applies this argument to language which he argues should be seen more holistically, 'not only the words we speak, but also other modes of expression whereby we define ourselves, including the "languages" of art gesture, of love, and the like' (Taylor, 1994, p. 32).

19  Again we could cite others as criticizing the pseudoscientific aspiration of philosophy, particularly virtue ethicists. Like Murdoch, virtue ethicists complain that this move has been reductionist and has led to philosophers being unable to address key moral and human concepts. For example, Michael Stocker argues, like Murdoch before, for the importance of love to moral theory (which is very difficult to fit into a pseudoscientific model) (Stocker, 1997).

20  For example, the virtue ethicists mentioned in previous footnotes.

21  As we move through Murdoch's vision of the good, the moral life, art and religion, what Murdoch intends by the term 'depth' will become clearer.

22  Indeed, Murdoch praises analytical philosophy for removing false certainties and consolations such as theism and 'theological fictions'. We will return to Murdoch's view of religion in Chapter 7.

23  This core conviction is presented dramatically in Murdoch's Platonic dialogue *Above the Gods* in the mouth of her youthful Plato, who states, 'Truth isn't just *facts* it's a *mode of being*' (Murdoch, 1987, p. 101).

24  Murdoch is not the only realist to assert 'moral colour' or its equivalence. For example, Jonathan Dancy argues that 'the world is *not motivationally inert*' (Dancy, 1993, p. 32).

25  We will return to what Murdoch means by 'beyond being' when we consider her central moral value – the good – in Chapter 4.

26  Although Murdoch is wary of using the term 'norm', as it tends to suggest ethics as derived from people's current thoughts and practices, which is descriptive rather than normative and tends towards a subjectivist (particularly projectivist) moral conception.

27  Moral life conceived of as a moral quest will be discussed in detail in Chapter 5.

# Chapter 4

# The Good

In the last two chapters Murdoch's opposition to the philosophies of her contemporaries was outlined; in particular, to their pictures of the self and to their uncritical adoption of the fact/value dichotomy. In contrast to these positions Murdoch presents her own picture of the self, in which the inner life and inner moral activity are fundamental, and through which the reality of moral values is known. In this endeavour Murdoch turns to experience to justify her case, as both the starting-point and means of verification for her philosophy. From experience she asserts the primacy of a moral background for all aspects of human knowing and evaluation. In the light of this all-encompassing moral background Murdoch claims that moral values are real and that it is by moral evaluation that we comprehend all aspects of the world. Moral knowledge is not only possible, but prior to all forms of knowledge. The key moral concept, as touched upon in the last chapter, is the good, from which all other moral knowledge is derived. In this chapter we will consider the nature and status of Murdoch's good and assess her arguments for this, her primary moral concept, around which her philosophy is built.

Murdoch's notion of the good as the central element of her moral philosophy first appeared in her book *The Sovereignty of Good* (1970a), in which the good is revealed as the guiding principle of the moral life and the ultimate reality. Murdoch returned to the good 22 years later in her largest and most detailed philosophical work, *Metaphysics as a Guide to Morals*. Murdoch's whole philosophy is derived from the good, not only her moral realism, but also her conception of the moral life and her understandings of art and religion, which we shall discuss in the remaining chapters. The good is the reality which, though difficult to define, is the determining principle of human life and proved by all aspects of life.

The good, like all moral values, is discovered in everyday life, and its recognition is part and parcel of life. Recognizing and comprehending the good is neither difficult nor mysterious, as Murdoch is swift to point out: 'there is no complicated secret doctrine' (Murdoch, 1970a, p. 74). For Murdoch, values are real and knowable. As Kerr comments, she presents the good as 'there, whether or not we perceive or pursue it. It is not impossible to get from what "is" to what "ought" to be' (Kerr, 1997, p. 78). However, though the good is primary for Murdoch, adjudging its status and nature is no easy task. Difficulty in defining the good arises in part from the 'unsystematic presentation of her ideas and the difficulty of the issues being considered . . . [which] . . . make it hard to be sure what she means by the Good' (Burns, 1997, p. 303).

72              *The Moral Vision of Iris Murdoch*

While the unsystematic presentation of Murdoch's ideas is a problem for her whole philosophy, in the case of the good the problem is more profound: one of content as well as form. Lack of a concrete definition is a constituent feature of the good because it lies beyond the sphere of human knowledge. We can know of the good and see intimations of it all around, but we cannot offer a comprehensive definition of it. This is because the task of the moral life, which is gradually to perceive the good more clearly, is a lifelong endeavour which can never be fully achieved.[1] Consequently, by virtue of the nature of the good, definition, especially definition of the analytical kind, is impossible. Yet, although defining the exact nature of the good is not possible, some aspects of the good can be known, because 'we ordinarily conceive and apprehend goodness in terms of virtues which belong to a continuous fabric of being' (Murdoch, 1970a, p. 30). Therefore, although imperfectly, one always has some sense of goodness, since

> the authority of the Good seems to us something necessary because the realism (ability to perceive reality) required for goodness is a kind of intellectual ability to perceive what is true . . . *The necessity of the good is then an aspect of the kind of necessity involved in any technique of exhibiting fact.* (Ibid., p. 66)

Thus one's experience of the good, though limited, makes partial description possible; if this were not the case, the good could not play such an overwhelming role in ordinary experience.

**Transcendence and Immanence**

Importantly, Murdoch constructs the good as both transcendent and immanent. Though this may appear controversial, Murdoch maintains that there is no contradiction in recognizing the good as both immanent and transcendent, because plainly the 'idea of good, perceived in our confused reality, also transcends it' (Murdoch, 1992, p. 405). Thus the good 'lives as it were on both sides of the barrier and we can combine the aspiration to complete goodness with a realistic sense of achievement within our limitations' (Murdoch, 1970a, p. 93).

Murdoch uses the term 'transcendent' in the Aristotelian sense, namely that of transcending the categories.[2] Good is transcendent in that it is never contained in a single object or action which one would describe as good, but always exceeds the confines of a particular situation. For Murdoch, the good constitutes the background and the moral colour of human life and, although part human experience, this 'inexhaustible reality' (ibid., p. 42) surpasses it. It is the 'ideal end-point' (ibid.). 'Transcendent', used in this context, does not have supernatural connotations, in that the good is not other-worldly, or dependent upon any 'thing' or 'being' outside the human world. Rather, it is a reality in the world and transcendence describes part of its nature.

## The Good 73

Simultaneously, Murdoch insists that the good has an immanent aspect. It is through this immanent aspect that the good itself is known, and she postulates that the 'idea of good (goodness, virtue) crystallises out of our moral activity' (Murdoch, 1992, p. 426). In other words, a partial recognition of the good itself is contained within the experience of goodness in ordinary life: every experience of goodness points to the larger good. In this vein Murdoch suggests that 'there is ... something in the serious attempt to look compassionately at human things which automatically suggests that "there is more than this"' (Murdoch, 1970a, p. 73). This recognition Murdoch describes as a 'spark of insight, something with, as it were, a metaphysical position but not metaphysical form' (ibid.). This 'spark' Murdoch argues should not be interpreted in a quasi-theological manner, but as pointing to the real and the good: 'it seems to me that the spark is real, that great art is evidence of its reality' (ibid.). Thus, for Murdoch, the transcendent good is evident all around, and knowing the transcendent good is, as we discussed in the last chapter, similar to other forms of knowing, hence, the 'all-important knowledge of good and evil is learnt in every kind of human activity' (Murdoch, 1992, p. 418). We know of the good and make judgments accordingly, for

at the level of serious common sense and of an ordinary non-philosophical reflection about the nature of morals it is perfectly obvious that goodness *is* connected with knowledge: not with an impersonal quasi-scientific knowledge of the ordinary world, whatever that may be, but with a refined and honest perception of what is really the case, a patient and just discernment and exploration of what confronts one, which is the result not simply of opening one's eyes but of a perfectly familiar kind of moral discipline. (Murdoch, 1970a, p. 38)

Thus, for Murdoch, goodness, reality and knowledge are connected, part of a true picture of human reality and it is by our knowledge of goodness and reality that our (moral) judgments are made.

These two characteristics are the most significant aspects of Murdoch's good, and her definition of these terms differentiates her realism from that of other contemporary philosophers.[3] Murdoch denies that transcendence and immanence are opposites, maintaining that any such dichotomy is false. She holds that transcendence and immanence are not mutually exclusive but connected, since the terms are used to highlight different aspects of reality; reality being coloured by the good. For her transcendence begins in immanence, otherwise it would not be perceptible to finite humans, as it is transcendence which gives particulars substance and which provides insight into the good. Thus the good is 'an idea, an ideal, yet it is also evidently and actively incarnate all around us' (Murdoch, 1992, p. 478). Hence the two aspects of the good flow into each other. The transcendent is recognized in its immanent aspects, for 'what is fundamental here is ideal or transcendent, never fully realised or analysed, but continually rediscovered in the course of the daily struggle with the world' (ibid., p. 427). The connection between immanence

74 *The Moral Vision of Iris Murdoch*

and transcendence is borne out by our experience, as we recognize in our experience of 'lower things the shadow of higher things, and thereby our continual (daily, hourly, minutely) sense of the connection between the good and the real can lead us to believe in the supreme reality of what is perfect: the unique place of God, or Good, in human life' (ibid., p. 398).

To illustrate her concept of the good as both immanent and transcendent, Murdoch refers to Plato's picture of the cave.[4] In Plato's imagery the good is 'unique, it is "above being"' and yet 'it fosters our sense of reality, as the sun fosters life on earth' (ibid., p. 399). Plato uses the image of the sun to elucidate his understanding of the good; the sun is presented in images and stories which are 'deliberately cast as explanatory myths and must not be mistaken for anything else' (ibid., p. 38). Hence the good, like the sun, is 'beyond' and transcendent, but it can be seen and known, in part, on an immanent level, just as the sun has influence and can be known in part from its effects. Therefore 'we do really know a certain amount about the Good and about the way it is connected with our condition' (Murdoch, 1970a, p. 97). Thus Murdoch uses the terms 'transcendent' and 'immanent' in order to signify the way in which an absolute concept, such as the good, can have relevance for finite beings like ourselves.

Murdoch's outright rejection of any division between transcendence and immanence and her insistence that they are not opposites but correlates has made her concept of the good difficult to grasp. Although dualism has been rejected by most contributors in the debate, underlying dualist assumptions are still present in much philosophical and theological thinking.[5] The legacy of dualism remains embedded in much of present-day thought and (despite post-modern assertions to the contrary) it still underpins many basic assumptions, such as the dualism of objective and subjective which remains in philosophy and other academic disciplines. In order for Murdoch to succeed, she must convince her readers of the fallacy of such an opposition, which one would think would be fairly straightforward, since scholars of moral philosophy have explicitly rejected dualist theories.[6] Nonetheless, such assumptions continue, and often philosophers remain trapped in dualistic mind-sets.

Instead of rejecting the dichotomy which a dualist worldview created, many theorists have tended to simply reject one side of the equation: the 'objective' side. Consequently, such theorists have denied the objective and insisted that all is subjective, a move which leads to relativism and non-cognitivism. Other schools of thought have gone in the opposite direction and rejected the subjective side of the equation, particularly in theology: for example, those who endorse divine command theories and hold to fundamentalist views of God and morality.[7] Such positions deny any subjective element in moral understanding and assert objective truths. As a result, both sides, while claiming to reject dualism, have not actually done so. Though they do not appear to propose dualist theories, their tendency to adopt one side of the dualism they claim to reject, rather than attempting a reintegration, ensures that the dichotomy remains in place. Murdoch rejects these approaches as ultimately

*The Good* 75

leading to misguided viewpoints. Adopting an objective stance leads to the old difficulties of unchanging dogma which is imposed upon human beings and which limits the possibility of truly moral action.[8] Alternatively, the claim that all is subjective, while releasing humanity from the control of 'outside' factors, opens the path to relativism, which for Murdoch results in a loss of the meaning and significance of moral value and ignores the phenomenology of moral experience. Both pictures Murdoch regards as false.

Therefore, in attempting to remove the division between transcendence and immanence, and represent them as correlates, Murdoch hopes to integrate both sides of dualism, a project which she deems necessary if one is to account for the full complexity of human experience. This argument is somewhat parallel to Murdoch's argument against the fact/value dichotomy and is likewise controversial because the dichotomy between subjective and objective still tends to predominate, either in its traditional form, or because of a one-sided emphasis. This underlying continuation of dualism, which informs and upholds many philosophical and theological assumptions, makes Murdoch's thesis problematic. However, if one grants Murdoch's rejection of the transcendent/immanent dichotomy, just as if one accepts her rejection of the fact/value divide, then it is possible to conceive of the good as both transcendent and immanent.

## Establishing the Good

If one accepts that transcendence and immanence are correlates, the different aspects of the good are accounted for. Having asserted the importance of both immanence and transcendence, Murdoch goes on to argue for the reality of the good. She does this using two main arguments: an argument from perfection and her own version of the ontological argument. These arguments go some way to setting out a philosophical defence for her position. However, ultimately, as we would by now expect, she believes that the fundamental support for her thesis is found in examining one's own experience. Therefore her use of the argument from perfection and the ontological argument are in some sense 'after the fact'; they are ways of philosophically articulating what she holds to be already known and proved by experience.

## The Argument from Perfection

Murdoch's argument from perfection revolves around the meaning of the term 'perfection', which clearly presents the relation between the immanent and transcendent elements of the good. Murdoch asserts that 'perfect' is a comparable term and can only be used in contrast with that which is imperfect.[9] That which is truly perfect is never attainable by finite beings such as ourselves, and hence perfection is always an ideal. However, though unattainable, the

76       *The Moral Vision of Iris Murdoch*

concept of perfection enables one 'to see that A . . . is really better than B' (Murdoch, 1970a, p. 62). The comparative nature of the term means that one can judge between actions and objects, for 'we learn of perfection and imperfection through our ability to understand what we see as an image or shadow of something better which we cannot yet see' (Murdoch, 1992, p. 405). This ability to contrast and compare means that it is possible to intuit what is not already visible, in that 'we *know* of perfection as we look upon what is imperfect' (ibid., p. 427). By extension, the good is known when one looks upon that which is not good.

Murdoch's claim, then, is that, though human beings cannot fully know perfection, we do know in which 'direction' it lies, something which is deduced from imperfect objects and situations which we encounter. This knowledge is immediate in that 'we are not usually in doubt about the direction in which good lies' (Murdoch, 1970a, p. 97). It is the concept of 'direction' towards that which is perfect which suggests that the good is real, because it is from recognizing imperfect instances of goodness that the reality of the perfect good is revealed. Murdoch argues that this transcending order of perfection is '*characteristic* of morality' (Murdoch, 1992, p. 427), for it is only in the light of perfection – which for Murdoch means what is perfectly good – that 'better' alternatives can be judged. Because perfection is not attainable, but always lies beyond and transcends any particular instance, it provides an ideal, a standard against which particulars can be assessed. Murdoch argues that perfection functions in any field of human activity (she uses art as an example). She holds that increasing understanding of any aspect of life 'involves an increasing revelation of degrees of excellence and often the revelation of there being in fact little that is good and nothing that is perfect' (Murdoch, 1970a, p. 61).[10] Murdoch argues that exactly the same revelation occurs in the moral realm, as 'we come to perceive scales, distances, standards and may incline to see as less than excellent what previously we were prepared to "let by"' (ibid.).

The fact that perfection can never be attained increases its capacity to inspire us. Murdoch argues that perfection inspires in a way that a mediocre standard does not, thus she recommends the command, 'Be ye therefore perfect' rather than 'Be ye therefore slightly improved' (ibid., p. 62) and asserts that 'for all our frailty the command "be perfect" has sense for us' (ibid., p. 93). Thus knowing of perfection, which cannot be seen, provides inspiration and knowledge, for 'the idea of perfection moves and changes us . . . because it inspires love' (ibid., p. 62). Therefore, although perfection is 'beyond . . . it exercises its *authority*' (ibid.). The realism of the good is fundamental to Murdoch's picture, as 'a purely subjective conviction of certainty, which could receive a ready psychological explanation, seems less than enough' (ibid., p. 64).

In this reading, perfection is an appropriate standard to judge any activity 'in terms of the kind of perfection which is appropriate' (ibid., p. 98), therefore at a particular level perfection is a situation-dependent concept. Accordingly, Murdoch concludes that one cannot say 'in general what perfection is, in the

## The Good

way in which one could talk about generosity or good painting' (ibid.). In this transcendence of particular situations Murdoch holds that the unity of the moral world begins to emerge, as does the explicit connection which Murdoch makes between the good and reality. In the universal applicability of perfection, we can see that 'morality, goodness, is a form of realism' (ibid., p. 59). This is because the standard of perfection is absolute, it lies in one direction and not in another, hence it provides our knowledge of the reality of the good. This again Murdoch considers proved by experience, and thus she states that 'the idea of a really good man living in a private dream world seems unacceptable . . . he must know certain things about his surroundings, most obviously the existence of other people' (ibid.). Murdoch's vision of a moral reality is one which is grounded in the concept of the good, and it is the good which connects the virtues: again proved by experience, since 'if we reflect upon the nature of the virtues we are constantly led to consider their relation to each other. The idea of an "order" suggests itself, although it might be difficult to state this in any systematic form' (ibid., p. 57). To illustrate her point, Murdoch uses the example of courage, arguing that, when we reflect upon courage and attempt to define it as a virtue, and to distinguish it from 'rashness, ferocity, self-assertion and so on, we are bound, in our explanation to use the names of other virtues. The best kind of courage (that which would make a man act unselfishly in a concentration camp) is steadfast, calm, temperate, intelligent, loving' (ibid.). Therefore Murdoch argues that we find good in the wide gamut of our experience exemplified in different virtues and aspects of life. Reflection on this experience leads to 'an increasing awareness of "goods" and the attempt (usually only partially successful) to attend to them purely, without self, brings with it an increasing awareness of the unity and interdependence of the moral world' (ibid., p. 70).

In asserting a unity of the virtues Murdoch is not asserting a strict hierarchy or permanent structure, indeed to do so would run contrary to her whole philosophy and her insistence on the fundamental uniqueness of individual human experience. Rather Murdoch is envisaging an implicit connection and relationship, in which virtues relate to each other because they are all related to goodness. Again here Murdoch takes her lead from Plato who, as she states,

> never in fact anywhere expounds a systematic unitary view of the world of forms, though he implies that there is a hierarchy of forms . . . what he does suggest is that we work with the idea of such a hierarchy in so far as we introduce order into our conceptions of the world through our apprehension of Good. (Ibid., p. 95)

This is a view that Murdoch endorses and she argues that a formal unity or systematic hierarchy is not possible: 'the scene remains disparate and complex beyond hopes of any system, yet at the same time the concept of Good stretches through the whole of it and gives it the only kind of shadowy unachieved unity which it can possess' (ibid., p. 97).[11] Because goodness/perfection cannot be fully realized and is part of all situations it is able to provide a kind of unity

78 *The Moral Vision of Iris Murdoch*

to the moral life as well as functioning as the absolute ideal to which moral striving is directed. In this way, then, the indefinability and mysteriousness of the good is 'connected with the unsystematic and inexhaustible variety of the world and the pointlessness of virtue' (ibid., p. 99). The good, as perfection, is inspiring and, in our partial recognition of it in daily life, it calls us to aspire, to stretch our limitations, and is also 'mysterious because of the immense distance involved' (ibid.). It is this distance, and its relevance to every aspect of life, which allows us to judge the direction in which the good lies; thus the good is 'the magnetic centre towards which love naturally moves' (ibid., p. 102).[12] The good, then, revealed by the function of the concept of perfection in experience, is shown to be real and inspiring in human life.

## The Ontological Argument

The second argument Murdoch employs in support of her realist conception of goodness is the ontological argument, which, like the argument for perfection, is about progressions of goodness. The ontological argument was first put forward as a proof of the existence of God by St Anselm (1033– 1109), and Murdoch reproduces this argument in great detail.

Anselm's thesis is formulated around his definition of God, namely that God is a 'being than which nothing greater can be conceived' (Anselm, 1968a, p. 4). His argument starts with the assertion that even the fool who does not believe in God can understand this definition.[13] If the definition can be understood then God must exist, otherwise any existing being would be greater, contradicting the initial definition. Thus Anselm's assertion is that 'there is no doubt that there exists a being, than which nothing greater can be conceived, and it exists both in the understanding and in reality' (ibid.).

This first form of the argument ran into difficulty immediately and was criticized by Anselm's contemporary, Gaunilo, who argued that merely because one can conceive of 'the greatest being' – a possibility which he questions – this does not mean that it exists in reality.[14] To illustrate his point, Gaunilo cites the now famous example that imagining a perfect island would not bring it into existence. For Gaunilo to be convinced he demands some other proof.[15]

In response to this criticism, Anselm restates his argument, explaining that his conception could only apply to the Supreme Being, because only the Supreme Being 'necessarily exists', arguing that, 'if such a being can be conceived to exist, then necessarily it does exist' (Anselm, 1968b, p. 14). This assertion of necessary existence, Anselm argues, can only be applied to the Supreme Being. He contends that experience of the Supreme Being is revealed all around, and is especially derived from experience of goodness, for 'by ascending from the lesser good to the greater, we can form a considerable notion of a being than which a greater is inconceivable' (ibid., p. 24). Hence, if one starts with an experience of goodness, one can then reason that good

## The Good

would be greater if it had no beginning or end, and it is this eternal concept of goodness which is the Supreme Being.

Anselm's introduction of 'necessary existence' has not satisfied critics, and has been disregarded to the extent that Schopenhauer called it 'a charming joke' (Murdoch, 1992, p. 392). Momentously, Kant apparently destroyed the validity of the proof with the observation that 'existence' is not a predicate, which returns the proof to being susceptible to Gaunilo's first criticism. However, Murdoch, along with other scholars, has returned to the proof with a renewed interest.[16]

Murdoch remains unconvinced by Kant's criticism, maintaining that 'only the first version is vulnerable to Kant's contention that existence is not a predicate' (ibid., p. 404). Murdoch concedes that Anselm's first formulation 'may indeed seem frail, only to be given substance by a belief or faith deriving from another source' (ibid.) and appears as 'a specious way of expressing a personal certainty which is already tacitly concealed in its premises' (ibid.). However, she views the second formulation differently and maintains that the replacement of existence by necessary existence creates a very different argument. She argues that 'necessary existence' is not an empty concept, and to corroborate this she introduces the work of Norman Malcolm, who claims, as Anselm did, that 'God' is different from any other concept.[17] Murdoch suggests, in line with Malcolm's work, that if God exists then he must have always existed. Hence, if the concept 'God' 'is meaningful, if it is not self-contradictory, God must necessarily exist' (ibid., p. 410). For Murdoch the notion of necessary existence is concerned with what constitutes our notion of 'God', and therefore the 'problem, in no trivial way . . . [is] . . . one of meaning' (ibid.). Her contention is that necessary existence concerns those elements of human life which are ever-present aspects of experience.

Murdoch contends that God does not fulfil these criteria, and therefore 'necessary existence' cannot be correctly applied to the Christian God. If the term were to be used of God, then God could not be 'a particular, a contingent thing, one thing among others; a contingent god might be a great demonic or angelic spirit, but not the being in question' (ibid., p. 395). Consequently, if necessary existence is to be used legitimately of God, then 'God is not to be worshipped as an idol or identified with any empirical thing; as is indeed enjoined by the Second Commandment' (ibid.). Thus Murdoch reckons that Anselm's second version of the ontological proof fails, not because necessary existence is not a predicate, but because it is wrongly applied to God, for 'no empirical contingent being could be the required God and what is "necessary" cannot be God either' (ibid., p. 425).

To reinforce her pronouncement that the ontological proof cannot apply to the Christian God (at any rate not to the object it has become), she turns to the work of J.N. Findlay, who dismisses 'forms of religion . . . (that) . . . attach a uniquely sacred meaning to existent things' (Findlay, 1968, p. 120).[18] Findlay observes that 'there are other frames of mind, to which we should not deny the name "religious", which acquiesce quite readily in the non-existence of

80            *The Moral Vision of Iris Murdoch*

their objects' (ibid.). Furthermore, he notes that part of what is attributed to God is the 'possession of certain excellencies we cannot possibly conceive away' (ibid.). It is these 'excellencies' which Murdoch contends the proof is really about, and she praises Findlay for bringing to light what she believes is the 'deep meaning' of the ontological argument, namely that 'morality and demythologised religion are concerned with what is absolute, with unconditioned structure, with what cannot be "thought away" out of human life' (Murdoch, 1992, p. 412).

Murdoch's hypothesis is that necessary existence cannot be applied to God, or to 'one empirical phenomenon among others' (ibid.), but that it can be used in relation to the good and morality. Murdoch argues that Anselm's proof is actually a proof of the reality, not of God, but of good, because 'what is in question . . . is something unique, of which the traditional idea of God was an image or metaphor and to which it has certainly been an effective pointer' (ibid.).[19] Consequently, her hypothesis is that the proof claims 'some uniquely necessary status for moral value as something (uniquely) impossible to be thought away from human experience, and as in a special sense, if conceived of, known as real' (ibid., p. 396). The correct interpretation of Anselm's proof is that it establishes the 'necessity and sovereignty of the Good' (ibid., p. 425), which is revealed in Anselm's description of how one conceives of God: namely, in the 'degrees of goodness' argument. Anselm's assertion that 'we recognise and identify goodness and *degrees* of good, and are thus able to have the idea of a greatest conceivable good' (ibid., p. 395) is similar to Murdoch's own argument from perfection. Thus, although the '*goodness* of God is . . . lost to view in logical discussions of the Proof' (ibid., p. 414), it is this which she holds is at the core of his work. Murdoch concludes, then, that the proof is really not about God but concerns the existence of goodness.

Hence, Murdoch regards the ontological argument as being about the necessity of the good, and by extension of moral value, which is derived from our 'most general perceptions and *experience* of the fundamental and omnipresent (uniquely necessary) nature of moral value, thought of in a Christian context as God' (ibid., p. 396). The proof claims necessary existence for the good, and her use of the ontological argument she believes effectively addresses 'one of the great problems of metaphysics . . . to explain the idea of goodness in terms which combine its peculiar purity and separateness (its transcendence) with details of its omnipresent effectiveness in human life' (ibid., p. 408). Thus she contends that the proof is a logical attempt to articulate 'the unique nature of morality' (ibid., p. 428), which for her is characterized by immanence and transcendence. It elucidates her contention that 'what is perfect must exist, that is, what we think of as goodness and perfection, the object of our best thoughts, must be something real, indeed especially and most real, not as contingent accidental reality but as something fundamental, essential and necessary' (ibid., p. 430).

To support her interpretation of the ontological argument Murdoch returns to experience. Indeed, she argues that, in addition to presenting the ontological argument as a logical proof, Anselm also argues from experience in his 'appeal to our sense of God (Good) as discovered everywhere in the world' (ibid., pp. 404–5). She contends that this argument from experience 'emerges . . . under the pressure of the logical argument' (ibid., p. 405) and 'experience shows us the uniquely *unavoidable* nature of God (Good or the Categorical Imperative)' (ibid.). Thus she asserts that the argument 'appeals to our moral understanding' (ibid., p. 396) and supports the logical claims for the necessity of moral value. The logical formulation of the proof is an attempt to systematize and to account philosophically for what is known in experience; to find a philosophical formula to assert that 'we can "think away" material objects from human existence, but not concepts of good, true, and real' (ibid., p. 425).

Murdoch returns to her starting-point of experience and argues that 'reflection upon our ordinary perceptions of what is valuable, what it is like to seek what is true or just in intellectual or personal situations, or to scrutinise and direct our affections, can thus also lend support to the argument about existence and essence which appeared at first as a kind of logical argument' (ibid., p. 398). For Murdoch, the ultimate ground for the conviction of the reality of goodness remains one's own moral experience, and it is from reflection upon this experience that logical proofs emerge. It is experience which tells us of the reality of the good, of 'its omnipresence, its purity and separateness from our fallen world, in which its magnetic force is nevertheless everywhere perceptible' (ibid., p. 405). The ontological argument provides a logical articulation of our awareness of the good, an awareness which is not 'something unusual, specialised or remote' (ibid., p. 398), but part of everyday life. In essence, her use of the ontological argument is an attempt to systematize and reveal in philosophical form the reality of the good.

Despite Murdoch's concentration upon one of the traditional proofs for the existence of God, she is at pains to stress that she is not wishing to replace God with good. Like God, the good provides 'a *single perfect transcendent non-representable and necessary real object of attention*' (Murdoch, 1970a, p. 55). Indeed, Murdoch is adamant that 'moral philosophy should attempt to retain a central concept which has all these characteristics' (ibid.). However, because the good is not an empirical object or a personal being, it is 'above the level of gods or God' (Murdoch, 1992, p. 475). Consequently, Murdoch's good, unlike God, is non-personal, and though it inspires and informs the moral life, the good is indifferent to human striving. Accordingly, the good does not 'play a real consoling and encouraging role' (Murdoch, 1970a, p. 72); 'God sees us and seeks us, the good does not' (Murdoch, 1992, p. 83). Furthermore, Murdoch contends that, because of the impersonal nature of the good, it is a better focus for attention, for one must 'love good for nothing' (ibid., p. 344). Unlike with a personal God, there can be no ulterior motives for being moral; there can be no hope of reward or fear of punishment and the moral life is pure and uncorrupted. Thus her contention is that 'good is not the old God in disguise, but rather what the old God symbolised' (ibid., p. 428). God provided a personality for moral value. Stripping away the personality of

82     *The Moral Vision of Iris Murdoch*

God, we are left with reality of the good, in the sense that the 'good represents the reality of which God is the dream' (ibid., p. 496). For Murdoch, the good offers a central focus which does not have the disastrous consequences for moral living and communication which many ideas of God do.[20]

## The Ontological Status of the Good

Given the prominent place of the good in Murdoch's philosophy, indeed as the cornerstone of her position, we must critically assess the validity of this concept. Therefore we will now reflectively consider her account of the good and examine the main obstacle to her (and her mentor Plato's)[21] realism: that of satisfactorily establishing the reality of the good without presenting it as an object.

Her introduction of the ontological argument is intended to establish the reality of the good as something more than simply an idea, or concept in the mind.[22] If the good was simply a concept or metaphor, Murdoch would not have introduced the ontological argument to support her cause, especially given the controversy which surrounds it, and the fact that necessary existence is generally dismissed out of hand. Murdoch's intention is precisely to claim ontological status for the good. In order to do justice to Murdoch's good, it is imperative to accept that for her the good does exist in some absolute sense. The alternative is to accuse her of using an ontological argument which she does not intend to be about ontological status.

This said, her use of the ontological argument is confusing, in that she uses it explicitly to preclude the possibility that the good is an object – the fact that the good is not an object forms part of her reason for claiming that the proof works for good but not for God – while at other points she refers to the good as an *object* of attention: the best object of attention, no less.[23] Yet she also states, with regard to the good, that 'of course we are dealing with a metaphor, but with a very important metaphor and one which is not just a property of philosophy and not just a model' (Murdoch, 1970a, p. 93). This suggests that, while the good is metaphorical, it is, in some non-specified way, more than a metaphor, something real, at least in the lives of individuals.

This apparent contradiction is never addressed by Murdoch; however, there are solutions to this dilemma which may be suggested. One explanation may be that Murdoch does not consider that the term 'object of attention', with regard to the good, refers to an 'object' in a material sense at all, a suggestion supported by statements like 'in an important sense goodness *must* be an idea' (Murdoch, 1992, p. 478). Perhaps Murdoch regards the good as an object only in the sense that it is the end-point of the search for perfection and goodness, and is real in our experience and thus a fixed point in our value systems and in the frameworks in which we live and conceive of the world. Indeed, given her rejection of the fact/value dichotomy and her insistence on a moral background proved by experience, such a claim would fit the wider context of her philosophy and be a not inappropriate conclusion.

In order to clarify this issue, it may be possible to draw insight from religion, a course which seems to be justified given Murdoch's own interest in the subject.[24] In Christianity there is a strong tradition, particularly arising from the mystical strains, that God must not be an object, and negative theology adopts much the same stance towards God as Murdoch does towards the good. For such believers, God is not an object but most certainly does exist. Clearly, Murdoch respects mystics and even suggests that some may have succeeded in achieving the end of the quest.[25] However, if Murdoch accepts the validity of such a view of God as a non-object, this threatens the distinction which she has made between God and good. Part of the problem with Murdoch's analysis is that she regards God as an object, and although certain believers may act as if this is the case, viewing God in such a way is explicitly precluded by Christian theology and tradition.[26] Not only does Christianity deny that God is an object, but 'Christian theologians who are orthodox enough to believe in God as Trinity would have caveats about referring to God as "*a* person"' (Kerr, 1997, p. 75). Thus the established position of Christian theology, and one which arose in part from the same source as Murdoch's own philosophy, Platonism, is that God, no less than Murdoch's good, should not be thought of as 'object'. Such reasoning provides an example of how it is possible to hold that 'something', or some 'entity' (it is difficult to find the correct word as 'thing' suggests 'object' but 'concept' implies a lack of reality) is both real and not an object. However, the difficulty of using this example is obvious, in that the example of God is precisely that from which Murdoch is attempting to distinguish the good. In fact, many critics take this position and declare that Murdoch has not succeeded in separating the two, but that she has simply replaced God with the good. Moreover, if the ontological argument can work for good, then it can also work for God.

Critics are correct to point out that Murdoch adopts a very narrow interpretation of Christianity. Furthermore, given the place she allots to religion and to religious thinking, theologians are underrepresented in her work.[27] Although this does not undermine her whole thesis, her lack of familiarity with theologians such as Augustine and Aquinas, and with different schools of thought, such as Christian Platonism, does lead her into error. As a result, she has misconstrued the ways in which God is conceived, and hence has simplified Christian views of God almost to the point of caricature. Consequently, Murdoch wrongly describes God as an object, and attributes to believers elements of belief and practice which many would find unacceptable, especially believers at the mystical end of the spectrum. However, although her conception of the Christian God may be naïve, there are elements of her criticism which do not disappear when these mistakes are rectified and which may yet serve to support her view of the good.

Although Murdoch has not fully taken account of theological conceptions of God and wrongly conceives of God as an object, her assertion that God is personal is not so easily dismissed. God, though not a person, is certainly 'personal', in that God has a character which is interested and intervenes in

84 *The Moral Vision of Iris Murdoch*

human affairs. Both good and God are personal in that they have supreme personal relevance for human individuals, though the good is disinterested. The impersonal nature of the good allows it to escape from the criticisms of the ontological argument and rescues moral value from the humanist critique of religious morality.

However, distinguishing between good and God merely because the good is impersonal (rather than the stronger, but flawed, assertion that the good is not an object as God is), weakens her argument. It brings into question the focus and reason for adopting her moral religion, and certain scholars have argued that, like Plato before her, Murdoch presents a philosophy in which the individual can find no fulfilment. Since the good is impersonal, achieving the end of the quest and seeing the good can have no practical relevance because all that is accomplished is knowing the impersonal good. Yet this reading makes assumptions which Murdoch would not endorse. She would argue that the good is highly relevant to practical decision making, indeed the most relevant component; as we saw in Chapter 3, moral knowledge is the most important form of knowledge, providing a background and context to all forms of human knowing. Furthermore, although the good is impersonal, in that it is not an entity with personality, it is not impersonal in the sense that it is irrelevant to the concerns of human beings.

The impersonal nature of the good is crucial for Murdoch because it precludes any possibility of coercion in the moral life. Unlike God, the good has no character and therefore does not 'wish' certain behaviour; one must be 'good for nothing'. By this means, Murdoch presents a moral source which is absolute but which does not bind the individual in any sense other than that it is part of the human condition. One must be good 'for nothing', yet underlying her whole thesis seems to be the hope that living a moral life is not pointless in the sense that the moral life is a better, truer, way of being. While Murdoch has discounted the possibility of an external *telos*, she clearly hopes that if one lives a moral life one will have a more fulfilled life. Her hope, though never explicitly articulated, is that the Universe, at least the human part of it, is not indifferent to human striving, and that moral effort does bring reward, in that it improves the quality of one's own life and of those around. The purpose and rewards of the moral life (being less deluded, seeing reality more clearly and thus being more fulfilled) will be discussed in detail in the next chapter. For now, all we need to note is that, although the moral life is ultimately for nothing, it is still the case, for Murdoch, that living a moral life, one which is less deluded and more real, is a better life to live.

## Reviewing Murdoch's Good

In arguing for the good, Murdoch has employed a number of means (her redefinition of the relation between transcendence and immanence, the argument from perfection and the ontological argument) and underlying all of

# The Good

these is the belief that the good is revealed to us in experience as an ever-present reality which draws one towards it. It is this conviction which leads her to the ontological argument. The ontological argument, while helping the reader to clarify the nature of the good, does not help her case for establishing the good. In introducing 'necessary existence', her intention is simply to assert that goodness is a constant certainty of the human condition and the enduring factor of the human quest. However, using the ontological argument – and especially necessary existence – to establish this takes the reader directly into the old debate about predicates and attributes which has surrounded the argument from its inception. Some claim that such associations do not aid her endeavours, for the terminology involved, such as possession of attributes, suggests the existence of an object or being to which attributes belong. Thus her invocation of the ontological argument to prove the good's status leads the reader back to thinking about the good as an object. Given these factors, one is left wondering if she might have achieved her aim more easily by avoiding Anselm's argument altogether, especially given the contempt in which many philosophers and theologians hold it, regarding it as little more than a word game. Her fundamental point is that the good is an essential part of experience. Those who cannot read her ontological argument without the associated criticisms may be best advised to disregard her ontological argument in favour of her other arguments – from perfection, and the Platonic degrees of goodness argument – which may be more helpful in establishing her realism and certainly less likely to give the impression that the good is an empirical object.

Yet however one feels about the ontological status of the good, it is clear that Murdoch's good has real presence in the lives of individuals. In its presence in experience it is real, and 'the decent man has probably always, if uncertainly and inexplicably, been able to distinguish between the real and the good' (Murdoch, 1970a, p. 93). It is in ordinary moral living, in 'efforts of attention directed upon individuals and of obedience to reality as an exercise of love' (ibid., p. 42), that the good is known. At this point '"reality" and "individual" present themselves to us in moral contexts as ideal end-points . . . this surely is the place where the concept of good lives. "Good": "Real": "Love". These words are closely connected' (ibid.). The reality of the good informs decision making and the construction of individual lives, and this for Murdoch is proved by experience. In support of this understanding, Murdoch asserts that 'the ordinary person does not, unless corrupted by philosophy believe that he creates values by his choices. He thinks that some things really are better than others and that he is capable of getting it wrong' (ibid., p. 97). The good then provides the background colour of all (moral) life, for, from Murdoch's perspective, 'apprehension of good is apprehension of the individual and the real, then good partakes of the infinite elusive character of reality' (ibid., p. 42). According to Murdoch, then, 'the authority of morals is the authority of truth, that is of reality' (ibid., p. 90). Yet how this reality is constructed remains, and perhaps necessarily so in Murdoch's reasoning, a mystery. Murdoch states that, in response to the question,

86 *The Moral Vision of Iris Murdoch*

'do you then believe that the Idea of Good exists?' I reply, 'No, not as people used to think that God existed.' All one can do is appeal to certain areas of experience, pointing out certain features, and using suitable metaphors and inventing suitable concepts where necessary to make these features visible. (Ibid., pp. 74–5).[28]

Therefore, although attempting to provide a clarified picture of Murdoch's good is difficult, its place in human moral endeavour is clear and the good remains the core of her philosophy; indeed, she believes it is fundamentally connected to a proper understanding of human being. So important is the good to her conception of moral knowledge and the moral life that Murdoch argues that, 'if a moral philosophy does not give a satisfactory or sufficiently rich account of what we unphilosophically know to be goodness, then away with it' (Murdoch, 1997 [1959a], p. 205). By presenting the good at the heart of philosophy, Murdoch believes she has returned not only moral values to their place at the heart of human living, but also moral philosophy to its proper function; 'the area of morals, and ergo of moral philosophy, can now be seen, not as a hole-and-corner matter of debts and promises, but as covering the whole of our mode of living and the quality of our relations with the world' (Murdoch, 1970a, p. 97). Murdoch comments that the Platonic picture with 'the image of the Good as a transcendent magnetic centre seems to be the least corruptible and most realistic picture for us to use in our reflections on the moral life' (ibid., p. 74). How the good functions in the task of moral living is the issue we will address in the next chapter.

## Notes

1 We will explore Murdoch's conception of the moral life as a continuing struggle to see the real in the next chapter.

2 A description of 'transcendence' as it applies to beauty can be found in the work of Maritain. Beauty is 'transcendent' in that it is present in all other categories for 'just as everything *is* in its own way, and is good in its own way, so everything is beautiful in its own way' (Maritain, 1974, p. 124).

3 Most contemporary philosophers would not use the terms at all. Instead, they would use the comparative though not identical distinction of objective and subjective. Indeed, most contemporary philosophers would eschew such language, not least for its religious connotations. However, as we shall see in later chapters, Murdoch embraces much religious language and practice as expressing fundamental aspects of human capacity and needs. She integrates these religious concepts and wishes into her moral philosophy.

4 Plato's myth of the Cave is found in the *Republic*, Book Seven. Murdoch uses Plato's image of the Cave as the fundamental image of the moral life, therefore discussion of the place of this image in Murdoch's philosophy will be left until the next chapter.

5 Dualism has been a strong characteristic of Western theology and philosophy. Formalized dualism took hold in the medieval period and the world divided into opposing spiritual and moral forces: mind/body, light/dark, mind/body, male/female, God/Devil, and of course Good/Evil. Many would argue that this formalized dualism had devastating consequences for the Western world, in particular for the treatment of women and the environment,

consequences which make modern thinkers extremely wary of endorsing a dualism of any kind.

6　Examples are found in much modern philosophy, particularly of the non-cognitivist type. For an example, see the work of J.L. Mackie, who rejects the possibility of objectivity and argues in favour of subjective (in the broadest sense of the word) conceptions. In theology, one finds it in the overt subjectivism of Don Cupitt.

7　Divine command theorists, particularly those who endorse strong versions of the thesis, such as B. Brody and P. Geach, offer examples of theological versions of objective theories of morality.

8　As pointed out so forcibly by the humanist critique of religion, which argues that the believer does not act morally for moral reasons (such as wishing to help another person or to do good), but from selfish reasons (hoping for reward, or in order to escape everlasting punishment). We will explore the humanist critique of religion, which Murdoch in part endorses, in detail in Chapter 7.

9　It may be suggested that the word 'perfect' is used in ordinary language simply as a description, without any consciousness that the object/person is not perfect in the fullest sense (absolutely entirely flawless and complete). However, this argument is peripheral to Murdoch's case, for on reflection when the term is used correctly it is comparative, and Murdoch's argument has validity.

10　This is very much Murdoch's view of art and she claims that 'the true artist is obedient to a conception of perfection to which his work is constantly related and re-related in what seems an external manner' (Murdoch, 1970a, p. 62). We will discuss Murdoch's views of art and the role of the artist in detail in Chapter 6.

11　The hierarchy which Murdoch suggests must not be systematized, which would imply that we can grasp perfection and goodness fully, an impossible task for contingent beings, hence 'the sovereign idea' cannot be 'in any sense "taped". In fact it is its nature that we cannot get it taped. This is the true sense of indefinability of the good' (Murdoch, 1970a, p. 62).

12　Of course we may be drawn to false goods: 'false love moves us to false good. False love embraces false death' (Murdoch, 1970a, p. 102). Here Murdoch introduces Plato's picture of eros as human desire, drawn to the good, but also drawn to less pure goals. If we do succeed in focusing on the good, and 'we try perfectly to love what is imperfect our loves goes to its object *via* the good to be thus purified and made unselfish and just' (ibid., p. 103). This process can be seen in the example of the mother-in-law's change of heart and will be examined in more detail in the next chapter, when we turn to the task of living the moral life.

13　The fool being taken from Psalm 14, where the fool says in his heart there is no God.

14　He argues that one has no means by which to picture a greatest being, because one has no experience of such a being. Thus, though one can imagine the 'greatest man', for example, because one has a general idea of 'man', one cannot picture the greatest being as one has no experience to draw upon.

15　For further detail, see Gaunilo (1968, p. 10).

16　For example, the scholars Murdoch employs in this discussion: Norman Malcolm, Charles Hartshorne, J.N. Findlay and so on.

17　Malcolm criticizes Kant's premise that 'if God exists (and it is possible that He does not) then He necessarily exists' (Malcolm, 1968, p. 155). The adoption of this premise, Malcolm argues, negates the true meaning of 'necessity' and presents 'a self contradictory position' (ibid.).

18　Incidentally, although Murdoch uses Findlay to support her rejection of any empirical being or object as the focus of the ontological proof, it is worth noting that Findlay takes

88                    *The Moral Vision of Iris Murdoch*

a very different approach to the ontological argument as a whole. He asserts that 'necessity in propositions merely reflects our use of words, the arbitrary conventions of our language . . . (and) . . . the Divine Existence could only be a necessary matter if we had made up our minds to speak theistically *whatever the empirical circumstances might turn out to be*' (Findlay, 1968, p. 119). Findlay, like most post-Kantian scholars, rejects necessary existence, seeing it as a trick of words, whereas for Murdoch it is not only real, but essential for establishing the good.

19    Murdoch's understandings of the Christian God and religion will be returned to in Chapter 7.

20    We will return to Murdoch's criticisms of religion in Chapter 7.

21    Plato was accused of presenting moral values as objects, and his critics, from Aristotle onwards, often envisaged the Platonic forms as objects, though not objects of the sensible world. By interpreting Plato's philosophy as a two-world theory, the forms were regarded as analogous to material objects, and hence thought of in a not dissimilar manner. Such a reading of Plato is rejected by Murdoch, and she is at great pains to avoid a similar interpretation of her own work. Consequently, she emphasizes that there is no other-worldly supernatural element to her thought and nothing which suggests that moral values exist as objects in some other realm.

22    Some commentators disagree, claiming that the good is never intended to be more than an idea in the mind; for example, see Kaalikoski (1997).

23    Attention for Murdoch is a mechanism to purify the thoughts and turn one's focus away from the self and illusion and towards something else. It is 'looking carefully at something and *holding* it before the mind' (Murdoch, 1992, p. 3). Attention to anything outside the self will aid the moral task to see the real; however, it is intended that one should gradually progress toward the good. This progression is paralleled to the progression in the Phaedrus, in which one moves from the beauty of the flesh to absolute beauty. Murdoch's concept of attention will be explored in detail in the next chapter.

24    We will return to Murdoch's conception of religion in Chapter 7: her wish to rehabilitate religious concepts and practice into a non-supernatural moral philosophy. For now we will simply use religion to shed light on Murdoch's concept of the good.

25    This will be explored further in Chapters 5 and 7.

26    As noted by Kerr, who comments that 'her knowledge of medieval theology evidently does not include the standard thesis that God is not to be regarded as an object in any kind' (Kerr, 1997, p. 75).

27    Murdoch neglects many of the most influential theologians, devoting 'more space to Don Cupitt than to Thomas Aquinas' (Jones, 1993, p. 689).

28    While this may seem unsatisfactory, Murdoch would claim that this is often all that philosophy can do; thus she states that 'no more, and no less, than this is done by the most empirically minded of linguistic philosophers. As there is no philosophical or scientific proof of total determinism, the notion is at least allowable that there is a part of the soul which is free from the mechanism of empirical psychology' (Murdoch, 1970a, p. 75).

# Chapter 5

# Living the Moral Life

In the course of the last two chapters we have explored Murdoch's moral realist conception and the central place of the value of the good in her schema. In this chapter we will go on to consider her vision of the moral life, which perhaps most demarcates her philosophy from that of her contemporaries, presenting the moral life as an all-encompassing way of being, in a manner we more usually associate with religious visions.

Murdoch's understanding of the moral life as a 'way' to be lived is in many ways the most singular, and for many the most inspiring, aspect of her moral vision which, like her conception of the good, owes much to her commitment to Plato. For Murdoch, the moral life is a totality and moral striving is the primary and unending task of the agent as he or she moves through life. The moral life is essentially a pilgrimage from illusion to reality, going on in the moment-to-moment judgments of daily life. Moreover, and perhaps surprisingly in the philosophical context, it is, in part, spiritual (although not supernatural) in nature.

This chapter will outline Murdoch's vision of the moral life in detail and its inspiration: Plato's image of the cave. It will set out the conditions of the quest, the limitations of the human condition, the danger of illusions and the progression of the moral life. Once this stage is set it will go on to explore the detail of how the moral life is to be lived: the notion of attention, her assumption, again following Plato, that there are levels of awareness through which the moral individual must progress, and the use of myths, metaphors and images in this ascension. The chapter will conclude with a discussion of the starting-points of the moral life: that of ordinary experiences of intellectual discipline, love and the appreciation of beauty in art and nature. The place of art in the moral life will be expanded fully in the next chapter.

## The Pilgrimage

In the previous two chapters, which discussed Murdoch's realism and her key concept of the good, we saw clearly that Murdoch envisages values and awareness of goodness as continually present in everyday life: 'good and bad "seep" through our moment-to-moment experiences' (Murdoch, 1992, p. 265). Such daily recognition of value in ordinary experience lies at the heart of our ability to structure and order the world. Accordingly, perceiving moral values and making the corresponding judgments (as discussed in earlier chapters) is not 'intermittent or specialised, it is not a peculiar separate area of our existence' (ibid., p. 495). Rather, in this picture, the moral sphere constitutes, in a very real sense, the whole of our existence; 'morality must engage the whole man' (ibid., p. 457). The moral world provides the context within which all thoughts, decisions and actions occur, the backdrop for all human living. The sense that what is true and real has to be strived for and is not, as we saw clearly in the discussion of fact and value, equatable or limited to scientific fact, is a starting assumption that Murdoch feels is revealed by experience and has roots in many philosophies and conceptions of life. In support of the assertion that reality lies behind superficial appearances, she turns for support not only to Plato, who is of course her first point of reference, but also to Kant and to Eastern philosophy's conception of the 'veil of Maya' (ibid., p. 298). Again she does not regard this as religious (in the sense of invoking a supernatural belief system) but rather asserts, 'that our awareness in all its variety, of our daily "world" is normally hasty and perfunctory, and may be deepened, revealing more truth and reality, is on reflection something obvious' (ibid.). Murdoch presents her own version of the quest using insights from Plato, Eastern and Western religions and from modern understandings of the human condition, particularly those taken from Freud and psychoanalysis, and thus pictures the human ego as essentially selfish and illusion-ridden.

The quest towards the good, real and true (which, as noted in the previous chapters, are connected and aspects of the same reality) involves overcoming the illusions which constitute human reality. The moral life then involves escaping the self and moving towards the good. The pilgrimage towards reality is enlivened by the good: the ultimately unattainable goal of the moral pilgrimage. In order to progress, 'we have to learn from our experience, as we move all the time in the continuum between good and bad. This is our everyday existence' (ibid., p. 507).

Murdoch's interpretation of Plato is fundamental to understanding her conception of the moral life. It would be no exaggeration to describe her philosophy at this point as an exegesis of, or meditation on, Plato's Cave. Indeed, from Plato she takes her foundational beliefs, that 'value is everywhere, that the whole of life is movement on a moral scale, all knowledge is a moral quest, and the mind seeks reality and desires the Good, which is a transcendent source of spiritual power, to which we are all related through the idea of truth' (ibid., p. 56). It is this holistic vision which Murdoch is attempting to translate and impart in the modern context: a vision of pilgrimage which is spiritual, but not supernatural or traditionally religious, an objective moral requirement which is absolute, but allows for the individual and individualized response and a holistic universal realism, but without dogmatism and coercion. The task she has set herself is immense and it is no surprise that this religious-sounding vision of the moral life is one of the least commented upon aspects of her philosophy, so out of fit is it in the current climate. Wary of the concepts of value and the self, present-day philosophy has no place for such grandiose visions and perhaps even less of a place for overtly proselytizing

*Living the Moral Life* 91

philosophies.[1] Post-Kantian philosophy has, in its move to descriptive, scientific models, denounced prescriptive philosophies. In her vision of the moral life, Murdoch departs almost entirely from the concerns of contemporary philosophy and their methodologies (of description and ever more detailed analysis) and from the concerns of most contemporary ethicists, those of 'right action' and the meaning of moral terms. Instead she returns to the Socratic description of ethics, that 'it is no ordinary matter that we are discussing, but the right conduct of life' (*Republic*, 352d, Plato, 1989, p. 603), a question which has been either regarded as too broad for philosophy or rejected on ideological grounds that philosophy should be descriptive and not prescriptive. Clearly, Murdoch is unimpressed by both these responses and, as we saw in Chapter 3, she regards such limited philosophies as failing to do philosophy at all. Thus, although unusual in modern philosophy, and for many uncomfortable, it is a broad and prescriptive philosophy that Murdoch is outlining in her vision of the moral life. It is in discussion of the moral life that we see how Murdoch's arguments for the self, for her brand of realism and for the good combine and support each other. Therefore, however unusual, her vision of the moral life needs to be addressed if the other aspects of her philosophy are to be fully understood.

## A Spiritual Quest

In light of the above we will begin our exploration of the moral life by examining Murdoch's assertion of the moral life as spiritual. Murdoch's insistence on the term 'spiritual' and her use of the term 'pilgrimage', a term which we normally attach to religious worldviews, as well as much of the language and images she invokes, suggests a religious conception of the world. Yet Murdoch is adamantly not religious in the traditional sense; as we found in the last chapter, her primary assumption is that 'human life has no external point or telos' (Murdoch, 1970a, p. 38). Moreover, the rest of her philosophy continually asserts the primacy of ordinary human experience as the starting-point and continual touchstone of true philosophy. Therefore the question we must answer is how to marry her spiritual vision, which does involve the language and trappings that we generally associate with religion, with her denial of the supernatural and her belief in the primacy of ordinary experience.[2]

In short, to accept Murdoch's vision, we must accept both premises (that the moral life is both spiritual and ordinary) which at first glance appear, if not contradictory, at least in some conflict. We must understand 'spiritual', like the recognition of moral values, as a basic human capacity, or as an ordinary capacity which only appears unusual because it has been gradually eroded from philosophical conceptions of the world. Just as a pseudoscientific, descriptive philosophical worldview cannot account for the ordinary, daily experience of value, neither can it account for ordinary, daily spiritual experience. It is again reductionist, and it reflects a failure of philosophy to

92       *The Moral Vision of Iris Murdoch*

recognize that 'spiritual reality is the same as ordinary reality' (Murdoch, 1992, p. 297).

In Murdoch's picture moral judgments are continual, 'like eating or breathing' (ibid., p. 458), and involve all aspects of human life. If this is so, Murdoch argues, morality must also include the spiritual. Again, following Plato, she describes living the moral life 'as moving through a continuum within which we are aware of truth and falsehood, illusion and reality, good and evil. We are continually striving and learning, discovering and discarding images. Here we are not forced to choose between "a religious life" and a "secular life"' (ibid., p. 250). For Murdoch, the spiritual is part of human knowing, something which modern moral philosophy has rejected or forgotten in its striving to be scientific, which again has impaired philosophy's ability to account accurately for human experience. In support of this contention she cites not only Plato but also Schopenhauer and Kant, suggesting that these philosophers 'attempt to think the spiritual without the supernatural' (ibid., p. 64). She also looks to Eastern philosophies and to Zen Buddism in particular as providing a parallel example of the moral quest, suggesting that in Zen 'one cannot separate cognition from an idea of truth as something to be reached by a spiritual or moral path' (ibid., p. 242). Thus, for Murdoch, the moral quest is always spiritual and transcendent, being an aspect of human lived reality. Again she is echoing Plato's understanding of the nature of morality of which she says: 'The Platonic "true knowledge" must also be understood in a moral–religious sense which pictures salvation or enlightenment as wisdom or true vision, brought about by a refinement of desire in daily living, and involving clearer perception, including literal perception of the world' (ibid., p. 175).

The transcendent element of the moral reality is most clear in Murdoch's conception of the good, but it is also evident in recognition of other values (again a position inspired by Plato (ibid., p. 224)). In our everyday experience of reality we perceive values and the good (in more-or-less accurate ways, depending on what stage of the moral pilgrimage we have reached) and this perception includes an awareness of transcendence. In our recognition of values we are recognizing transcendence: for example, in the moral values which inform and shape any given situation but are not contained by it. To illustrate this point, Murdoch looks to Plato's description of this perception found in the *Meno*. In this dialogue, Socrates questions a slave boy about his understanding of mathematics, and the boy, who has had no schooling, is able to follow Socrates's description and recognize and comprehend ideas (in this instance mathematical ones). The slave boy exhibits *anamnesis*, in that he can identify and articulate ideas even though he has not been taught them. Murdoch uses this example to show how it feels when we recognize values: as if there is 'a power working at the barrier of darkness, recovering verities which we somehow know of but have, in our egoistic fantasy life, "forgotten"' (ibid., p. 320).

In the *Meno* knowledge is presented as remembering what the soul once knew. Murdoch regards the postulation of the soul's pre-existence, not as a

*Living the Moral Life* 93

literal belief, but as a metaphorical device to depict the experience of recognizing values and reality. We have an affinity for perceiving the world in a moral manner and thus intuit values even when we do not completely comprehend the full reality of what we are coming to know. In her terms the picture of 'remembering' is used by Plato as a means to impress upon us the familiarity of moral knowledge and its place in everyday life. So in a pictorial manner the idea of remembering captures the feel of moral recognition. Murdoch retells Plato's use of remembering to convey the experience of attaining moral knowledge thus:

> We can only learn what we already know, what we can, as it were, remember. If we have ideas of good or perfection in an imperfect world these must be derived from a higher source. We have to find our certainties for ourselves, in ourselves, and we must believe in our duty and ability to discover and make our own truths which we first intuit or make out as shadows. We can only be sure of what we have thus personally found and appropriated. (Ibid., pp. 434–5)

What Murdoch is trying to convey by citing the *Meno* and Plato's doctrine of *anamnesis* is the fundamental and instinctive moral nature of the world. We automatically sense the moral factors of a situation. Our task is to recognize them ever more clearly and respond accordingly as we progress in our individual pilgrimage.

A similar thoroughly moral picture, Murdoch argues, is found in Kant, particularly in his construction of the Categorial Imperative. Murdoch reads Kant as attempting to describe 'the moral confidence which can only be consulted in each individual bosom, not blindly accepted on external authority, and his Ideas of Reason, which constantly inspire us to seek truths which we intuit but have not fully discovered' (ibid., p. 435). The concept of gaining knowledge through intuiting the reality of a truth which we know is there but we do not fully comprehend – 'we often long to understand a truth which we already intuit' (ibid., p. 398) – is central to Murdoch's vision of the moral life and moral pilgrimage. Therefore the moral quest is characterized by striving more clearly to understand that of which we are dimly aware of and to which we are drawn, namely moral value and, especially, the good. In this recognition and striving we are living the moral life and 'are changed by love and pursuit of what we only partly see and understand. This activity is our awareness of our world' (ibid., p. 222). It is recognition of the human (moral) external reality, but personalized in our individual discovery and verification.

Despite the esoteric nature of this description of attaining knowledge, Murdoch suggests that it is in fact 'an idea with which we are familiar in personal relationships, in art, in theoretical studies. I have faith . . . in a person or idea in order to understand him or it, I intuitively know and grasp more than I can yet explain' (ibid., p. 393). Thus she suggests that 'we have no difficulty in combining imperfect cognitions with ideas of perfection which haunt them. These are ordinary states of affairs' (ibid., p. 473). Murdoch

94 *The Moral Vision of Iris Murdoch*

illustrates the ordinary nature of this manner of gaining knowledge by using examples from art and intellectual disciplines. For example, at times when one struggles to comprehend a certain idea or gain a particular insight, 'the artist or thinker concentrates on the problem, grasps it as a problem with some degree of clarity, and waits. Something is apprehended as *there* which is not yet *known*. Then something comes; as we sometimes say from the unconscious' (ibid., p. 505). Gaining moral knowledge is not dissimilar to attaining other forms of knowledge, but rather is a familiar method by which we comprehend the world. In this vein Murdoch argues that 'an ability to think seriously and honestly, works to support what is already innately known. Goodness joins with knowledge, moral vision is cognitive' (ibid., p. 436).

It is this intuitive and transcendent element involved in the recognition of morality which Murdoch describes as 'spiritual'. She is using the term to capture the holistic nature of the endeavour, the continual commitment and striving, as well as the sense of growth and accomplishment when an only vaguely sensed idea is grasped. Providing a clear and concise description of this familiar, if cloudy, process is not easy (as discussed with reference to the good), hence the need for images such as Plato's *anamnesis*, which Murdoch regards as a mythical but intuitively accurate description of 'this strange familiar yet mysterious continuum which is so difficult to describe' (ibid., p. 495). It is for this purpose, then, in order to expand our conception of the world within which we experience morality and make moral decisions, that Murdoch deliberately introduces the usually religious term, 'spiritual', declaring that 'this word certainly seems to me to be at home in the moral sphere, suggesting creative and imaginative activity of our mind, spirit, in relation to our surroundings' (ibid.). The spiritual nature of the moral quest is not, for Murdoch, an optional extra, for 'we all, not only can but *have* to, experience and deal with a transcendent reality, the resistant otherness of other persons, other things, history, the natural world, the cosmos, and this involves perpetual effort . . . most of this effort is moral effort' (ibid., p. 268).

Such a notion of the moral life Murdoch recognizes is out of fit with many of her contemporaries and much current moral philosophy, which tends to advocate scepticism about 'anything *including the past*, which can be intuited as transcendent and somehow existing separately in its own right' (ibid., p. 6). However, in her vision, a broad conception of human reality is essential, for the pilgrim of the moral quest 'perceives the real world, a true and just seeing of people and human institutions, which is also a seeing of the invisible through the visible, the real through the apparent, the spiritual beyond the material' (ibid., p. 475).

The spiritual conception of the quest also emphasizes the individual moral agent, who is 'at every moment mobile between good and bad and attracted in both directions' (ibid., p. 336). The individual grows and changes, for 'moral progress (freedom, justice, love, truth) leads us to a new state of being. This higher state does not involve the ending, but rather the transformation of the "ordinary" person and the world' (ibid., p. 165). Essentially the attraction of

# Living the Moral Life

the good and the all-consuming nature of the moral quest is described as spiritual in order to communicate the continuing and all-consuming nature of the moral life. The term 'spiritual' recognizes the unavoidable call of morality and thus 'the absolute demand remains' (ibid., p. 506). The feeling of 'demand', often interpreted as religious, is for Murdoch moral demand (emphasized by other moral realists too[3]). The essential spiritual element of the moral quest is such that Murdoch claims that the 'moral (or spiritual) life is both one and not one' (ibid., p. 483): one in that the moral quest as a way is undeniably spiritual, not one in that the moral quest does not need to be connected to a religious (as the term is traditionally understood) quest. In a similar manner she argues that 'the ordinary way is the way. It is not in that sense theology, and the mysticism involved is an accessible experience' (ibid., p. 509). The quest then is spiritual in that spiritual comprehension is part of our ordinary interaction with the world and necessary and fundamental if we are to hold an accurate picture of human life. Such an assertion, for Murdoch, should not be controversial when considered in the context of her realism, as the experience she describes 'in ordinary life is a familiar one, is that of certainty or (its different face) necessity, connected with the sense of a pure untainted source of spiritual power. Herein our most ordinary modes of cognition become connected with strong convictions and vision' (ibid., p. 430). Given the central place of the spiritual in all areas of life, Murdoch wishes it to be recognized again in moral philosophies and other explorations and explanations of human life, asserting that 'I see no reason to predict a "loss of spirit". The human capacity to seek, and enjoy, the good and the true is versatile and endlessly creative' (ibid., p. 471).

## The Inspiration of the Cave

In Murdoch's vision of the moral life her reliance on Plato is vivid, and her picture of the moral universe is thoroughly Platonic. In her reading, Plato presents the moral life as

> a spiritual pilgrimage inspired by the disturbing magnetism of *truth*, involving *ipso facto* a purification of energy and desire in the light of a vision of what is *good*. The good and just life is thus a process of clarification, a movement towards selfless lucidity, guided by ideas of perfection which are objects of *love*. Platonic morality is not coldly intellectual, it involves the whole man and attaches value to the most 'concrete' of everyday preoccupations and acts. It concerns the continuous detail of human activity, wherein we discriminate between appearance and reality, good and bad, true and false, and check or strengthen our desires. (Murdoch, 1992, p. 14).

This description of Plato's vision of morality and the moral life is, in essence and substance, Murdoch's vision. She looks to Plato (and her particular interpretation of Plato) constantly, for inspiration and for the content of her

96        *The Moral Vision of Iris Murdoch*

philosophy. In particular, Murdoch is inspired and captivated by Plato's mythical picture of the moral pilgrimage, described in his myth of the Cave, which is found in the *Republic*, Book Five. She describes the Cave as a 'parable' which 'portrays a spiritual pilgrimage from illusion to reality' (ibid., p. 10). This myth is so central to Murdoch's whole philosophy, from her picture of the moral life to her conception of the good, that it is worth retelling in some detail.

In the dialogue Socrates describes an underground chamber in which there are prisoners who have been held there since childhood. These prisoners face the back wall of the cave, fastened by their legs and necks so that they are unable to turn and can only look straight in front of them. Behind the prisoners burns a fire (which is the source of light in this underground world), and between the fire and the prisoners runs a road, along which people are walking and carrying things. The shadows of these people going about their business are reflected onto the back wall of the cave and naturally the prisoners assume that the shadows they see are real objects and they conclude that the voices and noises they hear originate from the shadows they see. Socrates then considers what would happen if a prisoner were able to turn around and suggests that, if 'one was freed from his fetters and compelled to stand up suddenly and turn his head around and walk and to lift up his eyes to the light, and in doing all this felt pain, and because of the dazzle and the glitter of the light, was unable to discern the objects whose shadows he formally saw' (*Republic*, 515c–d, Plato, 1989, p. 748). The pain involved in this transformation would lead to bewilderment of such a degree that the prisoner would be likely to reject the revelations and wish to return to his old position, believing the shadows on the wall to be more real than the objects and people now confronting him. Moreover, if the prisoner was forced to look directly into the fire he would suffer even more pain and would be blinded and so unable to distinguish objects from each other and therefore he would wish to return to a darker level where he could see clearly. The next stage of the prisoner's journey, if he were not allowed to return to his shadow gazing and 'someone should drag him thence by force up the ascent which is rough and steep' (*Republic*, 515e, Plato, 1989, p. 748), would be out of the cave into the sunlight. The process would again be painful and the prisoner would again be blinded and unable to see that things he was now told were real. Eventually, the (ex-) prisoner would become accustomed to the light in the real upper world and able to recognize the world and its objects as real. The process of awareness would be slow:

> At first he would most easily discern the shadows and, after that, the likeness or reflections in water of men and other things, and later, the things themselves, and from these he would go on to contemplate the appearances in the heavens and heaven itself, more easily by night, looking at the light of the stars and the moon, than by day and the sun's light . . . and so finally, I suppose, he would be able to look upon the sun itself and see its true nature, not by reflections in water or

*Living the Moral Life* 97

phantasms of it in an alien setting, but in and by itself in its own place. (*Republic*, 516a–b, Plato, 1989, p. 748)

The final and highest point of the journey is reached, after much pain and perseverance, when the prisoner is able to lift his head and face the sun itself. Only at this final stage of the quest, facing the sun itself, is it possible for the prisoner to comprehend the whole landscape; only at this point could the prisoner conclude that it is the sun 'that provides the seasons and the courses of the year and presides over all things in the visible region, and is in some sort the cause of all these things that they had seen' (*Republic*, 516b, Plato, 1989, p. 749). At this stage he realizes the lowliness of his former state and pities those still mistaken about the nature of reality, and 'would choose to endure anything rather than such a life' (*Republic*, 516e, Plato, 1989, p. 749). If this (ex-) prisoner returned to the cave he would again become blind, this time from the darkness, and would appear to the remaining prisoners to be a fool as he would be unable to distinguish the shadows on the cave wall clearly. The prisoners would conclude that 'he had returned from his journey aloft with his eyes ruined and that it was not worth while even to attempt the ascent' (*Republic*, 517a, Plato, 1989, p. 749). These prisoners, unable to comprehend any knowledge or values beyond their own, would resist ascent to the point that they would kill anyone who tried to take them out of their illusory world.

Murdoch uses Plato's myth of the Cave in the same way that she believes he does, as a metaphor of the moral life, which entails levels of moral awareness and perception.[4] At lower levels one has only inklings of the higher states of awareness, hence the difficulty of clear and distinct definition and the need for 'metaphorical moral thinking' (Murdoch, 1992, p. 183). Murdoch regards Plato's picture of the Cave as perfectly capturing the intuitive and spiritual aspects of the moral life for 'we, inside the cave, are intuitively aware of many things whose presence and proximity we may "feel", but which we cannot, or cannot yet fully explain or inspect' (ibid., p. 228). Thus Plato's Cave is for Murdoch 'an endlessly instructive image' (ibid., p. 399), 'a spiritual guidebook, a myth of the soul' (ibid., p. 388), which 'presents fundamental ideas metaphysically in the form of myth' (ibid., p. 236). Yet, crucially, although mystical in form, Plato's images are not removed from ordinary life, but rather explain, in a metaphorical way, familiar forms of knowing, although resistant to definition in the predominant pseudoscientific empirical language preferred by modern philosophy. For Murdoch, then,

The Cave is a religious myth suggesting, what is also accessible to any careful not necessarily philosophical reflection, that there are discernable levels and qualities of *awareness* or *experience* (we need this terminology), which cannot be reduced to acquaintance with neutral factual propositions or analysed in terms of dispositions to act. (Ibid., p. 183)

## Illusions and Delusions

Murdoch's vision of the moral life as a pilgrimage from illusion to reality is inspired by, and is almost a direct retelling of, Plato's myth of the Cave. It is a presentation of the moral life which she feels 'offers us a recognisable picture of the human scene' (Murdoch, 1992, p. 59).

Given her allegiance to the Cave it is no surprise that Murdoch has a relatively dark vision of the human condition, one which is equivalent to the lowest, shadow-gazing, level of the Cave. The lowest level of the Cave, in Plato's terms *eikasia* or *phantasia*, represents the level at which human beings are unable to see what is real. Murdoch updates this level of the Cave for the modern context using the language of psychology and arguing that we are blinded by the wishes and desires of our own egos (ibid., p. 317). That we are illusion-ridden and egoistic is a fundamental premise for Murdoch.[5] She takes it as read that human beings in their lowest (natural) condition 'are ruthless egoists and that the world which we take as all-important and *real* is a valueless and *unreal* world' (ibid., p. 72). Murdoch asserts that the selfish and egoistic elements of the human condition (found not only in Plato, but also in Christianity and Eastern philosophies and religions) must be recognized in any accurate representation of human life. Indeed, the fact that recent philosophies have tended to ignore this reality is one of the reasons Murdoch considers they present a false and over-optimistic conception of morality (Murdoch, 1970a, p. 54).

Murdoch regards recognizing the ego-bound illusion-ridden nature of the human condition as an essential part of realism. Accordingly, her fundamental assumption is that 'human beings are naturally selfish' (Murdoch, 1992, p. 78), which 'seems true on the evidence, whenever and wherever we look at them' (Murdoch, 1970a, p. 78). The natural selfishness of human beings means that any moral philosophy which wishes to portray an accurate 'picture of humanity must portray its fallen nature' (Murdoch, 1992, p. 509). Murdoch does not regard this starting-point as unduly pessimistic (especially when one takes into account the illumination provided by the good), but rather realistic, for 'nothing is more evident in human life than fear and muddle, and the tumultuous agitation of the battle against natural egoism. The ego is "unbridled"' (ibid., p. 260). Murdoch relies heavily on psychology (in particular the work of Freud[6]) to provide a modern formulation of our illusion-ridden condition. She uses Freud's picture of the 'psyche as an egocentric system of quasi mechanical energy, largely determined by its own individual history, whose natural attachments are sexual, ambiguous and hard for the subject to understand or control . . . objectivity and unselfishness are not natural to human beings' (Murdoch, 1970a, p. 51).

Accordingly, much (even most) human action, when morality is ignored, is entirely selfish, 'moved by a mechanical energy of an egocentric kind' (ibid., p. 52). The desires of the ego run contrary to those of the committed moral pilgrim. While it is the moral agent who seeks the real, the ego wishes to escape reality and all external demands (including those made by other people) to protect itself in fantasy; 'it constantly seeks consolation, either through imagined inflation of the self or through fictions of a theological nature' (ibid., p. 79). In this illusion-ridden state human beings are 'largely mechanical creatures, the slaves of relentlessly strong selfish forces the nature of which we scarcely comprehend' (ibid., p. 99). We protect ourselves from seeing the real by aggrandizing the self and hiding from the realities of other people and the world; in this self-protective endeavour 'our minds are continually active, fabricating and anxious, usually self-preoccupied' (ibid., p. 84). As human beings, then, it is our 'natural impulse to derealise our world and surround ourselves with fantasy' (Murdoch, 1992, p. 503). To this end we rationalize situations and create justifying narratives in order to shield our fragile selves from reality and its demands (Murdoch, 1970a, pp. 84, 165). In this self-protective, thoroughly egotistical, illusory state we are unable to see outside the self to the real, for the 'fantasy (self) can prevent us from seeing a blade of grass just as it can prevent us from seeing another person' (ibid., p. 70).

The power of the ego to delude the self is almost unchallengeable in Murdoch's conception of its most deluded state. Even in cases of bereavement and suffering, times when the self is forced to confront reality and circumstances which cannot be fantasized away by creative retelling, the danger of further delusion is ever present. For example, Murdoch argues that bereavement (the death of a loved one) may force the ego to recognize realities outside the self and provide an opportunity for growth. Alternatively, however, the ego may respond, not by facing the harsh reality, but by frantically creating protective illusions and false coping mechanisms serving further to wrap the agent in illusion and false consolation. Murdoch suggests that such defensive image creation is common in suffering, as 'it is difficult to suffer well, without resentment, false consolation, untruthful flight' (Murdoch, 1992, p. 130). Thus, while capable of shattering illusions and diminishing the ego, suffering may also provide a means of strengthening the fantasy of the ego, for example by utilizing 'ideas of guilt and punishment . . . the most subtle tool of the ingenious self' (Murdoch, 1970a, p. 68). The aim of the ego in creating such fantasies is to protect itself from the real and to retreat back into the safety of illusion as quickly as possible; in the terms of the Cave myth, to retreat to a lower, more comfortable, level of the Cave. Therefore the moral task is to dismantle the veil which 'separates us from the order and true multiplicity of the real world' (Murdoch, 1992, p. 165). Our task is to break through the fantasy and begin to see what is outside the self and the ego; 'the enemy is the fat relentless ego' (Murdoch, 1970a, p. 52).

Although perceiving reality is a personal moral task, in which knowledge of the good and moral values must be discovered by the individual, Murdoch is keen to stress that true knowledge is far more than self-knowledge (although seeing oneself truthfully is part of seeing reality). Murdoch is critical of the current trend which suggests that the totality of truth can be found by inner searching alone. Indeed, her primary criticism of mysticism (which, we shall see in later chapters, she regards in a favourable light) is that it may be the 'ultimate deification of egoism' (Murdoch, 1992, p. 70). The danger of self-knowledge is that one may be falsely satisfied with self-knowledge alone and so fail to progresses in the moral quest. Moreover, self-knowledge alone can never be true knowledge because true knowledge involves the uncomfortable recognition of realities that are not the self: the reality of other people and, of course, the moral reality. Furthermore, exclusively seeking self-knowledge is potentially dangerous as it may masquerade as real knowledge and offer 'plausible imitations of what is good' (Murdoch, 1970a, p. 68). Murdoch regards self-examination where self-knowledge is the only goal as sadomasochistic, resulting in a corrupted vision of reality, which is still, if not more so, irredeemably sunk in illusion.

If we return to the image of the Cave, Murdoch regards this limited form of knowledge (self-knowledge) as equivalent to the second level of the Cave. The prisoners have recognized the reality of the fire and the sight fascinates and consumes them. They are captivated by the fire and cannot be drawn away. They remain at this low level of awareness, deluded by the secondary light of the fire, which 'represents the self, the old unregenerate psyche, that great source of energy and warmth' (ibid., p. 100). In order to progress morally, we must escape the delusions and illusions of self and 'break the barriers of egoism' (Murdoch, 1992, p. 297). We must not be confused by the fire, but strive to feel the true warmth of the sun, of reality beyond our ego and the delusions of the self. Or, to use the words of Eastern philosophies, rather than the language of psychology, we must 'look through the veil of Maya, lose our egoistic personal identity and overcome the divide between subject and object' (ibid., p. 59).

Likewise Murdoch is critical of philosophies and therapies which not only locate reality within the self, but which strive to harmonize good and evil within the soul. Murdoch argues that 'we must *see* evil, and reject any pact (Heraclitus, Jung) between evil and good' (ibid., p. 447).[7] Again Murdoch asserts her realism, arguing that 'self contained soul experience obscures, and is no substitute for, the struggle with an *alien reality* which engenders and imposes and develops absolute distinctions between good and evil and truth and falsehood' (ibid., p.135).[8] In our aim to move towards the real and the good we must distance ourselves from evil as, for Murdoch, 'there is no harmonious balance whereby we suddenly find that evil is just a "dark side" which is not only harmless to good, but actually enhances it. Evil may have to be lived with, but remains evil, and we live too with the real possibility of improvement' (ibid., p. 506). Her stern rejection of harmonizing philosophies puts Murdoch's vision into sharp contrast with many of the philosophies of our time, especially the widely embraced tenets of therapy and self-help which suggest that we should strive for a balanced psyche, summarized by the mantra 'know thyself'. Knowledge of the self for Murdoch is a constituent part of perceiving the real accurately but it must not be seen as the end-point of the quest. Thus, like Plato, she sees a profound and absolute 'contrast between states of illusion (selfish habits or egoistic fantasy) and honest clarified truthful serious thinking . . . [which] . . . suggests a moral picture of the mind as in a continuous engagement with an independent reality' (ibid., p. 399). The ego is to be overcome; not made peace with. The moral task Murdoch sets before us is uncompromising and must be without illusion. It is not an easy task and its goal, achieving a true vision of reality, is (almost) unachievable. However, we can progress towards the good. Our ego can be gradually reduced, and in consequence reality seen more clearly, for, in striving to see reality in all its forms without (or with less) illusion, our egoism decreases as a result of an 'increased sense of the reality of, primarily of course other people, but also other things' (ibid., p. 52).

At its simplest, then, for Murdoch, 'morality is loss of egoism' (ibid., p. 468), which involves checking selfish desires in order to purify the self and see reality clearly. As we ascend towards the real, our world will become larger and the clouds of delusion gradually lift. Incrementally, we will be able to see other people, the world and ourselves ever more clearly, instead of seeing shadows based partly (even mostly) on our own projections. Thus the 'good (better) man is *liberated* from selfish fantasy, can see himself as others see him, imagine the needs of other people, love unselfishly, lucidly envisage and desire what is truly valuable' (ibid., p. 331). This, of course, is an ideal picture which it is unlikely (perhaps even impossible) for a human being to achieve fully. However, it does provide a vision of the type of life we are aiming for and, certainly, in destroying selfish desires and attempting to see the real, we can progress some way along this path.

## Levels of Awareness

In progressively negating the ego and attaining a truer, more accurate, and therefore more moral, vision of reality, we progress, as in Plato's image of the Cave, through levels of awareness: from illusion to clearer vision and ultimately to a true perception of reality and the good. In Plato's Cave, from a lower level the next level of awareness appears as a shadow, therefore one can vaguely imagine what it would be like to live at the next level. To illustrate this Murdoch turns to religion, philosophy and art and suggests that 'we see a shadow or image of religious joy in some mystical writings and in some (few) philosophical writings, and then one is tempted to say some art' (Murdoch, 1992, p. 124). The difficulty in perceiving higher realities means that those who are more enlightened are likely to be regarded with suspicion and misunderstood, for 'it is *difficult* to imagine ways of life which are much above our own as being morally demanded. They exert no magnetism and cannot be seen except in terms of senseless deprivation' (ibid., p. 318). The difficulty in conceptualizing higher levels is illustrated by the problems we have in picturing the good person and describing their characteristics. Murdoch suggests that those we consider good we are 'likely to find . . . obscure, or else

102                    *The Moral Vision of Iris Murdoch*

on closer inspection full of frailty. Goodness appears to be both rare and hard to picture' (Murdoch, 1970a, p. 53). However, although goodness is hard to picture and it is difficult to envisage what it would be like to live at higher moral levels, the good does draw us and 'we are constantly in process of recognising the falseness of our "goods", and the unimportance of what we deem important' (Murdoch, 1992, p. 430). Thus, by striving to see clearly at our own level, we realize its limitations and begin the process of attaining higher, better conceptions of the good and correspondingly higher levels of awareness. As described in the last chapter, we know the direction of the good and, therefore, however vaguely, know that we can be better. We see the shadow of the next step of the pilgrimage and are capable of recognizing (when looking) those who are more virtuous than ourselves (at least if they are not too far removed from our own level). Murdoch takes solace in this and offers it as testament to her vision, maintaining that 'it is at least something if we notice and want to be commended by virtuous people, or have an intuitive sense of what we would be like if we were better' (ibid., p. 332). In whichever stage of the pilgrimage we are at, if we are honest and strive to see reality as clearly as our current state will allow, we will wish to progress, for 'we know when we are being satisfied with superficial, illusory, lying pictures which distort and conceal reality' (ibid., p. 462). If we recognize that we could be better, we will then strive to master illusion and so progress to the next level, where the process will continue. We are drawn by the magnetism of the good and thus have 'senses of direction and absolute checks' (ibid., p. 238).

In this depiction of the moral life Murdoch, at her most Platonic, fully endorses the spiritual pilgrimage of the *Republic*, asserting a 'scale of (increasingly) refined personal awareness' (ibid., p. 174). As we ascend through the levels of the moral pilgrimage we gradually reject the desires of the selfish ego, improve our quality of consciousness, purify our ability to be virtuous and develop 'confidence in our own inner life of thought and judgement and in our real existence as individual persons capable of truth' (ibid., p. 221).

**Inspiration and Images**

Murdoch's moral life is available to all; we all recognize moral values and are all aware of the pull of the good. But it has to be worked at and striven for: 'there is a way (a possible pilgrim's progress), but individuals have to *learn* how to use it' (Murdoch, 1992, p. 148). It is an ascension through levels of awareness where lower goods are gradually rejected for higher goods and the ego is overcome and reality ever more clearly perceived. Thus the moral life, like the spiritual life, 'is a long disciplined destruction of false images and false goods until (in some sense which we cannot understand) the imagining mind achieves an end of images and shadows (*ex umbris et imagininibus in veritatem*), the final *demythologisation*' (ibid., p. 320). However, although the ultimate end-point of the moral pilgrimage is to see reality and to destroy

*Living the Moral Life* 103

false images, images provide inspiration and help us on our way. Hence Murdoch's description of the moral life as an 'iconoclastic pilgrimage, through the progressive destruction of false images' (ibid., p. 507).

Images are crucial for describing, communicating and inspiring one to the moral life. The primary image, for Murdoch, is of course Plato's Cave. She also suggests that religious images, though ultimately false if taken as objectively true, can be inspiring and useful in the moral quest (as will be further discussed in Chapter 7). Indeed, images are essential in our attempts to inexpertly intuit higher levels of awareness which, as previously discussed, particularly with regard to the good, are difficult to describe in exact and non-metaphorical ways. Murdoch praises Plato's use of images and describes his myths as 'instructive metaphor' (ibid., p. 180), and 'pictorial explanations' (ibid., p. 475). Metaphors and pictures are not for Murdoch merely alternative ways of presenting metaphysics, they are philosophy themselves. If pictorial modes of communication are excluded from the vocabulary we use to define and interpret the world, as they arguably are, at least in their more mythical manifestations, from much recent and modern philosophy, then we will lose the ability to talk about the moral life at all (a parallel argument to her argument for the inner life and for the rejection of the fact/value dichotomy). Murdoch argues that it is 'impossible to discuss certain kinds of concepts without resort to metaphor, since the concepts themselves are deeply metaphorical and cannot be analysed into non-metaphorical components without a loss of substance' (Murdoch, 1970a, p. 77). Myths and metaphors are obviously important in Murdoch's and Plato's schemas as they allow pictorial explanations of a reality which cannot be accurately described until one reaches the end-point of the quest. Moreover, even if one had reached the end of the quest, any description of reality from this final perspective would be unintelligible at lower levels. Therefore pictures, metaphors and images are not only useful in describing the moral quest but are essential in depicting and providing inspiration for the moral life. Furthermore, images serve at an everyday level to counteract the illusion-ridden nature of the human condition and to lighten the somewhat bleak picture, for they provide insights and reveal the possibility of moral growth. In this regard she states:

> On the road between illusion and reality there are many clues and signals and wayside shrines and sacraments and places of meditation and refreshment. The pilgrim just has to look about him with a lively eye. There are many kinds of images in the world, sources of energy, checks and reminders, pure things, inspiring things, innocent things attracting love and veneration. We all have our icons, untainted and vital, which we, perhaps secretly, store away in safety. There is nothing esoteric or surprising about this, people know about it, it is familiar. (Murdoch, 1992, p. 496)

Our choice of metaphors is fundamental. Certainly Murdoch's choice of Plato's Cave is definitive, as 'metaphorical preferences are not mere matters

104 *The Moral Vision of Iris Murdoch*

of temperament. Dominant metaphors in metaphysics have large implications' (ibid., p. 462). The metaphors and pictures we use to describe the world demarcate the limits and possibilities within which we can be active in the world. Our choice of metaphor defines the 'images of our thinking and our moral life' (ibid.) and as such are foundational for self-definition. For example, as noted above, Murdoch considers images which present the moral life as striving for harmony and balance as bad choices. She regards such images as inaccurate and, moreover, dangerous, as they encourage the agent to accept illusion for knowledge. It is to be happy with the fire and fail to strive for the sun.

The creation and use of pictures is, for Murdoch, a continual human practice, by which we construct our world as 'all our most ordinary thinking, in the moral activity of every day, involves familiar picturing' (Murdoch, 1992, pp. 462–3). There is nothing strange about invoking images, rather it is the most common means of human explanation and 'every individual has a collection of such things which might be indicated by various names and images ... our moral consciousness is full of such imagery, kinaesthetic, visual, literary, traditional, verbal and non-verbal' (ibid., p. 336). Images, then, are 'an inexhaustible and familiar field of human resources' (ibid., p. 335) which provide mechanisms according to which we recognize ourselves and our relationships with others. Such image making and using

> is a familiar aspect of our moment-to-moment, minute-to-minute, hour-to-hour 'consciousness' ... our busy minds are ... not often empty or idle. Such activity constitutes, in my picture of the matter, a large part of our fundamental moral disposition, it is a function of what we really value, what we love and are magnetised by, and of what we are capable of noticing. (Ibid., p. 330)

How we use images is fundamental to the moral life, for 'there is a continuous breeding of imagery in the consciousness which is, for better or worse, a function of moral change' (ibid., p. 329). It is by pictures that we progress, or fail to progress, in the quest. Pictures enlighten, inspire and cast a shadow from the next level of the pilgrimage. Such metaphors function as 'moral illuminations or pictures which remain vividly in the memory, playing a protective or guiding role: moral refuges, perpetual starting-points' (ibid., p. 335). It is the task of the moral agent to use these pictures as a means for moral progress and disregard them when they have served their purpose and we have achieved a clearer picture of the good. As we progress towards reality so must the images we use to drive and inspire us progress for 'image making or image-apprehending is always an imperfect activity, some images are higher than others, that is nearer to reality. Images should not be resting places, but pointers to higher truths' (ibid., pp. 317–18). The images we choose to use are defining and moral change is connected to our preferred imagery: 'changes in our desires go along with changes in instinctive imagery' (ibid., p. 347). Images then must be used and discarded, they must never be regarded as the real itself

*Living the Moral Life* 105

or they will degenerate into idols. We must use our chosen images to grow, and then 'take leave' of them (ibid., p 454). We progress in the moral pilgrimage by 'moving beyond our images and . . . deliberately moving out into a "blank" or "void"' (ibid., p. 329), the time when we have discarded our old images but not yet clearly perceived new images to help and guide us.


## Attention

In addition to using good (or at least better images) there are other aids to the moral pilgrim. As we have seen, the natural human condition, as Murdoch depicts it, is relatively bleak. Human beings are naturally selfish, they are sunk in illusion and struggle desperately to protect the self and to remain in their comfortable deluded state. Countering this state of egoism and illusion is demanding, and breaking away from the ego and facing reality is extremely arduous. Images can inspire and sustain us in the moral life, as can certain habits and practices. In particular, Murdoch advocates the practice of 'attention', and it is this concept and its place in the moral life we will now consider.

The concept of attention is, exactly as its name suggests, attending in a serious way to an object or person, a 'looking carefully at something and *holding* it before the mind' (Murdoch, 1992, p. 3). The concept of attention, like all Murdoch's philosophy, has Platonic influence, and the attitude of attention can be seen in the *Meno* (as discussed earlier in this chapter) in the slave boy's 'remembrance' (*anamnesis*) which 'comes as the reward as a sort of morally disciplined attention' (ibid., p. 23). In Murdoch's retelling of the myth, the slave boy, in attempting to answer the geometrical query, 'is orientating himself towards, bringing his attention to bear upon, something dark and alien, on which the light then falls, and which he "makes his own". He "sees" an object invisible but grasped as "there", he is able to concentrate and attend' (ibid., p. 400). In this sense attention is the process by which one is able to move to a higher level of the cave and progress upon the pilgrimage, by waiting and struggling for a fuller knowledge of reality. The term 'attention', which Murdoch adopts to describe this particular quality of looking at the world, she takes from Simone Weil, who advocates selfless attention and obedience in perceiving the world (ibid., pp. 108–9); in Weil's words, attention is to 'perceive without reverie' (ibid., p. 218).

Attention is a device both to be used in the moral life and to be valued for itself as a good quality of consciousness. Attention shifts one's focus away from the self. It is a kind of secular version of prayer or meditation.[9] Murdoch praises prayer, which she defines, not as 'petition, but simply attention to God which is a form of love' (Murdoch, 1970a, p. 55), for its capacity to 'induce a better quality of consciousness and provide an energy for good action' (ibid., p. 83). The techniques of prayer and meditation (both Christian and Eastern) are advocated as they help those who practise them to be 'more calm, more

106 *The Moral Vision of Iris Murdoch*

"collected", less given to egoistic passions, in many ways more "unselfish"' (Murdoch, 1992, p. 248), all of which are necessary qualities to proceed in the moral quest. It is these capacities of prayer which Murdoch wishes to maintain in the secular context and she advocates the practice of meditation, 'a withdrawal, through some disciplined quietness, into the great chamber of the soul' (ibid., p. 73) and advises that it should be taught to children (ibid., pp. 3, 337). Such practices of 'meditation (prayer, attention, with or without God) may enlarge our being by giving power and reality to good impulses' (ibid., p. 468). Thus she suggests that attention can be adopted in the secular world as a substitute for prayer. This would be 'true mysticism which is morality, a kind of undogmatic prayer which is real and important' (Murdoch, 1970a, pp. 101–2). Attention in this form, although it parallels the role of prayer in religion, is not, Murdoch insists, a 'quasi-religious meditative technique, but something which belongs to the ordinary life of the moral person' (ibid., p. 69). Attention focuses the energy of the ego away from the self; it is a technique for the 'purification and reorientation of energy which is naturally selfish' (ibid., p. 54).

Attention, then, provides a way to break through the ego and to see the real more clearly. It is a means of purifying our desires and engendering moral change. Attention helps to 'change our orientation, to redirect our desire and refresh and purify our energy, to keep on looking in the right direction' (Murdoch, 1992, p. 25). The suggestion that attention is a tool by means of which energy can be turned from the selfish self to other more valuable vistas is for Murdoch neither unusual nor esoteric. Rather, she considers that we all experience the difference between qualities of attention (or perhaps, in more popular language, between ordinary time and 'quality' time). To illustrate this conviction, Murdoch uses an example of a tourist who 'does not *look* at the famous monument, but fiddles with his camera to get a good "view" which he can display later to his neighbours' (ibid., p. 264). This tourist is not giving proper attention to the monument and thus has a lower level of awareness (and so presumably enjoyment and fulfilment) than a tourist who gives the monument full attention and therefore sees clearly. Myriad situations such as this reveal the 'difference between anxious calculating distracted passing of time when the present is never really inhabited or filled, and present moments which are lived attentively as truth and reality' (ibid.). Attention then can be recognized in ordinary everyday experience of the world for 'we are all the time building up our value world and exercising, or failing to exercise, our sense of truth in the daily, hourly minutely business of apprehending, or failing to apprehend, what is real and distinguishing it from illusion' (ibid., p. 304).

For attention to aid the moral quest it would seem that it can be focused on anything that is not the self: 'by the details of our surroundings, we can be touched and surprised into an ability to change, to move "out of ourselves", by all sorts of attention to other things and people ... overcoming the barrier between self and the world' (ibid., p. 299). Murdoch illustrates the change that attention can bring with the following example:

*Living the Moral Life* 107

I am looking out of my window in an anxious and resentful state of mind, oblivious of my surroundings, brooding perhaps on some damage done to my prestige. Then suddenly I observe a hovering kestrel. In a moment everything is altered. The brooding self with its hurt vanity has disappeared. There is nothing now but kestrel. And when I return to thinking of the other matter it seems less important. (Murdoch, 1970a, p. 84)

In taking us away from the self, attention to any object (in this example the kestrel) is beneficial, although some objects of attention are better aids to the moral life than others; 'there are good modes of attention and good objects of attention' (Murdoch, 1992, p. 301). We shall discuss towards the end of the chapter various helpful objects of attention which are useful as instigators of the quest and continue to be beneficial throughout the moral life, namely, art, beauty, intellectual disciplines and love. The supreme object of attention is, of course, the good.

## Right Action from Clear Vision

From our description of perceiving moral values and living the moral life (particularly the concept of attention and the place of images in Murdoch's schema) it is clear that for Murdoch visual imagery and metaphors are crucial. Everything is described using metaphors of vision, which is not surprising as, for Murdoch, '*how* we see our situation is itself, already, a moral activity' (Murdoch, 1992, p. 315) as perception itself is already a mode of evaluation: a concept we discussed in detail in Chapter 3 with reference to the moral background or moral colour of any situation. Before we can act in the world we must see it: 'I can only choose within the world I can *see*, in the moral sense of "see" which implies that clear vision is a result of moral imagination and moral effort' (Murdoch, 1970a, p. 37). How much or how little (or how clearly) we see depends on our progress along the moral pilgrimage. To return again to the example of the Cave, what we can see, in terms of both our ability and the objects to be perceived, depends on our level in the Cave. The prisoners in the lowest level cannot turn their heads and their vision is limited to the shadows in front of them. At the next level they can see more; in the firelight of the Cave they can see other people and the reality of the fire. The ascension through levels of ability to see and the quality of the objects that can be seen continues until the pilgrim reaches the end of the quest and can see the good and recognize the relative position of all the lower levels (although he can no longer 'see' clearly the objects and values that were important to him at these levels). Moral 'sight' is the paramount metaphor of Murdoch's moral vision and defines one's ability to recognize and act accordingly, for 'the selfish self-interestedly casual or callous man *sees* a different world from that which the careful scrupulous benevolent just man sees; and the largely explicable ambiguity of the word "see" here conveys the essence of the concept of the

108 *The Moral Vision of Iris Murdoch*

moral' (Murdoch, 1992, p. 177). Thus morality is about broadening our vision, about seeing as clearly and disinterestedly as possible; it is about the images we choose and the way we choose to imagine ourselves and the world (for, just as perception is not morally neutral, neither is imagination: ibid., p. 314).

Imagination and sight are connected by visual metaphor, and both can be fantasy and illusion or efforts to move towards the real. For, 'when we settle down to be "thoroughly rational" about a situation, we have already, reflectively or unreflectively, imagined it in a certain way. Our deepest imaginings which structure the world in which "moral judgements" occur are already evaluations' (ibid., pp. 314–15). Therefore seeing morally is an active endeavour and the way we see and imagine affect what we can see and imagine. In Murdoch's terms:

> The world is not given to us 'on a plate', it is given to us as a creative task. It is impossible to banish morality from this picture. We *work*, using or failing to use our honesty, our courage, our truthful imagination, at the interpretation of what is present to us, as we of necessity shape it and 'make something of it'. We help it to be. (Ibid., p. 215)

Endeavouring to see more clearly is a continuous moral effort. Our moral attitude and engagement with the world is connected to 'what we "see things as", as what we let, or make, ourselves think about, how, by innumerable movements, we train our instincts and develop our habits and test our methods of verification' (ibid.). Clear (moral) sight then is the essence of the moral quest – 'it matters how we see other people' (ibid., p. 463) and the world – and moral improvement is measured by how clearly we see. If we recall the example of M and D cited in Chapter 2, we can see Murdoch's conception of morality as vision and attention at work. In the example, M is 'an intelligent and well-intentioned person, capable of self-criticism, capable of giving careful and just *attention* to an object which confronts her' (Murdoch, 1970a, p. 17), namely D, her daughter-in-law. The mother exhibits moral striving and shows how attention to D cuts through her illusions and allows her to see D more clearly. The mother-in-law deliberately attempts to see D from a just and loving perspective. In so doing the mother-in-law gains a broader vision of the world, not only seeing D more clearly, but grasping wider issues, such as the relationship of D to her son. M has to strive against her own ego to expand her vision, she has to work to become moral, and this effort is rewarded by clearer sight, for 'when M is just and loving she sees D as she really is' (ibid., p. 37).

In the example of M and D we can see clearly Murdoch's vision of moral change and how one progresses in the moral life. Importantly, for Murdoch, moral change is a process, which is slow and difficult and requires the forming of habits and a continual striving for the real. Moral change is not a question of effort of will but rather continuing effort which results in an improvement in the quality of consciousness. Therefore moral change is not a matter of 'will power', but brought about incrementally by a 'long deep process

*Living the Moral Life* 109

of unselfing' (Murdoch, 1992, p. 54). It is the slow practice of attention, of seeing what is real and true, which produces morally good acts; 'moral acts do not usually, and cannot essentially, rest on pure arbitrarily "willed" decisions' (ibid., p. 325).

For Murdoch, then, moral progress is the continual and gradual change of our whole being and outlook, the way we consider ourselves, the world and others; thus 'we can change what we are, but not quickly or easily, there is such depth and density in what needs to be changed' (ibid.). We strive to see more clearly, using tools like attention and by examining, utilizing and then rejecting images and pictures, and thus gradually moral change occurs as 'new modes of outlook (metaphor) and new desires come into being' (ibid., p. 330). Moral choice and action derive, not from willed decisions, but from moral vision. As choice is possible only within the world we can see our options depend, not on our 'strength of will but . . . [on] . . . the quality of our usual attachments and . . . the kind of energy and discernment we have available' (Murdoch, 1970a, p. 92). Thus moments of moral choice or perceived moral crisis are not the significant moments they are sometimes thought to be, for 'it is what lies behind and in between actions and prompts them that is important, and it is this area which should be purified. By the time the moment of choice has arrived the quality of attention has probably determined the nature of the act' (ibid., p. 67). Moral choice for Murdoch is relatively unimportant; what is important is our constant moral pilgrimage, our building up of good habits and our continued attention to the real. The importance of clear vision to our ability to make judgments means that those who have not striven to see the real and encouraged good practices of attention will have very limited choices when the moment of decision arrives. The limiting of choice, by the quality of attention of the moral agent, is an obvious consequence of locating morality in the moral background rather than in the moment of choice. Complete moral freedom Murdoch regards as illusory; moral action depends on constant moral effort and she argues that, 'if we consider what the work of attention is like, how continuously it goes on, and how imperceptibly it builds up structures of value round about us, we shall not be surprised that at crucial moments of choice most of the business of choosing is already over' (ibid., p. 37).

Such a picture of the moral reality does not imply a lack of freedom. Indeed, as we saw in Chapter 3, in Murdoch's comments on Derrida's structuralism, Murdoch fears and rejects deterministic philosophies; rather, she asserts a more realistic, limited freedom which 'implies that the exercise of our freedom is a small piecemeal business which goes on all the time and not a grandiose leaping about unimpeded at important moments' (ibid.). It is this conviction, that it is not action but the moral colour of the situation, which is derived from the 'experiential stream as a cognitive background' (Murdoch, 1992, p. 267), which is fundamental to Murdoch's philosophy. Moral change is about a gradual move away from illusion and the ego and towards the real, and we do this by constant moral effort, by forming good moral habits and habitual ways of checking the ego and refocusing on the real. The moral task – 'to come to

110 *The Moral Vision of Iris Murdoch*

see the world as it really is' (ibid., p. 91) – involves creating good habits, strengthening attention and forcing ourselves 'to have good desires and remove or weaken bad ones' (ibid., p. 395).

Therefore habits and dispositions have a place in the moral life. However, habits, such as obeying rules, are not enough to constitute a full moral life in Murdoch's terms. Rules and duties are central to morality, particularly public morality, in that they can strengthen the moral life, especially in difficult circumstances. Murdoch accepts that the concept of duty is '*indispensable*, though it cannot stand alone; it is a formal way of asserting both the orderly pattern-like nature of morality, and its uniquely absolute demand, quite different from that of inclination' (ibid., p. 303). Duty for Murdoch, then, is a kind of fall-back position, for times when we are struggling with our ego and finding it difficult to see the real. Duty is necessary for fallen beings like ourselves who are sunk in illusion, but it is a concept which becomes less important as we progress in the moral pilgrimage and our own egoistic desires are reduced, for 'a totally good being would not experience the call of duty, might be said to lack or not need the concept, since all acts and decisions would emerge from virtuous insight' (ibid.). In other words a clear vision of the real would produce right action without conflict with the now negated ego; thus 'truthful vision prompts right action' (ibid., p. 295).

In sum, then, we progress in the moral pilgrimage as we check the desires of the ego and expand our moral vision, gradually expanding the vista of true sight. Moral progress and change is hard; we must alter 'our motives, our desires, our reasoning' (ibid., p. 300), in other words our whole selves. But moral change and moral progress are possible. We can ascend in the moral pilgrimage, for 'truth and progress (or some truth and progress) are the reward of some exercise of virtue, courage, humility and patience' (ibid., p. 400). If we attend properly, then the quality of our moral background and perception will improve. From a higher awareness right action will follow, for action flows from vision; it confirms 'for better or worse, the background of attachment from which it issues' (Murdoch, 1970a, p. 71). Thus it is the background attachment, the colour of the moral life, the place on the moral pilgrimage which constitute the true moral status of the agent. Living the moral life is progressing along the pilgrimage – a slow and difficult journey, but one that is rewarded by the gradual growth of vision.

## Inspirations to the Moral Life

Having looked at the nature of the quest and what it entails, we will now consider various starting-points which inspire us to the moral life and which are found in our daily experience. In beginning and continuing the moral pilgrimage, the fundamental duty of the moral agent is to transfer attention away from the self and towards the real. As we saw in our discussion of attention, there are better and worse objects of attention, the best object of

*Living the Moral Life* 111

attention (though arguably available only towards the end of the quest) being of course the good. However, there are objects of attention which are likely to inspire towards the good and which certainly draw one away from the self, a fact which Murdoch regards as uncontroversial: 'it is . . . a psychological fact, and one of importance in moral philosophy, that we can all receive moral help by focusing our attention upon things which are valuable' (Murdoch, 1970a, p. 56). The three sets of objects of attention which are likely to aid (or inspire to) the moral quest are beauty (which for Murdoch, unlike Plato, includes art), intellectual disciplines and love.

If we begin with beauty we can again see Murdoch's debt to Plato, who regarded beauty as 'the only spiritual thing we love immediately by nature' (Baldanza, 1974, p. 27).[10] Plato presents the instinctual love of beauty in the *Phaedrus*, where it is presented as part of the doctrine of *anamnesis* or recollection and remembered most readily of all the 'ideas', for

> beauty, as we said, shone bright amidst these visions, and in this world below we apprehend it through the clearest of our senses, clear and resplendent. For sight is the keenest mode of perception vouchsafed us through the body; wisdom, indeed we cannot see thereby – how passionate had been our desire for her, if she had granted us so clear an image of herself to gaze upon – nor yet any other of those beloved objects, save only beauty; for beauty alone this has been ordained, to be most manifest to sense and most lovely of them all. (*Phaedrus*, 250d, Plato, 1989, p. 497)

Following Plato, Murdoch too asserts that beauty is the most accessible starting-point of the moral quest and most obvious instigator of moral change (Murdoch, 1970a, p. 85). She recognizes that claiming that attending to nature or to art may to many seem unconnected to the moral life, but argues, in the same vein as Plato, that this is because we love beauty by instinct. Murdoch, in a decisive break from Plato, also believes that art can also provide this starting-point and inspiration, for 'great art teaches us how real things can be looked at and loved without being seized and used, without being appropriated into the greedy organism of the self' (ibid., p. 65). Therefore art, like beauty, can take the individual out of the self and focus attention on the real. However, the role of art is more complex and we will discuss Murdoch's view of art in detail in the next chapter. For now it is enough to note that art and beauty can bring about moral inspiration and aid in the moral life and we can easily (as, for instance, in the example of the kestrel) imagine how this occurs. Therefore Murdoch describes beauty as the 'traditional name of something which art and nature share, and which gives a fairly clear sense to the idea of quality of experience and change of consciousness' (ibid., p. 84).

The second starting-point of the moral quest discussed by Murdoch is that of 'intellectual discipline'. Again the important aspect in making the activity of intellectual discipline moral is that attention is focused away from the self and towards the real. We can find a similar conviction in Plato who praised *techne* (craft) and the sciences, particularly mathematics, for Plato one of the highest

112    *The Moral Vision of Iris Murdoch*

forms of knowledge, which Murdoch remarks is not surprising given the mathematical progress made by the Greeks in Plato's time (Murdoch, 1992, p. 179). Murdoch's preferred example of intellectual discipline is that of learning a foreign language (Murdoch, 1970a, p. 89; 1992, p. 478); which presumably is from Murdoch's own experience and not intended to suggest that any intrinsic value is attached to one discipline over another.[11] In intellectual disciplines the relationship is not reciprocal (like the good, that which we study is indifferent), the student has to attend to a disinterested reality which draws one away from the self. To cite Murdoch's example, 'love of Russian leads me away from myself towards something alien to me, something which my consciousness cannot take over, swallow up, deny or make unreal' (Murdoch, 1970a, p. 89). For this reason Murdoch thinks 'any serious learning is a moral–spiritual activity' (Murdoch, 1992, p. 338), as studying draws attention away from the self and serves to 'stretch the imagination, enlarge the vision and strengthen the vision' (Murdoch, 1970a, p. 90). Consequently, intellectual disciplines and the act of studying provide 'introductory images of the spiritual life' (ibid.).

The final starting-point of the moral quest, and one which is double-edged, is that of love. Love does function as a starting-point for the moral quest, and perhaps the most dramatic one: 'falling in love is for many people their most intense experience, bringing with it a quasi-religious certainty, and most disturbing because it shifts the centre of the world from ourself to another place' (Murdoch, 1992, pp. 16–17). In this sense love is a very effective focus of attention. It destroys the ego as it is swallowed up in the overwhelming devotion to the beloved. However, love is also a dangerous starting-point and teacher for the moral quest because not only may it lead to the good but it may return one firmly to the ego if one attempts not to attend to the other but to devour the other. Falling in love may produce two outcomes: it 'can occasion extreme selfishness and possessive violence, the attempt to dominate the other place so that it be no longer separate; or it can prompt a process of unselfing wherein the lover learns to see, and cherish and respect, what is not himself' (ibid., p. 17). The dual nature of love as it functions in the moral life (a potentially great teacher or great deluder) takes us again back to Plato and his concept of Eros which is 'the highest form of spiritual energy, but lower unredeemed Eros as a plausible tempter' (ibid., p. 127). Eros as dual desire is described mythically by Plato in the *Symposium* as the child of poverty and plenty:

> it has been his fate to be always needy; nor is he delicate and lovely as most of us believe, but harsh and arid, barefoot and homeless, sleeping on the naked earth, in doorways, or in the very streets beneath the stars of heaven, and always partaking of his mother's poverty. But, secondly, he brings his father's resourcefulness to his designs upon the beautiful and the good, for he is gallant, impetuous, and energetic, a mighty hunter, and a master of device and artifice – at once desirous of full wisdom, a lifelong seeker after truth, and an adept in sorcery, enchantment and seduction. (*Symposium*, 203c–d, Plato, 1989, pp. 555–6)

*Living the Moral Life* 113

Thus Eros represents human desire, drawn towards the good but also capable of being drawn to less worthy objects, a spiritual energy or force which can help us in the quest if properly directed, but also capable of being egotistical and selfish and driving us away from the quest. Eros as energy is 'mixed and personal, godlike yet not divine, capable of corruption aspiring to wisdom, a needy resourceful desire' (Murdoch, 1992, p. 343). Love therefore in certain forms can teach 'unselfing' and attention, for 'one kind of love can be a figure or analogon for another, and any love can stir up, and reach down into, the breeding places of imagery' (ibid., p. 346).[12] Thus love, like beauty and study, can lead us away from the self and forward on the moral quest from illusion to reality.

**Conclusion**

In this chapter on the moral life all the separate aspects of Murdoch's moral vision discussed in the preceding chapters converge. Only in the context of her vision of the moral life as a way of living does it become clear why she argued so vehemently for the self and the inner life, against the fact/value dichotomy and for a transcendent/immanent good. All these arguments are controversial and, when taken separately, it sometimes appears that Murdoch is pushing too far when a slightly less ambitious argument would have been successful. However, when one considers her vision of the moral life, one sees the necessity of her previous arguments. Many of the claims that Murdoch makes regarding the moral life are even more difficult to sustain in the current climate, not least her insistence on the spiritual nature of the moral life; however, she attempts to redefine the spiritual. Murdoch is demanding a commitment and a change in life which is more like a religious commitment than the endorsing of a philosophical argument. Perhaps it is for these reasons that Murdoch's vision of the moral life has been used far less by moral philosophers than her realism, which has provided inspiration and impetus to current realist philosophies. Nonetheless, although many would not wish to go as far as to endorse (and ultimately, if seriously endorsed, undertake) Murdoch's pilgrimage as a personal ideology, without recognizing the breadth of her vision one cannot fully understand the type of philosophy Murdoch is putting forward. She is advocating a particular moral vision of the world which involves advocating how one should live in that world. As will be clear by now, Murdoch regards this project as being at the heart of philosophy. Where modern philosophy fails to offer a vision, Murdoch shows how we should live.

Yet it is not necessarily the challenge of Murdoch's philosophy to change one's moral conception and vision which is daunting, but rather that this type of philosophy, which stretches from moral realism, to aesthetics and into religion, is so thoroughly unfamiliar that it is difficult to grasp. In the next two chapters we will complete our picture of Murdoch's moral vision by considering in detail two of these areas: those of aesthetics and religion. Such exploration

# 114 *The Moral Vision of Iris Murdoch*

will not only clarify her vision, but will further explain her insistence on placing such non-scientific aspects of human experience at the heart of her moral vision.

## Notes

1  Although, as discussed, in Chapter 3, Murdoch would regard structuralism as not only proselytizing, but also destructive of all competing philosophies.

2  A full outline of Murdoch's vision of religion will be discussed in detail in Chapter 7. For now, all we need to recognize is the spiritual nature of the moral quest, where 'spiritual' is considered to denote an ordinary human capability.

3  The ability to account for 'moral demand' is regarded as a strength in the realist argument. Realists argue that the experience of 'moral authority', 'moral demand', and the ability to account for moral conflicts and conversions, means that realist arguments are supported by moral experience in which all such phenomena occur. For example, Geoffrey Sayre-McCord argues that moral experience supports realist conceptions as we do 'seek evidence for our opinions; we act as if there were something to discover, as if we could be mistaken, as if there is a fact of the matter; and we even talk of moral claims being true or false, and of people knowing better (even while doing the worse)' (Sayre-McCord, 1988, p. 9). In light of the current debate, which is in part inspired by Murdoch, her argument from experience and her wish to recognize the experience of moral demand stands within the current discussion.

4  Murdoch's interpretation of Plato's Cave is again open to question. There are tomes of scholarship interpreting the Cave, either on its own or in connected with the 'Divided Line' (which comes between the discussion of the good and the Cave in the *Republic*). There are arguments about whether the Cave is really concerned with levels of awareness and whether it is really possible to progress through levels of awareness or whether the Cave actually represents two separate cognitive worlds (Cross and Woozley, 1966; Annas 1981). Yet again, although Murdoch's interpretation can be criticized, for the purposes of understanding her philosophy we can accept her reading at face value (that of being an instructing and inspirational image and metaphor), and indeed we have to in order to understand Murdoch's conception of the moral life, levels of awareness as progressive and to some extent perceptible from other levels of awareness.

5  Egoistic is not intended to be read as psychological egoism (as we can fight and change the situation) nor as ethical egoism. Rather simply a self-centredness and self obsession, in the sense of being preoccupied, at least most of the time, with our own concerns and wishes.

6  Murdoch finds in Freud's psychoanalysis a deluded and self-deluding consciousness, which she regards as presenting a secular version of the true human condition. In religious pictures this has been previously presented in Christianity as 'original sin' and in Buddhism as the 'veil of Maya'.

7  Conradi reports Murdoch's 'growing antagonism towards psychoanalysis and psychotherapy which might delay the pilgrim' (Conradi, 2001, p. 493).

8  The 'alien reality' being that which is not the self, the moral reality, which is real and 'out there'.

9  Although Murdoch suggests 'attention' as a secular version of prayer, for Simone Weil, from whom Murdoch takes this concept, it was, of course, religious.

*Living the Moral Life* 115

10  Beauty, for Plato, is a 'form' or 'idea', which is intimately connected to goodness and truth. What Plato understood his forms to be is controversial and has been discussed from Aristotle (with whom Murdoch disagrees) onwards. They have been regarded as little more than ideas in the mind (a concept which Murdoch sometimes seems to endorse with regard to the good), the postulation of a separate world of original forms of which everything in this world is an imperfect copy (the so-called 'classical' two-world theory) (Ostenfeld, 1982, p. 76). Indeed, the forms in the early dialogues, the so-called 'Socratic forms' are regarded as little more than 'common elements among qualitatively identical groups' (Moravcsik, 1992, p. 52). Plato 'nowhere in the dialogues has an extended discussion of forms in which he pulls together the different lines of thought about them and tries to assess the needs they meet and whether they succeed in meeting them' (Annas, 1981, p. 217). In addition, Plato does not argue for the forms, he simply assumes them, usually introducing them to support or explain another issue. Given this perennial confusion regarding Plato's 'forms' and although Murdoch's interpretation (not only of beauty, but also of the good) is open to question, it is reasonable to accept her somewhat vague use of the forms, as both myths and realities, as discussed in Chapter 4 in relation to the good.

11  Conradi reports that Murdoch and Frank Thompson seemed to compete in attempting to learn languages and that, in addition to Russian and Italian, which they both learnt, Frank 'picked up Serbo-Croat, Bulgarian, Polish and modern Greek, faltering only with Arabic. She [Murdoch] goes beyond him only once, arriving at the Turkish Embassy and demanding to be taught Turkish' (Conradi, 2001, p. 153).

12  Again this is an understanding of love taken directly from Plato, most notably from the *Symposium* in which Socrates describes how the recognition of beauty in one instance – that of the particular – can lead to recognition of beauty in all instances, and 'having reached this point he must set himself to be the lover of every lovely body, and bring his passion for the one into due proportion' (*Symposium*, 210b, Plato, 1989, p. 562). Eventually the lover will recognize not only the outer beauty, but beauty as seen by the mind, and 'find in contemplation the seed of the most fruitful discourse and the loftiest thought, and reap a golden harvest of philosophy' (*Symposium*, 210d, Plato, 1989, p. 562). The final stage is the perception of beauty itself which is 'an everlasting loveliness which neither comes nor goes, which neither flowers nor fades, for such beauty is the same on every hand, the same then as now, here as there, this way as that way, the same to every worshiper as it is to every other' (*Symposium*, 210e–211a, 1989, p. 562).

Chapter 6

# Art and the Moral Life

At the end of the last chapter we noted that art, as part of beauty (along with intellectual discipline and love), can provide a starting-point for, and inspiration to, the moral life. However, the role Murdoch allots to art is far broader, and in this chapter we will consider the function of art and the aesthetic in Murdoch's moral vision.

In asserting that art is crucial to aiding the moral quest, Murdoch is parting company from her great mentor, Plato. Plato is highly critical of art and wished to exclude artists from his ideal republic. Murdoch's position could not be more different from Plato's; yet even here, when she is arguing against Plato's views, Murdoch continues to employ the same Platonic arguments which inform and inspire the rest of her philosophy. In this discussion Murdoch is both a 'Platonist and critic of Platonist aesthetics' (Hepburn, 1978, p. 270). Given the importance of the Platonic vision in Murdoch's philosophy, we will begin this chapter with Plato's criticisms of art. Murdoch's rebuttal of these criticisms form the basis for her own view of art. In fact Murdoch accepts much of Plato's critique of art: her disagreement lies not in Plato's fears about art, but in his willingness to apply his criticisms to all art. Murdoch believes Plato's criticisms are applicable only to 'bad' or 'mediocre' art which she divides from 'good' or 'great' art, which she goes on to justify on Platonic lines.

Having noted Plato's criticisms, we will then go on to explore Murdoch's case for art, namely that art can function in the same way as Platonic beauty. Accordingly, we will consider art's function as a good object of attention (as discussed in the last chapter), art's capacity to reveal what is real, art as training for the moral life, the moral function of literature, the analogy of art and morals, and the capacity of art to provide access to transcendence, perhaps the only readily available access to transcendence in the modern secular context. Finally, we will turn to Murdoch's own status as a novelist and briefly consider her attitude towards her own artistry and its relation to her philosophy and moral vision.

## Plato's Objections to Art

The role Murdoch attributes to art is similar to the role that Plato attributes to beauty, as discussed in the previous chapter, namely that it is a good object of attention which can provide imitations of the good and so serve as a

118                    *The Moral Vision of Iris Murdoch*

starting-point for, and inspiration to, the moral quest. Murdoch suggests that Plato (and indeed Kant, who took a similar attitude to Plato's on this point, regarding the beautiful as a symbol of morality but not art in general[1]) was motivated by the wish to 'keep morality "safe" from art' (Murdoch, 1992, p. 9). Plato's (and Kant's) motives for mounting an attack on art are various, 'moral, psychological, political and metaphysical' (ibid., p. 18). In addition, she attributes Plato's and Kant's criticisms of art to their 'puritanism' and general mistrust of pleasure (Murdoch, 1997 [1976], pp. 397, 400, 401). Yet, this said, she does find merit in many of their criticisms and it is to Plato's critique of art that we will now turn.

Plato's attack on art is uncompromising, even though Murdoch claims that he 'clearly loved art, especially music and poetry' (Murdoch, 1992, p. 18) and indeed was himself a 'great artist' (ibid., pp. 18, 317; 1997 [1978], p. 13; 1997 [1976], p. 396). In Book Three of the *Republic*, Plato memorably declares that, in his ideal republic, the poets, particularly emotive (and one would venture to say 'good' – aesthetically if not morally) would be escorted to the borders:

> we should send him away to another city, after pouring myrrh down over his head and crowning him with fillets of wool, but we ourselves, for our souls' good should continue to employ the more austere and less delightful poet and taleteller, who would imitate the diction of the good man. (*Republic*, 398a–b, Plato, 1989, pp. 642–3)

In this short passage, many of Plato's reasons for disapproving of art are contained or at least implied. Fundamentally, art is not good for us as individuals striving to be good, nor is it good for the state in attempting to maintain order. Plato's general concerns can be subdivided into five main criticisms. First, art corrupts the individual and is linked to the lowest part of the soul; second, art is irreverent towards religion; third, art is politically irresponsible; fourth, art is appearance rather than reality; and fifth, art masquerades as beauty and so undermines the moral quest.

The first criticism is that art corrupts the individual and encourages the lowest part of the soul to grow. The artist, and here Plato is mostly concerned with poetry and the theatre – indeed he sets his rejection of art within the old 'quarrel between philosophy and poetry' (*Republic*, 607b, 1989, p. 832) – tends to picture and glorify the bad man rather than the good (who is dull and simple and therefore not interesting enough to provide the subject matter for drama). Plato contends that, when we enjoy the portrayal of evil men, we indulge in vicarious emotions and situations which we would abhor in real life and so allow the soul to 'relax its guard' (Murdoch, 1992, p. 13; 1997 [1976], pp. 391, 421). Plato regards experiencing such emotions, even vicariously, as dangerous and detrimental to the good man. Plato argues that, however harmless it might seem, indulging in such emotions, even imaginatively, is dangerous:

> In regard to the emotions of sex and anger, and all the appetites and pains and pleasures of the soul which we say accompany all our actions, the effect of poetic

*Art and the Moral Life* 119

imitation is the same. For it waters and fosters these feelings when what we ought to do is to dry them up, and it establishes them as our rulers when they ought to be ruled, to the end that we may be better and happier men instead of worse and more miserable. (*Republic*, 606d, 1989, p. 832)

Thus art, in the form of poetry and the theatre, gratifies and feeds the lowest, desirous, part of the soul to the detriment of the higher part of the soul.

Plato's second and third criticisms, that art is irreverent and politically irresponsible, can be connected, because they are both concerned with maintaining a stable and well-ordered society. Plato criticizes art for portraying the gods as laughing and irreverent (*Republic*, 389a, 1989, pp. 633–4), which is a source of political and social instability. Therefore artists should not be allowed to engage in creating what they wish (or in Plato's terms what they are inspired to create: *Phaedrus*, 245a, 1989, p. 492), but only that which creates order and stability. For example, in the *Timaeus*, with regard to music, Plato asserts, that it has been given to us 'for the sake of harmony' and not

with a view to irrational pleasure, which is deemed to be the purpose of it in our day, but as means to correct any discord which may have arisen in the courses of the soul, and to be our ally in bringing her into harmony and agreement with herself, and rhythm too was given by them for the same reason, on account of the irregular and graceless ways which prevail among mankind generally, and to help us against them. (*Timaeus*, 47d–e, Plato, 1989, p. 1175)

Thus, for Murdoch's purposes, these two criticisms can be put aside as they do not relate directly to her immediate concerns. It is not Murdoch's intention, as it was Plato's, to create a blueprint for a new social and political order. Consequently, she regards these criticisms as concerned with public order and public morality, not with art as a creative medium itself nor with the personal moral quest. She quickly dismisses these criticisms as irrelevant to the personal pilgrimage to the good, concerned only with 'the results of its . . . [that is, art's] . . . consumption expressed in terms which are obviously moral or political rather than aesthetic' (Murdoch, 1997 [1976], p. 396). Murdoch's lack of direct concern with 'public morality' means she does not engage with these criticisms in any great detail. However, if she did, again in this aesthetic debate, she would be likely to disagree with Plato because of her fear of totalitarianism.[2] Indeed, she asserts that art, in its creative ability and truth-telling capacity (both of which we will discuss in detail later in this chapter), is an important guarantee of freedom. For this reason art is often mistrusted by tyrants and politicians who fear art's revolutionary capacities and wish to control it for their own purposes: those of creating order and encouraging feelings and attitudes to maintain the power of the state (Murdoch, 1992, p. 90).[3] Plato's final criticisms of art, that art is concerned with appearance and not reality and that art apes beauty and so undermines the quest, Murdoch cannot dismiss so easily and it is these that she must counter if she is to claim that art is beneficial and a source of good for the moral pilgrim.

120                    *The Moral Vision of Iris Murdoch*

Plato's fourth criticism, that artists deal in appearance and not reality, is most memorably put in Book Ten of the *Republic*. Here Plato presents the artist as being three removes from reality: the 'form'[4] (in this case of a bed) is the original; the second remove from reality is the bed made by the craftsman, who copies the form and has real knowledge (that of measurement and craftsmanship); finally, at the third remove from reality, the artist copies the bed made by the craftsman and has no real knowledge. The artist then is 'the imitator of the thing which ... others produce' (*Republic*, 597e, 1989, p. 822). This is not only true of the painter and sculptor but also of the poet, who 'will attempt, seriously and in the presence of many, to imitate all things' (*Republic*, 397a, 1989, p. 641). A similar conclusion is drawn in the *Ion*, where Socrates questions Ion (a Homeric poet) about his knowledge. Socrates points out that Ion has no real knowledge about the matters of which he so authoritively speaks, including the knowledge of generalship, which is the knowledge Ion tentatively claims, although he admits that he has never exercised this knowledge. Murdoch wishes to defend Ion with the claim that he has 'a general knowledge of human life, together of course with a technical knowledge of poetry' (Murdoch, 1997 [1976], p. 393) – an argument we shall return to. For Plato, then, far from helping the moral pilgrim by illuminating the moral life and revealing the real, 'art naively or wilfully accepts appearances instead of questioning them' (ibid., p. 390). To return to the image of the Cave (Murdoch's key Platonic inspiration), Plato pictures artists as sunk in image-ridden illusion, in *eikasia*. Artists are the prisoners in their lowest condition, chained and shadow-gazing.

Artists, pictured in this manner, clearly have no access to the real and the good, which brings us to Plato's final criticism, that artists pretend to have, and to give access to, truth. Herein lies the biggest danger of art for Plato, that it masquerades as beauty – which is, as we saw in the previous chapter, connected to the good – and consequently art is a danger even to the good man who is striving for the real. Art is 'pseudo-enlightenment' (ibid., p. 423) and in the lure of art 'the pull of the transcendent as reality and good is confused and mimicked. The true sense of reality as a feeling of joy is deceitfully imitated by the "charm-joy" of art' (ibid., p. 444). In this pretence, of offering knowledge, art deceives and obscures the real and the good and, though honestly attempting to pursue the good, the pilgrim is tricked and falsely satisfied with a lower form of life. Art, then, 'practises a false and degenerate *anamnesis*, where the veiled something which is sought and found is no more than a shadow out of the private storeroom of the personal unconscious' (ibid.). This is in fact a similar criticism to those we discussed in the last chapter, used by Murdoch against those who falsely believe that self-knowledge is true knowledge, and are satisfied with the fire and so cease to seek the sun. Indeed the (false) consolations of art Murdoch links to the egoism of both the artist and the spectator. When seen in this light art seems irredeemable (a most dangerous enemy to the moral life), capable of 'deluding even the decent man by giving him false self-knowledge based on a healthy egoism: which is

*Art and the Moral Life*                                        121

mistaken for the sun, and where one may comfortably linger, imagining oneself to be enlightened' (ibid.).

Given Plato's uncompromising attitude to art and Murdoch's dedication to Plato, one might wonder why Murdoch is so adamant that art is, or can be, a positive weapon in the arsenal of the moral pilgrim rather than a shortcut straight back to *eikasia*, as clearly she believes it can be. Yet Murdoch perseveres in her defence of art, or at least some art, and argues that (some) art is capable of fulfilling a role akin to the role Plato attributes to beauty in the moral life. While Murdoch recognizes the validity of many of Plato's criticisms, she attempts to rehabilitate art and indeed argues that 'Plato himself supplies a good deal of the material for a complete aesthetic, a defence and reasonable critique of art' (ibid., p. 449). Moreover, Murdoch counters that Plato's recourse to images and metaphors is fundamental in his presentation of the good and the moral life (as discussed in the preceding chapter) and the arguments in favour of using images and metaphors can be used to defend art. For, in his use of images and literary devices, Plato 'acknowledges high imagination as creative stirring spirit' and so 'implicitly allows a redemption of art' (Murdoch, 1992, p. 320).

## False Consolations of Art

Although, ultimately, Murdoch wishes to redeem art and provide a place for it in the moral life, she feels the weight of Plato's criticisms. Further, as discussed in the last chapter, Murdoch is too well-aware of the illusion-ridden, egoistic nature of the human condition not to recognize the consoling possibilities of art. Thus Murdoch takes Plato's criticisms of art to heart and considers many of his warnings 'apt today. Popular literature and film argue the dullness of the good, the charm of the bad. The violent man is the hero of our time' (Murdoch, 1992, p. 13). Murdoch even goes so far as to equate the Cave directly with the 'technical excellence of television' (ibid.), which leads us to 'accept scrappy images and disconnected oddments of information for insight into truth' (ibid.). Not only does Murdoch take Plato's criticisms seriously, but she is also willing to accept them as valid with regard to much art. Accordingly, she states that 'much art, perhaps most art, perhaps all art is connected with sex . . . art is close dangerous play with unconscious forces' (Murdoch, 1997 [1978], p. 10). In addition, when commenting on Plato's criticisms, she recognizes that 'of course much bad art deliberately and much good art incidentally is in league with lower manifestations of erotic love' (Murdoch, 1997 [1976], p. 399). Drawing on Freud's, as well as Plato's, criticisms, Murdoch accepts that art can be 'private consolation' (Murdoch, 1997 [1978], p. 14) and that it presents us with the 'most comprehensible examples of the almost irresistible human urge to seek consolation in fantasy' (Murdoch, 1970a, p. 64) (a tendency which, at its most extreme, is pornography[5]).[6]

122            *The Moral Vision of Iris Murdoch*

This tendency of art towards fantasy, rather than reality, Murdoch regards as part of the nature of art. Again she is close to Plato here, for 'stories (art forms) are almost always a bit or very false' (Murdoch, 1992, p. 105). In particular, art consoles us and comforts us about death because art plays with the idea of death and pain and presents, not real pain, but 'art pain or relative pain' (ibid., p. 141). To illustrate her point Murdoch takes the example of death in the Arthurian legends and argues that they do not portray real death and thus are not truly tragic: 'the Grail is a sexual symbol; whereas absolute pain, experienced or (if that is possible) justly perceived or portrayed, removes all sexual interest' (ibid.). In offering such consolation and fantasy Murdoch, like Plato, considers art to threaten fundamentally the moral life. Art has a tendency to pretend to truth while pedalling falsehood. The attempt to produce true art is beset with temptations of consolation and fantasy: 'melodrama, sentimentality, anything which makes the drama into a lie' (ibid., p. 105).

Given this, it would seem that producing true art (art which does not lie) is difficult; all stories are at least a little false. In light of this and her acceptance of much of Plato's critique of art, Murdoch's wish to reinstate art as a positive source of inspiration and a resource for the moral life would seem to be doomed to failure. Yet Murdoch perseveres. Her solution is to accept that much, even most, art is exactly what Plato says it is. It is self-consoling fantasy which provides both comfort and illusory knowledge to those who have never left the Cave and, perhaps worse still, it fools those who have begun the moral journey into returning to the Cave. Much art causes us to mistake the fire for the sun. Yet, although Murdoch admits this with regard to most art, she argues that it is not the case for all art. Thus Murdoch's response is to divide good or great art from bad or mediocre art. To bad/mediocre art she applies Plato's criticisms, while denying their validity to good/great art; to which she attributes all the truth-telling, morally inspirational qualities of Plato's beauty. Nonetheless, despite Murdoch's ambitious claims for good/great art in the moral life, Plato's criticisms continue to haunt her and she reminds the reader that 'even good art may make us feel too much at ease with something less than the best, it offers a sort of spiritual exercise and what looks like a spiritual home, a kind of armchair sanctuary which may be a substitute for genuine moral effort' (ibid., p. 91).

**Dividing the Aesthetic**

The method Murdoch uses to divide good art from bad art is almost tautological in that bad art is art that fulfils the role that Plato outlined (it is egotistical self-consoling fantasy that imitates moral and spiritual achievement) whereas good art performs the opposite function: it draws attention away from the selfish ego, towards the good and the real and so actively aids the moral life. Murdoch does not define good art as such; in fact she rejects the need of an abstract definition, suggesting rather that we define great art and outline our aesthetic

*Art and the Moral Life*   123

in accordance with 'great works of art which we know to be such independently' (Murdoch, 1997 [1959a], p. 205). We are to define 'great art' by means of specific examples, thus we 'start by saying that Shakespeare is the greatest of all artists, and let our aesthetic grow to be a philosophical justification of this judgement' (ibid.).[7] Murdoch reasons that adopting this methodology will result in a definition of art in its highest manifestation: the alternative form of definition, which covers all art objects, Murdoch dismisses as nothing more than 'a sort of lower common denominator' (ibid.).

Shakespeare is used by Murdoch as a benchmark for great art because his 'plays are pre-eminently about the difference between illusion and reality, and the battle between good and evil, they shine with a positive sense of goodness' (Murdoch, 1992, p. 142). We can see the extent of Murdoch's dedication to Shakespeare in her suggestion that the '*light* which illuminates the atmosphere of the Platonic dialogues' (ibid.) is also found in Shakespeare's plays. Essentially, Shakespeare produces great art because he shows us what is real. His personality, his own selfish ego, is almost entirely hidden in his plays – 'he is the most invisible of writers' (Murdoch, 1997 [1959b], p. 275) – enabling him to create characters other than his own; 'the pages of Shakespeare abound in free and eccentric personalities whose reality Shakespeare has apprehended and displayed as something quite separate from his own' (ibid.). This ability to create free characters Murdoch calls tolerance and she regards it as evident in all great art, particularly novels. Murdoch cites other artists who achieve this non-egoistic vision, for example, Tolstoy, George Eliot and Jane Austin, although her intention is not to give a comprehensive list of examples (ibid., p. 276).

According to Murdoch, Shakespeare's achievement is that his art does not overly console but rather shows true reality. In *King Lear*, regarded by Murdoch as his best tragedy (and perhaps the only successful tragedy since the Greek tragedies), Shakespeare presents real death, rather than the usual art-death, which is connected to egoism and sex: 'Sex is absent from *Lear* as is the notion of an ordeal, sadomasochistic suffering, transcended redemptive suffering or magical release' (Murdoch, 1992, p. 143). In *Lear* particularly, Murdoch judges that Shakespeare succeeds (in comparison to most art which merely consoles) in portraying the unavoidable reality and finality of death: 'we are placed, as it were right up against it; close to a real awareness of death, of the senseless rubble aspect of human life' (ibid., p. 142). As well as showing us the reality of death, Murdoch argues that Shakespeare also succeeds in revealing, in his evil characters (Iago and Macbeth), the horror and banality of evil, that 'evil is terrible and also very close' (ibid., p. 103).[8] Ultimately, Shakespeare is a great artist, because his vision is directed to the real and the good and it is this vision, not his selfish ego, which is the source of his artistry. He sees the reality of death, of evil and of good, and yet does not lose the detail of individual lives in portraying these realities: he 'comprehends human nature from its deepest evil to its highest good, together with its funniness, its happiness and its beauty' (ibid., p. 142).

124 *The Moral Vision of Iris Murdoch*

In addition, Murdoch asserts that, for art to be great art and not to provide false consolation, a work of art must not be complete (it is not enlightenment itself but a pointer on the way). It is an 'illusory unity' or 'limited whole' (ibid., p. 36). We must beware of the artistic (and Murdoch would add the metaphysical) desire for wholeness (Murdoch, 1997 [1972], p. 251; 1992, pp. 2, 37, 48, 87). Therefore, to ensure that art does not become fantasy, or a tool of fantasy, a work of art must not be 'too complete, the object must be pierced, the circle broken' (Murdoch, 1992, p. 98). A 'broken whole' must be achieved which does not console too much and reveals the real disunity as well as the illusory unity of the work (ibid., p. 88). Again Murdoch looks to Shakespeare and *King Lear*, which she describes as 'a very high instance of a broken pattern' (ibid., p. 87), which ensures that the client takes note of the reality beyond. Great art (again Murdoch uses the example of tragedy and particularly *King Lear*) 'must be in a positive, even thoroughly uncomfortable, sense a broken whole; the concluding process of the idle egotistic mind must be checked' (ibid., p. 104).

Good art, then, can and does exist and it holds within itself the means to check the ego and attend to reality and so offers 'a pure delight in the independent existence of what is excellent . . . it is a thing totally opposed to selfish obsession' (Murdoch, 1970a, p. 85). Given this definition of great art, great art being that which shows the real and is truth-telling, it is clear that it is very rare, especially when we consider how difficult seeing reality is in Murdoch's picture. Yet, this said, Murdoch maintains that good art is still 'easier and more natural than really good life' (Murdoch, 1992, p. 333). Most art will not reach Murdoch's standards of great/good art, hence she states that 'a great deal of art, perhaps most art, actually is self-consoling fantasy' (Murdoch, 1970a, p. 85). Moreover, many artists do not aim to capture reality, which Murdoch claims results in 'vast commercial and pseudo-intellectual proliferations of rubbish which usurp the name of art' (Murdoch, 1992, p. 179).

Consequently, art remains ambiguous in Murdoch's schema, a great revealer and a great deceiver, for 'even great art can be a potent source of illusion' (ibid., p. 9). Clearly, there are difficulties with Murdoch's definition of great art. While many would no doubt agree with her regarding Shakespeare's greatness, they would profoundly disagree with her reasons for his greatness. For Murdoch, whether art is great or not depends entirely on whether it aids, or complies with the constraints of, the moral life. While Murdoch herself is critical of those who wish to use art to promote moral codes and social structures, and she continually insists on the creative freedom of the artist, she could be criticized for a narrow, even moralistic, view of art. However, such a reading would be reductionist, as clearly Murdoch admires and requires the artist to be free and, not insignificantly (perhaps even primarily), is an artist herself. Nonetheless, her definition of art is controversial, a difficulty which is compounded by her piecemeal and unsystematic presentation. However, for present purposes, we need simply to accept her contention that art can be divided along these lines in order to consider the place of art in her vision of the moral life. For, despite the dangers of art, which Murdoch recognizes as real and many, she claims that the benefits of great art more than justify its use by the moral agent, as great art can be 'used to silence and annihilate the self' (Murdoch, 1997 [1970], p. 228).

## Access to Truth

Having discussed the division of great/good art from bad/mediocre art, we will now explore how Murdoch puts great art to work in the moral life. Essentially, great art is an invaluable aid to the moral life; it inspires us to begin and continue in the moral life; it helps us to escape the illusions of the selfish ego; and it reveals reality, so hastening our moral progress. At its highest, art is almost identified with the moral, for 'art is truth, art is some kind of truth, art is true' (Murdoch, 1997 [1972], p. 244). Murdoch supports this presumption, in the now familiar manner, of looking to experience: '"Truth" is something we recognise in good art when we are led to a juster, clearer, more detailed, more refined understanding. Good art "explains" truth itself' (Murdoch, 1992, p. 321). Art's proper function is to be 'truth-seeking and truth-revealing' (Murdoch, 1997 [1978], p. 11) and the artist's duty is to be 'truth-telling in his own medium' (ibid., p. 18). The artist's quest is analogous to (and even at times identical to) the moral quest, as 'serious art is a continuous working of meaning in light of the discovery of some truth' (Murdoch, 1992, p. 211), an argument we will return to later in this chapter.

Truth, then, is crucial for rehabilitating art and reinstating it into Murdoch's Platonic picture of the good life, as 'it is concern with truth . . . that allows good art . . . to be seen as a mode of access to moral goodness' (Lloyd, 1982, p. 62). By revealing what is true, art helps us to progress in the moral life, as it helps us to 'refine and extend our conception and grasp of truth' (Murdoch, 1992, p. 313). Moreover, because art appeals to us at many levels (like Plato's beauty we respond to it immediately, whether it be visual, pictorial or musical), art is able to reveal aspects of reality which are hard for us to discover in other ways. Art's great gift to the moral pilgrim is to give us speedy access to 'what is deeply and obviously true, but usually invisible' (ibid., p. 90). The task of art, then (if we recall the discussion of Chapter 3) is no different from the task of philosophy; both are, or should be, about explaining the (moral) nature of the world.

This capacity of art to show us that which is real, but which we often struggle to see, is a conviction which Murdoch repeats many times in her various writings.[9] For Murdoch, good art does not, as Plato suggested, falsely ape the real or the good, but actually offers a way to the good. Art functions, for Murdoch, just as beauty did for Plato, a position she puts forward in her own fictional platonic dialogue on the subject, *Art and Eros*, in which it is said that 'good art is wisdom and truth. Art is looking at the world and explaining it in a *deep* way and when we understand the explanation or even half understand

126 *The Moral Vision of Iris Murdoch*

it we feel oh – such joy – and I think that's what *beauty* is' (Murdoch, 1987, p. 27). Of course attributing this statement taken from a fictional dialogue directly to Murdoch is dangerous (a quandary we shall return to later in this chapter when we discuss her novels), but, given the grand spiritual claims that Murdoch is making for art, this exclamation in the dialogue seems perfectly to sum up the view she has expressed in the more restrained (although at times only slightly) language of her explicit philosophical writings.

The role Murdoch allots to art is highly ambitious. While bearing in mind the danger of art, she does wish to claim that art almost uniquely offers us easy, or easier, access to the real and so the good. This exalted position Murdoch is outlining for art is exactly the view that Plato feared. Plato recognized that art could appear to reveal truth, but saw this as a mirage. Therefore what for Plato is illusion for Murdoch is real. Against Plato Murdoch argues that art is not the illusory shortcut that he feared and that in fact good art does give access to the real and so the good. For Murdoch, art is indeed a moral teacher; it teaches one how to be moral and so helps moral progress rather than usurping it. Moral effort is still required. In addition, she asserts that art is a pointer to the real, a revealer, not the real itself (a position which is not dissimilar to her argument about the function of images in the moral life, as we discussed in the last chapter and return to in the next).

**Moral Training**

The effort required in focusing on art as an object of attention (as discussed in the last chapter) is moral effort, in that the attention is focused away from the self and towards the other. The attention involved in art is 'good' as it is disinterested and thus is akin to the best form of attention, attention to the indifferent good (unlike, for example, most types of love): 'great art inspires because it is separate, it is for nothing, it is for itself' (Murdoch, 1992, p. 8). Functioning in this way, art is the equivalent to Plato's beauty and teaches one about the reality of the good. Attending to good art 'is an education in the beautiful which involves the instinctive, increasingly confident sorting out of what is good, what is pure, what is profoundly and justly imagined, what rings true, from what is trivial or shallow or in some way fake, self-indulgent, pretentious, sentimental, meretriciously obscure and so on (Murdoch, 1997 [1976], pp. 458–9). Art, like beauty in Plato's schema, offers an inking of reality and goodness. Art provides a glimpse of the real which encourages one in the moral quest and, in addition, art itself provides techniques (in the form of attention) to aid the quest. It is for this reason that Murdoch describes art as 'moral training' (Murdoch, 1992, p. 3), because attention to art teaches respect for the other and good qualities of awareness and so is an invaluable tool in the moral life (so much so that Murdoch advocates that children should be taught to attend to art objects). In this sense learning to attend to art is like learning to attend more generally, it is a tool for focusing away from the self

*Art and the Moral Life*                                          127

(and because of its revelatory capacity a particularly rewarding tool). Art is fundamental to Murdoch as 'training in art is largely training in how to discover a touchstone of truth' (Murdoch, 1997 [1978], p. 26). Attending to art is good for us because, like beauty, 'it stirs us to the effort of true vision' (ibid., p. 14) even to the extent where we overcome the selfish ego and reach 'a point where the distinction between subject and object vanishes in an intuitive understanding' (Murdoch, 1992, p. 339).

Art objects are capable of being 'a great source of revelation' (ibid., p. 85) which reveal truths about ourselves and the world. Art teaches us about aspects of reality which we struggle to face, preferring to console ourselves with fantasy: 'art illuminates accident and contingency and the general muddle of life . . . so as to enable us to survey complex or horrible things which would otherwise appal us' (ibid., p. 8). Art at its highest (which for Murdoch is tragedy, as we discussed above with relation to Shakespeare) is able to reveal, unromanticized, 'the true nature of sin, the futility of fantasy and the reality of death' (ibid., p. 105). Art, then, is a 'revelation of reality' (Murdoch, 1997 [1976], p. 454) which teaches us about the human condition in a manner which we can comprehend and endure, 'in a form which can be steadily contemplated; and indeed this is the only context in which many of us are capable of contemplating it at all' (Murdoch, 1970, p. 87). In providing access to the real, great art provides an opportunity to explore the reality of the human condition in all its gory and potentially glorious detail, as well as helping us see the moral reality. The ability of art to make space for human reflection (moral training) is a point which Murdoch returns to again and again. She constantly comments on the capacity of art to allow (particularly moral) reflection, teaching and revelation (Murdoch, 1992, pp. 8, 122, 161; 1997 [1972], p. 256).

## The Novel and the Moral Life

To illustrate how art provides moral training and reflection we will consider, in a little more detail, the way that good literature, specifically the novel, fulfils this role. It is perhaps not surprising that, for Murdoch, the novel is a crucial learning ground. Not only, as we discussed in the previous chapter, does she put great store in images and metaphors, but she is of course a (perhaps great) novelist herself. Like all good art, good novels for Murdoch 'concern the fight between good and evil and the pilgrimage from appearance to reality' (Murdoch, 1992, p. 97). Murdoch contends that, although in the present climate the struggle between good and evil may be 'covert, unclear, secret, ambiguous' (Murdoch, 1997 [1972], p. 255), it is still this struggle that underlies the structure of good novels.[10]

In literature, as in life, Murdoch contends that one 'cannot avoid value judgements. Values show and show clearly in literature' (Murdoch, 1997 [1978], p. 21). This is a process which involves the author and the reader.

128 *The Moral Vision of Iris Murdoch*

Murdoch argues that the 'author's moral judgement is the air that the reader breathes' (ibid., p. 28) and a good author (as we discussed with regard to Shakespeare) will be a 'just and intelligent judge' (ibid.). The great novelist will be tolerant and create free and realistic characters, something that, as Murdoch points out, presumably from her own experience, is not an easy task: 'anyone who has attempted to write a novel will have discovered this difficulty . . . is one going to be able to present any character other than oneself who is more than a conventional puppet?' (Murdoch, 1997 [1959b], p. 283). The failure to present free characters Murdoch sees as a 'spiritual failure' (ibid., p. 284) because it is profoundly important that characters are real and not simply foils of the selfish ego, as Antonaccio states; for Murdoch, 'it *matters*, in literature, morals and politics, how we portray the human person' (Antonaccio, 1996, p. 117). Literature then is 'soaked in the moral, language is soaked in the moral, fictional characters swim in a moral atmosphere' (Murdoch, 1997 [1972], p. 254). Our engagement with novels as readers is fundamentally moral; we 'rightly criticise novels in which characters' thoughts (as well as actions) exhibit a lack of moral sensibility which seems called for by the story' (Murdoch, 1992, p. 169). To illustrate this further, Murdoch relays a number of familiar examples, which are worth quoting at some length:

> What do we think about Hamlet? What do we think about Fabrice del Dongo, or Madame Bovary? Or what about D.H. Lawrence's treatment of Clifford Chatterley compared to his treatment of Mellors? Does Tolstoy meanly abandon characters such as Sonia and Karenin? . . . Can Mauriac get away with a character as incoherent as that of Thérèse? Is Fanny Price in *Mansfield Park* really a rather nasty girl or is she a nice girl? (Murdoch, 1997 [1972], p. 254)

Such (moral) criticism is a natural response to the novel, part of our endless interest in other people and how to live (ibid., p. 253), and it is in this critical task that our moral awareness is broadened, for we 'read great novels with all our knowledge of life engaged, the experience is cognitive and moral in the highest degree' (Murdoch, 1992, p. 97). Therefore in the task of reading we judge the character, the author, the society and so on from a moral point of view, it is a place where we can explore and 'practise' moral judgment. In Murdoch's words, 'a great work of art gives one a sense of space, as if one had been invited into some large hall of reflection' (Murdoch, 1997 [1978], p. 28). In this way, then, novels can show us the truth, about ourselves, other people and the world, and provide a context in which we can explore moral values and judgments: a 'moral training ground'. We then apply the lessons we have learned and our experience of moral deliberation to our daily moral judgments about real people and situations. Art is a kind of 'testing ground' for morality and reveals the real; art is 'a form of revelation, and the great artist is the man or woman who, on canvas or in print, can increase our awareness of reality' (Dunbar, 1978, p. 523).

## Art and Morals as Analogous

In addition to arguing that art can help one to see the real, Murdoch also at times presents art as analogous to morality (Murdoch, 1970a, p. 59); indeed, she even goes so far as to say that 'art and morals are, with certain provisos . . . one' (Murdoch, 1997 [1959a], p. 215). She clarifies this statement by saying that 'the essence of both of them is love. Love is the perception of individuals, Love is the extremely difficult realisation that something other than oneself is real. Love, and so art and morals, is the discovery of reality' (ibid.). Clearly, there are great similarities in Murdoch's ethics and aesthetics and, like the moral agent, the great/good artist is on the same quest from illusion to reality (Murdoch, 1997 [1976], p. 456). In addition, both art and morality are 'imaginative cognitive activity' (Murdoch, 1992, p. 341); the energy of the artist, like that of the moral pilgrim, is 'spiritual energy' (ibid., p. 505); and both moral agent and artist must strive to understand that which he or she is only vaguely aware of (ibid., p, 328). When considered from this perspective, 'the activity of the artist or the thinker may be taken as an image (or analogy) of, or a case of, the moral life' (ibid., p. 505). For the great artist, like the successful moral pilgrim, exhibits virtue, in the form of 'patience, courage, truthfulness, justice' (ibid., p. 86). Moreover, the enemy of good art is the same enemy as that of the moral pilgrim, namely, illusion. Considered from this perspective, Murdoch suggests that the 'practice of any art is, of course, a moral discipline in that it involves a struggle against fantasy, against self-indulgence' (Murdoch, 1997 [1972], p. 255). For Murdoch, then, the discipline of the artist provides an analogy for the moral life and, in some circumstances, appears to be the moral life. Given the place of attention in the moral life and her praise of intellectual discipline, it is not surprising that Murdoch finds much to recommend the dedicated, striving artist, just as she would praise the dedicated scholar or the truthful unrequited lover. Yet the capacity of art to reveal the real makes the artist closer to the moral agent than other practitioners because their goal is the same.

This said, Murdoch does not suggest that the successful artist is also the successful moral pilgrim as, because of the 'quasi-spiritual satisfactions' (Murdoch, 1992, p. 429) and temptations of art, the good man is probably not an artist. Therefore, although Murdoch wants to employ art as an analogy for the moral life, art and morality are not (or at least not all the time) equivalent. Despite her praise of art and the artist, Murdoch declares that 'of course art and morals have a different status, altogether a different place in human life' (ibid., p. 333). Yet, this said, and although she notes that moral and aesthetic imagination are different from each other, she deems them, at times, 'hard to distinguish' (ibid.). The difference between the two lies not only in the ambiguity of the aesthetic life – its temptation to illusion as well as reality – but also in the necessity of morality. We all need to be moral, whereas we do not all need to be artists or necessarily to enjoy art: 'good life is required of us in a sense in which good art is not' (ibid.). Morality is required, art is not: and

130            *The Moral Vision of Iris Murdoch*

at one point Murdoch suggests that art is merely 'a kind of treat' (Murdoch, 1997 [1976], p. 454). (Although, given the immense difficulty of the moral life, for the moral pilgrim not to make use of art's help in the moral life could be regarded as a little rash.)

Despite these provisos, that art is not necessary to the moral life, Murdoch continues to use the analogy and to draw similarities between art and morality. Indeed, having noted the differences between art and morality, she extends the analogy, suggesting that in a sense we are all artists. Particularly in the way we derive pictures of ourselves, others and the world, something that human beings do in narrative form (Murdoch, 1997 [1978] p. 12; 1992, pp. 85, 332). For example, 'when we return home and "tell our day", we are artfully shaping material into story form' (Murdoch, 1997 [1978], p. 6); this story of ourselves is 'a little evaluative work of art' (Murdoch, 1992, p. 94). If we take this 'extended sense of the aesthetic in which "we are all artists"' (ibid., p. 334), what Murdoch means to stress is that creative imagination is central to daily life. Understood in this manner, Murdoch is pointing out that the aesthetic element in human understanding of the self and others is, like moral value, ubiquitous: 'art is not a small domain, it is everywhere' (ibid., p. 131).

Murdoch's insistence on art as important to the moral life, when understood in this wider sense, is not a requirement to create or enjoy great art (which could be rightly criticized as elitist and culturally relative, not least in her definition of great art) but, in a broader sense, is about recognizing the importance of creative imagination (which is the opposite of egoistic fantasy) in the moral life. Thus Murdoch argues that the 'concept of imagination on reflection is an essential one, not least perhaps because it can strengthen or clarify the sense in which "we are all artists"' (ibid., p. 322). Creative imagination can help us to move away from the self, as well as, presumably, aiding our illusion-ridden fantasy creation. Yet our imagination (for example, employed when we read a novel and judge the stories and characters) allows us to explore values and so become morally more attuned in life as well as in imagination. Murdoch regards imagination as an essential tool in the task of moving away from the self and attempting to see the other, for example, when we 'imagine someone else's plight' (ibid., p. 334). In this description of the importance of creative imagination in the moral life, Murdoch's analogy makes more sense and we can understand her claim that 'looked at in this way life can be seen as full of aesthetic imaginative activity which is also, scarcely distinguishably, moral activity' (ibid.).

**The Great Revealer**

Murdoch's claims for art are high; great art can inspire us to the moral life, provide moral training and provide an analogy of the moral life. Such lofty and controversial claims already outline a major role for art in the moral life. Yet Murdoch goes further still with her final claim, that art also gives access

*Art and the Moral Life* 131

to the spiritual and transcendent. Again this is equivalent to the role of beauty in Plato's schema. Murdoch contends that, in pointing to reality, great art 'points beyond itself' (Murdoch, 1992, p. 88) and acquires a significance, not necessarily intended by the author, in which 'the "brute particular" is transcended and retained (known)' (ibid., p. 339). In the experience of art, the magnetism of the good can be glimpsed as 'the art object conveys, in the most accessible and for many the only available form, the idea of transcendent perfection . . . it is an image of virtue' (ibid., p. 8). Art then 'symbolises morality' (ibid., p. 313), it is 'goodness by proxy' (Murdoch, 1970a, p. 87), it 'seems like a picture of goodness itself, a sort of semi-sensory image of a spiritual ideal' (Murdoch, 1992, p. 9). The revealing capacity of great art here is more than revealing the other, it is the capacity to show us the reality of the good, the end-point of the quest; it shows us 'the absolute pointlessness of virtue while exhibiting its supreme importance' (Murdoch, 1970a, p. 86). These claims are grandiose indeed. Murdoch is suggesting that, while not achieving knowledge of the good themselves, artists are able to reveal the good, for 'the good artist, while showing us what is not saved, implicitly shows us what salvation means' (Murdoch, 1997 [1976], p. 456). The essence of art's high spiritual call is summed up in Murdoch's Platonic dialogue *Art and Eros* (again we should bear in mind that this is not philosophical writing as such):

> Good art explains to us how the world is changing and judges change, it's the highest wisest choice of morality, it's something spiritual – without good art a society dies. It's like religion really – it's our best speech and our best understanding – it's a proof of the greatness and goodness which is in us. (Murdoch, 1987, p. 45)

Given this high praise for art, it is no surprise that Murdoch considers that art is 'far and away the most educational thing we have, far more so than its rivals, philosophy and theology and science' (Murdoch, 1997 [1976], p. 461). This assertion that art is a better teacher than philosophy or religion and other disciplines is often repeated in her work (Murdoch, 1970a, p. 88; 1992, p. 305). Art reveals the nature of the world and the nature of morality; for example, the deaths in literature (which are few, for as we have discussed, portraying real death is hard) 'show us with an exemplary clarity . . . by a juxtaposition, almost an identification, of pointlessness and value' (Murdoch, 1970a, p. 87). Murdoch argues that, in this truth-telling role, which calls us towards the good, 'the writer has always been important, and now he is *essential* . . . it may be that in the end the novelist may prove to be the saviour of the human race' (Murdoch, 1997 [1970], p. 232). In novels, as we have seen, the reality of the individual consciousness and the ubiquity of moral value continue and in a sense are proved – for stories both speak to and constitute our experience. As Murdoch's Socrates states in *Art and Eros*, 'good art tells us more truth about our lives and our world than any other kind of thinking or speculation – it certainly speaks to more people . . . perhaps the language of art is the most universal and *enduring* kind of human thought' (Murdoch, 1987, p. 63). Thus,

132          *The Moral Vision of Iris Murdoch*

in a secular age, art may be the last repository of the spiritual (or at least the easiest to gain access to). As we discussed in the last chapter, Murdoch regards the spiritual as a basic human capacity, although in the current context it is difficult to define and difficult to express. Art, for Murdoch, continues to offer access to the spiritual in a predominantly secular society.

## Murdoch's Artistry

Having explored Murdoch's aesthetics and outlined the supreme importance of art as 'one of the greatest aids' (Allen, 1993, p. 24) in the moral pilgrimage from illusion to reality, we would be remiss if we did not touch upon Murdoch the artist. Not only is Murdoch better known as a novelist than as a philosopher, but the vast majority of her writing is fiction. She has published 26 novels, in comparison to five philosophical books (and that is if one classifies her Platonic dialogues, '*Art and Eros*' and '*Above the Gods*', published together as *Acastos*, as a philosophical rather than literary work). Given the importance Murdoch places on art as an educator and revealer, the obvious question is whether Murdoch uses her novels to communicate her moral vision in preference to her philosophy. The question is particularly pertinent in the light of her claim that art is the best form of communication and education, better than other modes of discourse, including philosophy. Much has been written about the presence of philosophy in Murdoch's novels and many have read them as a vehicle for her philosophical ideas. For example, A.S. Byatt comments that Murdoch's novels 'certainly *appear* to centre on the ideas' (Byatt, 1970, p. 184) and that 'some *idea*, which could well be called philosophical, provides much of the unifying framework for each of Miss Murdoch's novels' (ibid.). In a like manner, Alasdair MacIntyre comments that her novels are full of philosophy: 'her characters sometime talk about Wittgenstein or quote Heidegger or Kant or go to dinner with Oxford philosophers' (MacIntyre, 1982, p. 15).

    In the light of such comments one could conclude that Murdoch's novels should be read in order to understand her philosophical ideas, or perhaps as an alternative to reading her philosophy, especially given her claim that art is the most educational form of discourse. However, to do this would be to deny Murdoch's own pronouncements on the matter, which explicitly preclude reading her novels in this way. Murdoch overtly rejects the notion of being a 'philosophical novelist'. In interviews on this topic, again and again, she has said that her novels should not be read as philosophy. For example, in an interview for *The Times* she states, 'I am not a philosophical novelist in the sense that Sartre or Simone de Beauvoir is' (1964, p. 15); a point later repeated more strongly: 'I would hate to write philosophical novels' (BBC, 1989). That Murdoch refuses to see literature as a vehicle for philosophy is perhaps not so surprising if we return to her definition of great art, in which the author must look away from the self, see the real and produce free characters (one of the

# Art and the Moral Life                                           133

qualities that made Shakespeare a great artist was his invisibility). If the author's intention is to comunicate philosophy it will be the author's ego which drives the characters and the story. To use novels intentionally to convey her vision would be to ignore her points about creative imagination and the author's need to exhibit tolerance. Thus we should not be surprised when Murdoch states that 'I am reluctant to say that the deep structure of any good literary work could be a philosophical one ... for better or worse art goes deeper than philosophy. Ideas in art must suffer a sea change' (Murdoch, 1997 [1978], p. 21). Accordingly, Murdoch is critical of the philosophical novelist for not creating free characters; for example, she criticizes Sartre as a novelist for his inability to see individuals clearly and for using his characters to make philosophical points. Consequently, she does not regard him as a great novelist, as he lacks 'an apprehension of the absurd irreducible uniqueness of people and of their relations with each other' (Murdoch, 1953, p. 75). Murdoch argues that philosophical novels fail as novels as they do not reveal reality – of other people and of the world – but only portray the philosophy of the author (despite this, Murdoch admires *Nausea*).

Murdoch admits that there is philosophy in her novels, and indeed it would be impossible for her not to, but she argues that this is because philosophy is what she knows about, just as 'if I knew about sailing ships I would put in sailing ships' (Murdoch, 1997 [1978], p. 20). In this manner, again in her interview in *The Times*, she accepts that inevitably philosophy seeps into her novels, stating that 'I suppose I have certain philosophical ideas about human life and character, and that these ideas must somehow find expression in my novels; but for the most part I am not conscious of this process' (1964, p. 15). Therefore Murdoch's claim is not that her novels do not convey her philosophy, but that they do not do so directly. She does not write novels in order to transmit a certain philosophical point. Indeed, she dismisses this method of writing, stating that 'I feel in myself such an absolute horror of putting theories or "philosophical ideas" into my novels' (Murdoch, 1997 [1978], p. 19). Rather than writing a 'philosophical novel', she would argue that she draws on philosophy, just as she draws on all her experience, in order to create free characters and to write their story.

Given Murdoch's protestations, it may seem best to leave the discussion here and take Murdoch at her word and separate her novels from her philosophy entirely. Certainly, it would be rash and, in light of Murdoch's very clear rejection of the idea, foolhardy to use her novels as a cipher for her philosophy. However, when one reads her novels, many of the themes of her philosophy are present. For example, Angela Hague observes that 'Murdoch's characters frequently voice her own philosophical tenets, and her recent fiction contains, not surprisingly, characters who echo her belief in the fundamental absurdity of the human predicament' (Hague, 1984, p. 46). Johnson suggests that her characters are 'subject to *eikasia* and particularly that form of *eikasia* which renders other people invisible' (Johnson, 1987, p. 9). Certainly, when one reads Murdoch's novels, the ability of human beings to be deluded and

134 The Moral Vision of Iris Murdoch

egotistical in the manner she describes in her philosophy is clear; through her characters she 'again and again warns against the dangers of fantasy and illusion' (Dipple, 1996, p. 139). To name but two examples, Charles Arrowby in *The Sea, The Sea* and Blaise in the *Sacred and Profane Love Machine* are both immensely selfish egotistical characters who, though thinking they are knowledgeable and reflective, are absolutely unable to see through their own self-delusion and rationalization. They fail completely to see the reality of other people, projecting their own desires and interpretations on the people around them. In all her novels the overwhelming power of human beings to delude themselves and the difficulty of perceiving anything without the terrible distortions of the selfish ego is clear. The tremendous difficulty of being good in a world sunk in illusion is also depicted. Therefore it does make sense to suggest that, for illustrations of the human condition, one could augment her philosophy by reading her novels.

Some critics have attempted to explore Murdoch's philosophical ideas directly in her fiction. For example, the place of the good in Murdoch's novels has been explicitly discussed by Sugana Ramanathan and Elisabeth Dipple. Both of them have considered what the good person would look like by studying the good characters in her novels. Significantly, the good characters (whom both Ramanathan and Dipple place as being some way along the pilgrimage, Ramanathan even suggesting which level of the cave they have reached: Ramanathan, 1990, p. 403) are generally relatively peripheral characters (with the exception of Anne Cavidge in *Nuns and Soldiers*): for example, Talis Browne in *A Fairly Honourable Defeat*, Brendon Cradock in *Henry and Cato*, James Arrowby in *The Sea, the Sea* and Theo in *The Nice and the Good* (Ramanathan, 1990; Dipple, 1982; Jasper, 1986). These characters are considered to be good by virtue of their perception; they can see other people and the world more clearly than the other characters can. However, just as the pilgrim returning to the Cave (those who have attained a higher level of awareness), they are often invisible and misunderstood by the other characters in the novel (even by Anne in *Nuns and Soldiers*, who is central to the plot). Moreover, these characters, via various means, whether by faith (both Western, Brendon Cradock, and Eastern, James Arrowby) or by a denial of the self in another manner, have significantly reduced the power of the ego.

Given that the preoccupations of Murdoch's novels are the preoccupations of her philosophy, it is hard at times not to see her novels as the philosophical novels Murdoch so desperately wishes to avoid. This is especially the case not only when general themes (such as the deluded egotistical nature of human life and the difficultly of attaining goodness) are explored in the novels, but when specific philosophical arguments and positions appear, which seem to be recastings of her philosophical arguments. For example, in the *Philosopher's Pupil*, there is a discussion of the ontological proof, which is one of Murdoch's key arguments for the good. In this passage she is criticizing her own philosophical position:

*Art and the Moral Life* 135

It's all done with mirrors like the Ontological Proof. You imagine a perfect love which emanates from a pure source in response to your imperfect love, in response to your frantic desire for love – then because this gives you a warm feeling you say you're certain . . . I suppose that's what's called faith. You feel it all coming beaming back. But you would need the God you don't believe in to make it real. It's all the same imperfect stuff churning to and fro. You want a response. You can't have a real one so you fake one, like sending a letter to yourself. (Murdoch, 1983, p. 192)

What are we to make of passages like this? Is it really not the case that behind this dialogue is Murdoch's worry over her own vision of the good, and whether she has really substituted God for good, which, as we have seen, Murdoch denies and vehemently argues against. It seems that it would be against the evidence, or in more Murdochian words, against experience, to deny that Murdoch's philosophy is present in her novels. However, this said, there seems to be no justification for reading her philosophy directly into her novels, or for extrapolating it from her characters (as particularly Ramanathan and perhaps Dipple could perhaps be said to have done). Certainly, in light of Murdoch's own protestations, it would seem to be unwise to attempt to read Murdoch's novels as if they were philosophy. Nevertheless, there is undoubtedly a connection between Murdoch's philosophy and her literature, even if this is simply that Murdoch's concerns about life are explored in these two very different mediums. Therefore studying Murdoch's novels is not necessary in order to comprehend her philosophy, and on no account should one treat her novels as an alternative and equivalent source of her philosophy. Yet reading the novels may enhance the reader's understanding of Murdoch's concerns. Indeed Martha Nussbaum advises that 'the reader who wishes to confront Murdoch's more subtle reflections about art, objectivity, fantasy, and love would still do best to reread that fine, disturbing novel, *The Black Prince*' (Nussbaum, 1978, p. 126). So, although reading Murdoch's novels will give insight into Murdoch's views about human nature and the good, it will not alone provide a full understanding of her vision, particularly as the stances of her characters – by virtue, one supposes, of their freedom – are very often not in accord with her own philosophical positions.

In sum, then, Murdoch's novels are likely to be of interest to the student of her philosophy, and undoubtedly they do provide insights into her vision of humanity and the world, but they should not be read as philosophy as such. As Murdoch states, the voice she uses and the aims and intention are different (Conradi, 1997).

## Conclusion

Murdoch's conception of art, as her understanding of moral values, the moral life and the spiritual, is broad. The aesthetic element in her description of human beings 'all as artists', suggests that creative imagination (for example, in empathy and sympathy, both in art and in reality), is a basic human capacity.

136         *The Moral Vision of Iris Murdoch*

Such a reading emphasizes the creative capacities of individuals and the value of their experience in a manner which is now familiar from our previous discussion. When considered from this perspective, her analogy of morality and art, her assertion that art is a good object of attention, her claim that art provides moral training and inspiration, and even her plea for the transcendence of art, help us to further understand Murdoch's vision and to comprehend the daily, familiar ways in which the moral pilgrim progresses.

This said, however, her understanding of art is beset by additional difficulties as her conception of the type of art which helps us in the moral life is so terribly limited. Her definition of great art is exceptionally small and, given the small number of examples, hard to comprehend and defend. Murdoch's definition of great art is highly controversial and out of step with contemporary aesthetic theories, as well as with artists' own testimonies about what they consider themselves to be doing. This, of course, is not a problem in itself; as we have seen, much of Murdoch's vision is overtly and consciously in conflict with prevailing contemporary ideologies. However, in the case of art, we seem to be in a little more difficulty, especially with the charge of elitism. For example, Murdoch's dismissal of television, which she equates with the lowest level of the Cave, has been justly criticized.[11] Here Murdoch seems to be out of step with her own vision, not only her much broader reading of aesthetics (in the sense that we are all artists), but also her continual insistence throughout her philosophy that proof of her vision can be found in ordinary experience. While many could agree that great art is truth-telling, they may not agree on what art is great. If it is with the function of truth-telling that Murdoch is concerned then someone from a different culture or background could be equally drawn away from the self by a piece of art (or even television) that did not fit Murdoch's very small classical canon.

The narrowness of Murdoch's definition of art seems to spring directly from her need to do justice to Plato's criticisms, which, as we have seen, she accepts with regard to most art. It is her need to satisfy Plato that leads her to such a narrow definition of art. Love too is double-edged, leading both to the good and to the self (as we saw in the last chapter). Yet Murdoch, like Plato, accepts love as a way to reach the good, even though it is also dangerous and can lead one in the opposite direction. Significantly, it is love of all sorts, if we recall the progression in the *Symposium*, which can eventually lead to the purest love, that of the good. Given this, it may be best to focus on the way that art can function with regard to the moral life. It is far easier to accept a more holistic vision (and arguably more in tune with the rest of Murdoch's philosophy) of art's place in the moral life than it is to accept her definition of great art. If we put to one side Murdoch's definition of great art, we can see quite clearly the ways in which art can help the moral pilgrim: as a focus of attention, as a revealer of truth, as a place where values can be explored and perhaps even as a route to transcendence. We can also accept, given Murdoch's understanding of the moral life, that art is also quite capable, as is love, of leading one further into illusion.

# Notes

1. Murdoch's discussion of Kant's aesthetics in her article 'The Sublime and the Good' (1959). In this article she describes his theory as one that 'distinguishes between the beautiful and the sublime, and in speaking of the beautiful he distinguishes between free and dependent beauty' (Murdoch, 1997 [1959a], p. 206). This is an aesthetic theory she ultimately disagrees with and instead asserts her own definition of great art, which we will discuss later in this chapter.

2. Murdoch's very twentieth-century fear of totalitarianism and strong wish to protect the individual would probably lead her in a completely different direction. Here we are speculating, but it would seem unlikely that Murdoch's blueprint for a just and good society would be Plato's republic.

3. She discusses this issue in relation to communism. She states that 'all tyrants try to mystify and may invent languages for that purpose. Bad artists are useful to tyrants, whose policies they can simplify and romanticise, as in Stalinist-style art' (Murdoch, 1992, p. 90).

4. As noted in the last chapters, there are many interpretations of Plato's forms and their nature and function is still highly controversial. The form of the bed here is a form from the 'middle period', which fits the two-world vision of forms.

5. Despite her praise for love, including sexual love, as an inspiration to the moral life, Murdoch also sees love (perhaps particularly sexual love) as a potential danger, leading to obsession and illusion. As Martha Nussbaum notes, 'it is frequently suggested, both in Murdoch's philosophical works and in her novels, that sexual desire and the bodily component in love are sins in the Dantean sense, that is, sources of egoistic self-delusion and self-immersion that persistently come between us and the reality of those we love' (Nussbaum, 1996, p. 37). Therefore, even though Murdoch does regard love as potentially revealing and inspiring, as Nussbaum recognizes, commenting on her novels that there are occasions when 'through sexual love her characters do find themselves jolted out of themselves, prepared to search, at least, for the real good that is in the world around them' (ibid., p. 46), its potential for illusion is, at least, equally strong. Obsessive, illusion-ridden love appears to be at its worst in pornography, about which Murdoch says: 'I am very hostile to pornography, I think it's really damaging and degrading' (Murdoch, 1997 [1978], p. 14).

6. Murdoch depends on the work of Freud to present a modern version of the illusion-ridden individual. She describes Freud as 'a self-styled modern disciple of Plato' (Murdoch, 1992, p. 20). Freud, like Plato, was critical of art for its capacity to encourage fantasy. As Murdoch describes his reasons, his criticism of art derives from the fact that 'we would normally be repelled by the private fantasies of another person, but the artist persuades us to accept his by disguising them cleverly, and by offering us formal and aesthetic pleasures which then incite us to release, upon our side, a play of personal fantasy which is normally inhibited' (ibid.).

7. It is from this first premise of her aesthetic that she concludes that Kant's aesthetic is misguided. Arguing that his aesthetic cannot account for the greatness of tragedy and therefore fails to regard Shakespeare as a great artist, she states that 'Kant thinks that art is essentially play. Now Shakespeare is great art, and Shakespeare is not play, so Kant must be wrong' (Murdoch, 1997 [1959a], p. 211).

8. Murdoch suggests that these characters show us 'evil as "duty", or "inevitable fate", the natural irresistible exercise of a depraved vision, taken for granted as an aspect of sexual cynicism or ambition, the circumstantial working of "original sin"' (Murdoch, 1992, p. 103). She goes on to elaborate on Macbeth's condition, as one which rings true both in life and

138 *The Moral Vision of Iris Murdoch*

in fiction that 'evil, once deeply entered into, seems "forced" to continue' (ibid., p. 104). Just as goodness is about habit and the moral colour, so is evil, yet even so she argues that 'evil people are not usually (morally) excused on the plea that "once started they couldn't stop"' (ibid.).

9  To cite a number of examples, Murdoch states that 'good art reveals what we are usually too selfish and too timid to recognise' (Murdoch, 1970a, p. 86); 'it reveals to us aspects of our world which our ordinary dull dream-consciousness is unable to see' (ibid., p. 88); in art we recognize 'what we vaguely knew was there but never saw before' (Murdoch, 1997 [1978], p. 12); literature is concerned with telling 'truths and drawing attention to a lot of things which might otherwise not be noticed' (Murdoch, 1997 [1972], p. 249).

10  Murdoch recognizes the changes in literature, particularly those brought about by structuralist literary criticism which insists 'that literature is required to be linguistically self-conscious, no longer taken in by the "referential fallacy" (looking through the page into another world), and to treat language as an experimental adventure playground' (Murdoch, 1992, p. 48). This philosophy supposedly creates non-evaluative works, and presents the novel 'as a network of meanings' (ibid., p. 205) to be studied as a text unrelated to the author. Murdoch dismisses this form of criticism in the same way that she did Derrida's structuralism (see Chapter 3) as the wish to be pseudoscientific and be experts with secret knowledge. While Murdoch accepts that such theories do undermine literature, she insists that literature will survive: 'however much novelists may try, for reasons of fashion or of art, to stop telling stories, the story is always likely to break out again in a new form' (Murdoch, 1997 [1970], p. 233).

11  For example, Simon Blackburn is horrified by Murdoch's vision and comments that 'television does not picture (model?) the unredeemed state of *eikasia*. Television gives us visual information that is in interesting ways extremely like the visual information we would get by a direct view of a scene, and this is not an apt metaphor for the state of the Prisoners in Plato's myth. Television does not give us shadows of copies of things' (Blackburn, 1992, p. 23).

# Chapter 7

# Religion and the Moral Life

We now turn to the last of the main themes of Murdoch's work, that of religion, and the place it occupies vis-à-vis morality. Murdoch is not religious herself, yet, 'in spite of her atheism, she has always been deeply interested in religion and the religious life' (Kaalikoski, 1997, p. 144). Throughout our exploration of Murdoch's moral vision we have noted the religious concepts she invokes: for example, attention – a device 'for the purification of states of mind' (Murdoch, 1970a, p. 83) – as a secular form of prayer, and use of the term 'pilgrimage' to describe the moral life. Indeed, even her presumptions about the illusion-ridden nature of the human condition owe much to religious thinking, a debt Murdoch acknowledges in her recognition that Christianity, Buddhism and Hinduism all assert that 'our guilt or sin is our existence itself' (Murdoch, 1992, p. 69). If we replace the religious terms 'sin' and 'guilt' with the secular term 'egoist illusion' we have the Murdochian picture. Yet, despite the religious-sounding nature of her moral vision, Murdoch is an atheist. Indeed, her philosophy is premised on the assumption that 'human life has no external point or telos' (Murdoch, 1970a, p. 79) and on the belief that 'there is no general and as it were externally guaranteed pattern or purpose of the kind for which philosophers and theologians used to search. We are what we seem to be, transient moral creatures subject to necessity and chance' (ibid.).

In the current context, where pseudoscientific philosophies prevail, Murdoch's interest in religion and religious concepts has been welcomed by theologians and she has been described as 'in the contemporary philosophical setting, a friend to theistic religion' (Gamwell, 1996, p. 175). Whether or not Murdoch is a friend to theistic religion remains to be seen – she certainly could not be described as a friend to the personal theistic God – yet she is undoubtedly a friend to the preoccupations and insights of religion. Murdoch's recognition that religion has something to offer philosophical visions of the world is unusual as 'the Christian God has been mainly absent from post-Kantian philosophy, the problems he poses relegated to theology' (Murdoch, 1992, p. 80). The absence of theological concerns from philosophy and the more general decline of a religious background framework Murdoch regards as highly significant, so much so that she asserts, 'the most important change that we have experienced in this century is the loss of religion as something taken for granted' (Murdoch, 1997 [1972], p. 255), a sentiment she repeats (Murdoch, 1997 [1978], p. 27). The loss of religion as a shared framework, Murdoch contends, has wide implications for literature, politics and philosophy, as concepts of the individual and moral value change: 'belief in a personal

140                    *The Moral Vision of Iris Murdoch*

God seemed a prime guarantee of general morality' (Murdoch, 1992, p. 81).[1] The consequences of such a paradigm shift cannot be over-estimated and Murdoch suggests that 'the relation of religion, morality and philosophy is perhaps the great intellectual problem of the age' (ibid., p. 135). Murdoch addresses this 'great problem', not by entering into specifically theological debates about the processes of secularization, but rather by focusing on the elements of religion and spirituality which are connected to her vision of the moral life. Murdoch, then, is not concerned with the decline of religion as such, but with the effect that the decline of belief has on our moral concepts and on our understandings of what it means to be human.

This chapter will begin by exploring Murdoch's presumption that religious belief is inevitably declining in the West as non-religious ideologies prevail. We will then assess Murdoch's wish to maintain some form of spirituality, the relationship between religion and art, and the role of religion in the moral life. The chapter will conclude with Murdoch's vision of a 'godless religion' and her wish to connect morality and mysticism.

## Decline of Traditional Christianity

Murdoch does not believe that Western religion, by which she means Christianity, can continue in its present form and she regards the present age as 'untheological' (Murdoch, 1997 [1970], p. 232), to the extent that 'Christianity is not so much abandoned so much as simply unknown' (Murdoch, 1997 [1970], p. 228). Murdoch acknowledges the impact of the humanist critique on modern views of religion and its result that 'many people hate religion, with its terrible history of irrationality, and would regard resort to religious rituals as a false substitute for real morals and genuine amendment of life' (Murdoch, 1992, p. 487).[2] Murdoch endorses much of this position and agrees that religion can be the enemy of morality, and in particular that religion can justify immoral actions and can undermine true moral motivation.

First, then, religion can be used to justify and even require acts which would be judged to be immoral by any human standards of morality, on the grounds that such acts are commanded by God. The classic example used in the literature is the biblical example of Abraham and Isaac. In this story Abraham is commanded to kill his child in order to prove his love for God, although, having proved his willingness, God relents and Abraham does not go through with the sacrifice. In this example, because Abraham believes he is commanded by God to sacrifice Isaac, an action which would normally be considered immoral becomes morally required, as morality in this schema derives directly from the commands of God.[3] The consequence of such a belief is that any act of immorality is not only morally permitted, but morally required, if one has been commanded by God to act in such a way: a view that has led to wars, genocide and much human suffering. Consequently, the humanist critique has accused religion of perverting morality because, by making moral values dependent on the commands of God, moral values are not objective, absolute or universalizable, but can be changed and overturned by the will of God. Indeed, the consequences of making morality dependent on religion have long troubled theologians, and even some divine command theorists accept that, because of the ability to God to make anything he chooses good (for example the sacrifice of Isaac), 'divine command theories . . . seem to wind up encouraging evil' (Quinn, 1978, p. 54).[4] Philip Quinn (a 'weak' divine command theorist, who believes that God commands only morally good actions) claims that actions such as Abraham's are only apparently immoral as God will 'appropriately compensate both the killer and the victim in the relevant felicific or beatific respects either here or hereafter' (Quinn, 1981, p. 60).[5] Such reasoning, which allows God's commands to change morality, is dependent on a theistic faith and is a position which is diametrically opposed to Murdoch's realist vision. For Murdoch, it is moral value which is absolute and unchanging. The belief that morality derives from God's commands is one which Murdoch totally rejects and here she echoes the humanist critique, stating that, 'organised, institutionalised religion is an enemy of morality, an enemy of freedom and free thought, guilty of cruelty and repression' (Murdoch, 1992, p. 487).

Second, not only does a morality which depends on the commands of God have the potential to result in horrendously immoral acts but, even when religious adherents do act morally (and generally religious moral codes are in accord with human morality), adherents act more from religious motives than from moral reasons, again threatening the fundamental authority and reality of moral values. The religious adherent acts from religious reasons (for example, from hopes of reward and fears of punishment, either in this life or the next) rather than in response to moral demand. Such a conception of the relationship between morality and religion Murdoch denies and, throughout her work, there runs the fundamental assumption that one must be 'good for nothing', simply in response to one's awareness of morality. To act morally for non-moral reasons is immoral, egotistical and deluded.

Consequently, forms of religiosity and belief which present morality as dependent on religion, such as divine command theories, are anathema to Murdoch. For moral action to be authentic, the individual agent must act for moral reasons, reasons which Murdoch believes are just as compelling for the theist as for the atheist. Thus she argues that even 'if God appeared physically before us on His throne and said "Do this" we would still be able to wonder if we ought to' (ibid. p. 303).[6] Moreover, to rely on an external source for moral action would not broaden the moral vision of the individual. For Murdoch, moral action derives from true moral vision which can only be achieved by realistic striving and therefore cannot be effectively mimicked by simply acting in the 'right' way. Morality is much more than right action and, accordingly, for Murdoch, a morality of following commands is not morality: although it may induce good habits and aid us when we struggle in the moral life, it can never be true morality which derives from the individual's clear vision.

142 *The Moral Vision of Iris Murdoch*

As a result, and in part because of the influence of the humanist critique, Murdoch regards traditional, literal belief as declining; indeed, she declares such belief 'impossible to a modern man' (ibid., p. 135). Like the humanist thinkers she draws on, she regards the decline of religious belief as an inevitable consequence of competing rational and scientific worldviews and she states that 'it may indeed be the case that deep slow changes (only roughly indicated by the "scientific temper of the age") render it difficult or impossible to think about religion in the old literalistic way' (ibid., p. 459). Murdoch does not regard this decline in belief and the accompanying moral uncertainty as a peculiarly modern phenomenon. In fact she regards the situation as relevantly similar to the situation that Plato was addressing: a time when belief in the gods was likewise declining in response to the rise of alternative explanations derived from the new mathematical and scientific discoveries.[7] Indeed, the similarities, particularly regarding religion and morality, between the periods are one reason that Murdoch believes that it is the 'Platonic view of the cosmos which speaks to our age' (ibid., p. 181). This conviction is dramatically presented in her Platonic dialogue, *Above the Gods*. The characters express their feelings about religion thus: 'This is a time of transition. Our civilisation is growing up, we're scientific and factual, we can analyse the old superstitions and see how they arose. God is not the measure of all things, man is the measure of all things' (Murdoch, 1987, pp. 72–3). She echoes this perception in her philosophical writings, suggesting that 'we increasingly see it . . . [religion] . . . as a historically determined phenomenon, and ourselves as emerging from an era where myths were regarded in an unreflective way as "real", into a scientific era' (Murdoch, 1992, p. 138).

The change in ethos between a religious past and a secular present is for Murdoch profound. She suggests that the inability to believe is caused, just as it was for Plato's Greeks, by the developments in new sorts of knowledge and a corresponding paradigm shift, and as a result 'we are now more self-conscious and critical about religion in a way which is new' (ibid.). For Murdoch, the present age is one of 'pseudo-scientific anti-human "philosophies"' (ibid., p. 425), it is 'a scientific linguistically minded age, wherein religion too is thrust aside' (ibid., p. 159). The dominance of the scientific paradigm mitigates against religious beliefs and consequently 'religion is rejected today on the simple charge that "it isn't true"' (ibid., p. 449). Traditional religious beliefs are incompatible with the prevalent scientific explanatory systems and, as a result, 'many people leave their churches because reason forbids belief, not only in God, but in saints, visions, revelations, mystical states and so on' (ibid., p. 249). Murdoch argues that the secular, scientific value framework precludes traditional belief systems and, as a result, belief 'in a personal God . . . increasingly inaccessible to the thinkers of today' (ibid., p. 38). In this context a religious construct of the cosmos becomes difficult to maintain, even for those who remain within the religious tradition. To illustrate this, Murdoch cites the work of Martin Buber, a Jewish thinker, who states that the 'God who formerly spoke to us is dumb' (ibid., p. 465) and who 'speaks of the

*Religion and the Moral Life*  143

present age as a period of darkness or silence which awaits a new revelation' (ibid., p. 461). Murdoch concurs with this view, stating that 'the present does certainly appear to be a time of "angels", of wandering fragmented spirituality' (ibid., p. 467). The scientific paradigm which characterizes the Western public context is one which not only makes religion difficult to believe in, but also (as we have seen) threatens fundamental concepts which have hitherto been taken for granted, such as the self, the inner-life and morality. For Murdoch, all these, essentially 'human', elements are connected, and uncertainty regarding one affects the others, and so she sees the present context as one in which '"facts" proliferate, values fade, religion fades, our sense of truth is shaken. A confidence carried for us by religion and art, seems no longer present' (ibid., p. 372).

## Reclaiming Spirituality

Here we see the essence of Murdoch's interest in religion. She is critical of religion along typical humanist lines, and feels that 'it is time to say goodbye to the old literal personal "elsewhere" God' (Murdoch, 1992, p. 420). Nevertheless she is wary of rejecting all forms of religion and religiosity as, in doing so, we might lose something of what it means to be human. Religion, or perhaps more accurately a certain religious orientation or spirituality, is something which Murdoch is keen should continue in some form. Spirituality, for Murdoch, as we saw in her vision of the moral life, is not about belief in a traditional God, but, like moral recognition, is a basic human capacity. It is part of what makes us whole human beings; it includes our history, sense of self and of course our recognition of values. She suggests that 'the ease with which children acquire and retain religious concepts may be taken as proof that we are all naturally religious or naturally superstitious' (ibid., p. 147). Even in the modern world, Murdoch argues that 'religious consciousness' (ibid., p. 341) may still be a natural human capacity although 'in a materialist, scientific, technological, television-dominated atmosphere, people do not have it, or do not *recognise* it' (ibid.). The loss of a means to articulate this religiosity has important repercussions for concepts of what it means to be human and affects 'the popular consciousness in the form of a sense of loss, of being returned to a confused pluralistic world from which something "deep" has been removed' (ibid., p. 7).

Murdoch argues that the mistake made by the humanist critique is not the rejection of traditional religion, with which she largely concurs, but the rejection of all forms of religiosity and spirituality. Therefore she states that 'opposition to religion is at its most dangerous when it argues that the age of Platonic–Kantian western philosophy is over' (ibid., p. 181). Such a change in worldview which denies all forms of spirituality Murdoch regards as dehumanizing and disastrous (in a similar manner to her criticisms of worldviews which threaten the view of humans as fundamentally moral beings) because areas of human

144 *The Moral Vision of Iris Murdoch*

expression, self-understanding and experience also disappear. A wholesale rejection of the religious worldview, then, denies many realities essential to human experience. As a result Murdoch suggests that 'when we say that "religion is disappearing" part of what is disappearing is both the occurrence of certain experiences, and also of our tendency to *notice* them and, instinctively or reflectively, to lend them moral or religious meaning' (ibid., p. 307). Spiritual experiences continue, but our ability to articulate and use them declines and it is this fundamental human experience which Murdoch wishes to reclaim, just as she wished to retain, in the concept of attention, a secular version of prayer in order to engender 'respect for persons and for nature' (ibid., p. 337) and so aid the moral life.

Murdoch's concern is that, as we move evermore into a scientific, technological paradigm, we do not reject the spiritual aspects of human life, for to do so would be to lose fundamental human capacities and modes of experience: to suffer from 'a lack of Eros' (ibid., p. 307). She perhaps best sums up this fear of loss dramatically in her Platonic dialogue on the subject of religion, *Above the Gods*, when Acastos (who often seems to be the mouthpiece of Murdoch's own views) declares:

> If we lose traditional religion now we may lose *all* religion because – it can't use the old language and concepts – and it can't make new ones . . . it's as if the gods can't speak to us any more . . . But I don't want worship and ritual and prayer and so on just to *go* – there's a valuable – precious – thing somewhere inside it all. (Murdoch, 1987, p. 86)

Murdoch is attempting to prevent this possible future, and she calls on us to recognize that 'human nature is the abode of spiritual intimation and spiritual imagery and we are not forced by "science" or "modernism" to live by the will, by a simple ability to leap right out of a bleak "factual" world' (Murdoch, 1992, p. 460). Thus the loss of spirituality is connected to the dehumanizing philosophies of the modern age and, while welcoming the decline of traditional (false) religion, she urges us to maintain the capacity to recognize and live spiritual, fully human, lives.

**Religion and Art**

However, although Murdoch is keen not to lose religiosity, she is still wary of religion, particularly, as one would expect, its capacity for consolation and delusion. Just as Murdoch feared the capacity of art to lead one into illusion, she fears religion's ability to do the same. Murdoch's position is summed up by Scott Dunbar: 'The Christian religion . . . at its most widely endorsed and popular level offers the most consoling moral framework this side of the eternal. In so doing, it too lacks realism about the human condition and fails to take the human pilgrim seriously' (Dunbar, 1978, p. 516). This summation does

*Religion and the Moral Life*                                      145

not exaggerate Murdoch's hostility to the consoling aspects of religion. For example, she asserts that most religious believers have simply accepted 'easy religious consolation' (Murdoch, 1992, p. 139). As we have seen, Murdoch regards seeing reality as a difficult task; the ego prefers to protect itself and be consoled, and 'almost anything that consoles us is fake' (Murdoch, 1970a, p. 59). Religion, like art, may, while masquerading as truth, be nothing more than 'private egoism' (Murdoch, 1992, p. 248); 'a fantasising protection of the ego, a deterministic myth, concealing change and obliterating freedom' (ibid., p. 103). Religion with its all-encompassing framework and eternal promises has more propensity to false consolation and illusion than anything else. Moreover, Murdoch regards Christianity and the way it has embraced art, with its personal God and central figure of Christ, as particularly guilty of false consolation (ibid., p. 81).

Consequently, Murdoch likens the consolations of religion to the consolations of art. As with art, Murdoch divides religion between 'high' true religion, and most religion which is 'power-seeking and magic' (ibid., p. 460), for, just as 'there is little great art' there is little 'true religion, little holiness, few saints, much superstition and sentimentality' (ibid., p. 130). Religion is not only like art in its double-edged nature, but it employs and uses art, so arguably is more dangerous than art alone, in that its consoling capacities are then added to the consoling capacities of art. Murdoch argues that Christianity particularly (unlike Judaism and Islam) has used art and presented 'God as a kind of super-art-object' (ibid., p. 81). The use of art in Christianity Murdoch traces back to the gospels, which she describes as 'easy to read . . . (even I would think for a complete stranger to them), because they are the kind of great art where we feel: it is so' (ibid., p. 128). Murdoch claims that Christianity continued to use art in the writings of Paul, to whom she attributes almost 'demonic power' (ibid.) whose depiction of Christ is 'like a personal creation and a work of art' (ibid., p. 82). Together, Paul and the gospel writers – 'five artists of genius' (ibid.) – provide Christianity with its 'dominant, attractive central character' of Christ, and so make Christianity 'itself like a vast work of art' (ibid.). These initial images and pictures were supplemented over the centuries and 'Western art, so solid and clear, has helped us to *believe*, not only in Christ and the Trinity, but in the Good Samaritan, the Prodigal Son, innumerable saints and a whole cast of famous and well-loved scenes and persons' (ibid.). Therefore Murdoch speaks of religious belief as a 'living work of art' (ibid., p. 131), and Christianity's central image of Christ crucified as 'more familiar in the west than the most ubiquitous advertising cliché' (ibid.).

The interweaving of Christianity and art is hard to unravel, so much so that it is difficult to talk about religion or a religious subject 'without employing the consolations and charms of art' (ibid., p. 126). In Christianity art and religion have combined and Christ has become the 'universal tragic character' (ibid., p. 125). In this merging of religion and art the dangers of both are clear. For example, Murdoch describes the story of Christ as one 'which we want to

146                    *The Moral Vision of Iris Murdoch*

hear: that suffering can be redemptive, and that this is not the end' (ibid., p. 128). Yet it is exactly at this point that the danger of consoling illusion is hardest to resist; both religion and art present 'the eclipse of death by creative suffering' (ibid., p. 133). Religion can hide the horror of reality and obscure the call of the good; for example, forgiveness may result either in 'amendment of life, or renewed security in carefree sinning' (ibid., p. 82). Thus Murdoch asserts that religion is 'for most people a consoling, though perhaps ethically efficacious, fiction' (ibid., p. 138), although only ethically valuable in the formation of habits; and therefore, as discussed earlier, religion is also a threat to moral living.[8] Likewise Murdoch is critical of the doctrine of purgatory as being similarly consoling as it 'combines the absolutes of sin and just punishment with the then justified and clarified disappearance of the idea of death' (ibid., p. 130).

For Murdoch, then, religion, as it is traditionally conceived, is the ultimate escapist illusion, for, as Murdoch insists, we are accidental contingent beings and 'it is a persistent illusion to imagine otherwise' (ibid., p. 144). It is with regard to death that the illusion of religion is most dangerous, as 'belief in God can function as another veil created by our anxiety to hide away what is terrible and absurd in life and reality' (Tracy, 1996, p. 74). For religion, like art, 'has the effect and intended effect, of concealing the fact of death and the absolute contingency of existence' (Murdoch, 1992, p. 139). Yet, although religion can be the ultimate illusion, as we have seen, she does not want to dismiss it entirely. As with art, Murdoch regards religion as double-edged. Whilst it can lead us into illusion (and an all-encompassing, dangerous illusion), like great art, high or true religion can also contain great truth and advocate true, non-illusory moral living, for religion 'lives between cosy sentiment and magic at one end of the scale and at the other a kind of austerity which can scarcely be expected from human beings' (ibid., p. 129). At one end of the spectrum religion is dangerously consoling and deluding (particularly when it is combined with art), yet at the other end of the spectrum religion can inspire to the moral life and, moreover, the true religious life, focused on the real, Murdoch identifies with the moral life (ibid., p. 441; 1997 [1976], p. 447).

**Religion and the Moral Life**

The similarity of religion and art does not end with the capacity to delude the individual with egoistic fantasy and so obscure reality. Religion is capable of leading the individual into illusion, yet, like art and love, it is capable of helping the moral pilgrim to see the real. So 'true' religion, as opposed to most religion, which is 'false', like art can be a great revealer, for 'there is an analogy between truth in art and truth in religion' (Murdoch, 1992, p. 130). Both art and religion console and degenerate into illusion, yet they also have 'some truth-content' (ibid.) and revelatory capacities.

*Religion and the Moral Life*　　147

Thus religion, like art, is a paradox. For religion, to be true, like tragedy 'must be about the deepest things, it must be *true*' (ibid., p. 98). It must not be (as Murdoch believes is shown vividly by Shakespeare) 'consolation (magic)' (ibid., p. 120) and, like great art and tragedy, religion 'must concern the absolute in a specifically moral way' (ibid., p. 140). For this to be the case, for religion to be true (and for art to be great), like tragedy, religion 'must break the ego, destroying the illusory whole of the united self' (ibid., p. 104). True religion, then, 'is about, or is, the change of being attendant upon our deepest and highest concern with morality' (ibid., p. 183). Thus, although religion is 'always menaced by magic' (ibid., p. 337), it can also transform magic and convey the truth of reality and morality. Moreover, in this form, religion which 'colours and fixes and bodies forth moral ideas' (ibid., p. 82) is able to communicate moral ideas in an accessible and instinctive manner, for 'religion symbolises high moral ideas which then travel with us and are more intimately and accessibly effective than the unadorned promptings of reason' (ibid., p. 484). The presentation of moral ideas in the picture system of Christianity, Murdoch argues, is perfectly suited to 'the image-making human animal' (ibid.), and for this reason 'religious belief may be a stronger motive to good conduct than non-religious idealism' (ibid.).[9]

In our discussion of the moral life we saw how important images can be, functioning both to inspire and to help individuals in their moral journey and to communicate pictures of the moral life. Religious images are no different in this regard, and can be used (as other images) as pointers to the real. Murdoch's positive regard for religious imagery is not surprising, particularly in light of her assertion that the true reality lying behind the myth of the Christian personal God is of the impersonal good. She contends that Christianity carries, in mythic form, truth about the reality of moral value and the nature and status of the good. As discussed in Chapter 4, Murdoch, like Plato, believes that 'religion cannot rest upon personal deity' (ibid., p. 144) but that 'the final demand or absolute is not itself a form of life, though as an object of (pure) love it can inspire (true) life' (ibid., p. 145). The Christian God, then, is like the gods of Hinduism and Buddhism which are explicitly (as Murdoch argues), 'shadows which indicate something beyond' (ibid.): 'beyond' being the reality of moral value and the good. Therefore the image of God or gods can be useful to the moral pilgrim, but only when perceived 'as a symbol of an absolute demand, as an internalised categorical imperative, a traditional image of commitment to religious values, rather than as an external supernatural loving Father to whom we speak in our prayers, and who wants to be loved by us in return' (ibid., pp. 143–4). Therefore, as long as we accept Murdoch's contention that lying behind religious myths is the truth of morality, religious images can be a great aid to the moral life.

What (true) religion offers the moral pilgrim, then, is a 'fleshing out', a 'humanizing', of moral ideas. Such fleshing out, in the form of pictures, images and stories, is, as we saw clearly in Murdoch's view of the moral life and art, a natural mode of comprehension and expression for image-making,

148 *The Moral Vision of Iris Murdoch*

story-telling, human beings. Religion makes morality personal, accessible and inspirational. Murdoch takes as one example the image of Christ's suffering which can, like other stories of suffering, inspire moral change, but 'the beneficiary must internalise the spectacle of suffering as a lesson whereby he is changed' (ibid., p. 131). Murdoch elaborates the power of this image using examples of suffering. The first example is of a mother's long-suffering love for her delinquent son, and the second of an ill or disabled person suffering well. In both of these examples, the 'patient good sufferer produces in the spectator shame, then love, then the creative energy required for amendment of life' (ibid., p. 132). Religious stories, in this case of Christ's suffering – which vividly illustrates 'how a moral–religious concept does work, how it demands and stirs practical thought at a deep level' (ibid.) – can inspire moral change (as with the patient sufferers in Murdoch's examples) and so aid the moral quest.

Metaphor, pictures and images are an important means of inspiration, communication and explanation, and therefore religious images too can be enlightening. In this vein Murdoch speaks of Christ as 'an icon . . . . exhibiting personal yet selfless love and proving that it is possible' (ibid., p. 346). Yet, although all stories and images, not only religious ones, can inspire moral change – 'If Christ can redeem then a figure in a story can have redemptive power' (ibid., p. 132) – Murdoch seems to suggest that religious stories can be particularly effective, in part because they are familiar stories in our culture and also because they embody particularly moral notions. Murdoch argues that, in religion, 'the furniture of the world is freely taken as spiritual pointers' (ibid., p. 346). It is this use of poignant images which speak to us at a deep level which Murdoch wishes to maintain for use by the moral pilgrim and she suggests that religious 'mythical pictures should be kept and used, not as literal factual information, but as enlivening spiritual images' (ibid., p. 403). Indeed, Murdoch claims that many Christians already instinctively use the religious images of their tradition in this way, rather than regarding these stories as literally true. However, the illusion and danger of religion must not be forgotten and the images (as all images) must be used and then discarded. The myth must not be taken too literally; if it is, rather than aiding the moral pilgrim, it will be nothing more than consoling fantasy and actually arrest moral progress; 'the picture of Christ may enlighten and inspire us, or enable us to stop thinking' (ibid., p. 306). The temptation of not recognizing the image as an image and treating it as reality is so dangerous that Murdoch, in a moment of uncertainty, asks 'but can we still *use* these great images, can they go on helping us?' (ibid., p. 146). Moreover, we must be careful, as discussed with regard to the moral life, about which images and myths we adopt. She reminds the reader that any inspiring myth is not sufficient, it has to be 'true'; it has to be rooted in morality, morally true rather than factually true.[10] Ultimately, Murdoch would like to argue that we can, and indeed should (but only in the way she outlines) find a way to reclaim and use religious images in the moral life, just as she was able to use Plato's images, particularly the Cave, as inspiring spiritual guides.

Religion, then, can be useful in the moral life in both its images and its rituals (such as prayer, which Murdoch advocates in the secular form of attention). Ritual, as was intimated with the concept of prayer, is useful to the moral life. Although not essential to the moral life, ritual may help us to embrace it and serve as 'vehicles of enlightenment, as exercises likely to strengthen good desires' (ibid., p. 433). The embodied nature of ritual, like art, is immediately comprehended by human beings, and as such 'the ritual object speaks directly to the soul, it is meant to be immediately ingested and is itself an image of the good' (ibid.). Morality without religion (or art) Murdoch fears is too abstract: 'the inner needs the outer because, being incarnate, we need places and times, expressive gestures which release psychic energy or bring healing, making spaces and occasions for spiritual activity or events' (ibid., p. 307). Murdoch then regards Christian images as potentially useful to the moral quest, as religion may 'make morality more attractive' (ibid., p. 382) and she argues that there is no need to reject it 'simply because (as it may be) we do not believe in God' (ibid., p. 329). For Murdoch, religion helps to make the moral comprehensible, as 'high morality without religion is too abstract, high morality craves religion' (ibid., p. 484). Therefore, like art, religion can both inspire the moral life, help us to see the real and provide useful tools for the moral journey.

## Murdoch's 'Godless Religion'

Having recognized Murdoch's wish to keep both a religious sensibility and some religious images and practices alive in a world without a literal belief in God, we will now go on to examine in more detail Murdoch's 'godless religion'. Murdoch's godless religion is one in which the supernatural (false) elements of religion are rejected; indeed, she asserts that 'religion involving supernatural beliefs (in a literal after-life etc.) was always partly a kind of illusion' (Murdoch, 1992, p. 431) and now, according to Murdoch, is impossible to maintain (ibid., p. 425). What Murdoch is seeking is a means to gain access to and portray the same (true) beliefs in the reality of moral value, which religion has both revealed and obscured, without recourse to traditional belief.

Murdoch presupposes that the movement away from traditional belief is already going on. Consequently, Murdoch's primary concern is not to show the falsity of traditional belief (she implies that this has already been done and she assumes that secularization will continue); rather, her concern is to ensure that, even as religious belief declines, religious sensibility or spirituality continues as an (now overt) aspect of the moral life. Some form of spirituality must be maintained, as to lose it would be to deny a basic form of human experience. Murdoch's constant preoccupation is to provide an accurate picture of human experience, and for her this includes recognizing religious experience as ubiquitous, and indeed 'the unavoidability of religion is a theme that pervades Murdoch's work, both her fiction and her philosophy' (Kerr, 1997, p. 74).

150      *The Moral Vision of Iris Murdoch*

Murdoch's 'godless religion' would look very different from any other religion and markedly different from Christianity as it would deny 'belief' in any 'thing' or 'person'. It would be likely to be an individual path (or pilgrimage) inspired by the Platonic vision of the good: as Kerr remarks, Murdoch believes that 'now there is no God for most of us to love . . . the only way forward is back to Plato' (ibid., p. 78). Images would be nothing more than individual guides to be used in the same way as Murdoch believes Plato uses images, in a non-literal manner, as 'ladders to be thrown away after use' (Murdoch, 1992, p. 318). Images, then, are to be used to inspire and explain, as they speak directly to the image-making beings we are, but they must always be regarded as inadequate half-truths in comparison to the reality which lies behind them: 'theological mythology, stories about gods, creation myths and so on, belong to the realm of image making and are at a lower level than reality and ultimate religious truth' (ibid.). By explicitly acknowledging the imperfect and temporal nature of our religious images, Murdoch suggests we could move to a 'theology which can continue without God' (ibid., p. 511), a sort of mysticism, ultimately to 'a non-dogmatic essentially unformulated faith in the reality of the good' (Murdoch, 1970a, p. 74).

In order to support this vision of a 'godless religion' which aids the moral life, Murdoch looks to demythologizing theologians such as Ian Ramsey, John Robinson and Don Cupitt, and praises their attempts at demythologization which she refers to as a 'great moral tonic' (Murdoch, 1997 [1970], p. 233). This branch of theology, Murdoch hopes, will provide a 'revival of religion' (Murdoch, 1997 [1972], p. 256) and result in a religion which does not regard the Christian 'stories' as literally true, and which respects the autonomy of the moral agent (Murdoch, 1992, p. 452). To demythologize effectively, Murdoch argues that religion must reject a personal God, with whom an 'I–thou'(ibid., p. 469) relationship can be established and certainly should reject any 'intimations of an elsewhere, and of an omniscient spectator and responsive superthou' (ibid., pp. 431–2). She asserts that these fictions can no longer function even at a symbolic level.

For Murdoch, then, 'the "demythologisation" of religion is something absolutely necessary in this age' (ibid., p. 460). Yet, although she wishes to rehabilitate religious images into her moral vision, she is not convinced that this is possible and asks, 'can western religion survive, retain continuity, without the old dogmatic literalistic myths?' (ibid., p. 135). Murdoch hopes that it can, and suggests that Christian theologians look to the East, especially to Hinduism and Buddhism, and to Plato and the 'Platonism which St Augustine introduced into Christianity' (ibid., p. 252). Murdoch is not certain that we should attempt to keep the terminology of God, nor does she think that we should extend 'our word "God" to cover *any* conception of spiritual reality' (ibid., p. 419). Murdoch's recommendation is to deny any literalistic interpretations, and to recast the Christian myth in ways akin to Eastern religion and her Platonism: 'we must now . . . internalise our God' (ibid., p. 137). In this vein she argues that 'a Buddhist-style survival of Christianity could preserve tradition, renewing

Religion and the Moral Life 151

religious inspiration and observance in a vision of Christ as a live spiritual symbol' (ibid.): 'a mystical Christ who is the Buddha of the west' (ibid.). However, although Murdoch would like this transformation, she is not sure it can occur, and wonders whether it is really possible for Christ to become like Buddha 'both real and mystical, but no longer the divine all-in-one man of traditional Christianity' (ibid., p. 136). Buddhism is significantly different from Christianity, and Murdoch recognizes that the change in Buddhism, from a historical to a spiritual Buddha, happened in pre-scientific times (ibid., p. 137). In addition, Buddhism and Hinduism, in Murdoch's view, have avoided the difficulties of a personal God, and she argues that, because of this, 'it may be easier to perceive, or come to perceive, these . . . [the Eastern gods] . . . as sources of spiritual energy, and not as literal–historical supernatural people' (ibid., p. 249). This rejection of the literal, Murdoch argues, means that 'the *reflective believer* in the east is supported by a long tradition' (ibid., p. 135) and thus there is less 'difference between the sophisticated and unsophisticated believer' (ibid., p. 249). In other words, in Murdoch's terms, there is less difference between true religion and superstition and so less crisis of belief when traditional models are threatened and consequently an easier transition to a non-literal belief system.

Murdoch's hope that Christianity in some form can survive is based on the historical recognition that religion thus far has contrived to make itself believable in new contexts, a comment she repeats often (ibid., pp. 126, 137, 229, 419, 425, 486). Given the importance Murdoch gives to spirituality and its necessary place in a full concept of human being, it is not surprising that Murdoch, even though she is highly critical of organized religion, finds it hard to imagine a world where there is not a structured place for spirituality. This sentiment is displayed dramatically in her own Platonic dialogue, *Above the Gods*, where the Socrates of her creation declares:

> I think religion will always be with us, and we shall continually remake it into something we can believe. You see, we want to be certain that goodness rests upon reality. And this desire will never go away, we shall always be searching for the gods. We want to love what is pure and holy, and to know that it is . . . inviolable, indestructible, *real*. (Murdoch, 1987, p. 40)

## A Mystical Christ

At the end of the demythologization process Murdoch hopes that some sort of religiosity will be left which will provide access to the transcendent moral reality. Christ would become a mystical Christ, 'a Christ who can console and save, but who is to be found as a living force within each human soul not in some supernatural elsewhere' (Murdoch, 1992, p. 419). It is hard to envisage how Murdoch pictures this mystical Christ. However, we can gain some sense of what she intends by considering a passage from her novel, *Nuns and Soldiers*.[11]

152 *The Moral Vision of Iris Murdoch*

Including a passage from Murdoch's novels to clarify her philosophy breaks the premise that using Murdoch's non-philosophical works to gain insight into her philosophy is at best a dubious methodology which should be resisted. Yet, despite this, and as we are looking for pictures which inspire the individual, we may regard this picture of a personal Christ as simply one such story and therefore can justify its inclusion at this juncture. However, one should not regard this passage as revealing Murdoch's image of a mystical Christ, but at best, and perhaps even this is too much, as an example of how a personal Christ, which we make our own, can function as an inspiration (and of course Anne's Christ is not ours, nor perhaps Murdoch's).[12] Therefore, although breaking the schema of the book, we shall consider this passage as a fictional illustration, an image, of how 'the mystical Christ . . . can be "met" with' (ibid., p. 487).

In the book, Anne, an ex-nun who has lost her faith, meets Christ in her kitchen, after waking from a dream. She knows him immediately: when he asks 'who am I?', in the traditional scriptural words of recognition, she answers, 'you are the Christ' (Murdoch, 1981, p. 295), an answer he receives with a 'quizzical almost humorous' (ibid., p. 296) expression. Murdoch's description of Christ is of an odd, nondescript, almost ugly and certainly unkempt man, only made beautiful by his mouth 'thoughtful and tender and the eyes large and remarkably luminous' (ibid., p. 295). In the 'dream', Christ, in a parallel story to that of Julian of Norwich, gives Anne a stone. Anne expects to be given a walnut, as Julian was, to explain the mystery of the godhead, but instead she receives a stone. Anne looks to 'her Christ' for answers, but she is disappointed, he denies the reality of himself and says, 'I prove nothing, Anne' (ibid., p. 298). It is she, Anne, who must make herself good and be good, and he tells her, 'you must be the miracle-worker little one. You must be the proof the work is yours' (ibid.).

What Murdoch is trying to convey in this passage is not clear (and nor would we expect it to be); indeed, to think of it as attempting to convey anything is to read too much into this fictional character's meeting with a fictional, mystical Christ. However, it does provide an example of how stories and visions of Christ can be inspiring without holding a literal belief in Christ. This passage shows that the power of the story of Christ for Anne (now a non-believer) can inspire her towards the true reality of the good, a reality which she must find for herself.

**Morality and Mysticism**

In Murdoch's wish to reclaim parts of religion she is hoping that spirituality can once again be recognized as part of morality, that we can create 'a religion without dogma' (Murdoch, 1992, p. 456). At this point (as possibly suggested in her use of attention) Murdoch is advocating a kind of secular mysticism, and asserting that 'there is, just as there used (with the old God) to be, a place

*Religion and the Moral Life* 153

of wisdom and calm to which we can remove ourselves' (ibid., p. 249). Indeed, Murdoch connects morality directly to mysticism, stating that 'the background to morals is properly some sort of mysticism' (Murdoch, 1970a, p. 74) and that 'morality leads naturally into mysticism and has a natural bond with religion' (Murdoch, 1992, p. 301). The mystical attitude which Murdoch associates with the moral life is one of continual awareness of the good and reality. In attempting to depict the type of religious morality she is recommending, she commends Buber's view of religion as a 'matter of continuous consciousness, a preservation of the moment, an entrance into the whole of reality' (ibid., p. 464). Murdoch praises mystics (both Eastern and Western) for their seeking after truth and their non-literal use of images: beyond the last image in Christianity 'we fall into the abyss of God' (ibid., p. 318). In this vein she claims that 'the mystical is an ever-present moral ideal, that of extending ordinary decent morals indefinitely in the direction of perfect goodness' (ibid., p. 355). This high level of religious vision Murdoch equates with the moral life, as at this point any 'distinction between religion and morals, whether offered to protect the one or the other, tends to be somewhat general and unrealistic' (ibid., p. 336).

Here we must remember that Murdoch is using the term 'religious' in her own peculiar way to signify 'a religious attitude and form of life, not a literalistic adherence to a particular dogma' (ibid., p. 301). For her, 'religion is not only a particular dogma or mode of faith and worship, but can exist and indeed exists, undogmatically . . . potentially everywhere, forming a deep part of morality' (ibid., p. 336). As Kaalikoski describes it, Murdoch uses the term 'spirituality' (and we could extend this to religion) to convey the fact that 'morality is connected with the whole of our being, every moment of our lives includes moral reflection . . . human consciousness is moral consciousness' (Kaalikoski, 1997, p. 149). Murdoch's meaning of religious is almost the same as her depiction of the moral life. She is referring to a way of being in the world, which has traditionally been found in the religious life, but which for her does not depend on any supernatural beliefs. Thus, for Murdoch, 'religion is not a special subject or one activity among others' (Murdoch, 1992, p. 418), but in its true form, as a representation of the moral, is about the whole of the human quest. True religion is about the nature of the good, and conducted in the proper manner 'praise and worship are . . . themselves a grasp of reality' (ibid.). Thus morality demands a spiritual awareness and Murdoch argues that 'moral philosophy must include this dimension whether we call it religion or not' (ibid., p. 481). Murdoch believes that 'agnosticism about God, an unknown God, or a complete denial of God does not . . . involve a surrender of the spiritually informed understanding of "all the world"' (ibid., p. 454).

At times it does not seem to matter too much to Murdoch how the spiritual or religious element of the moral is continued, a conclusion borne out by her completely ambiguous description of herself as 'a neo-Christian or Buddhist Christian or Christian fellow traveller' (ibid., p. 419). Yet, clearly, she is attached to Christianity at least to some extent – not least because she is steeped,

154     *The Moral Vision of Iris Murdoch*

politically, culturally and morally in the Christian worldview – and she wishes it to survive. Nonetheless, Murdoch does not believe that the loss of God affects the mystical (as the mystical was never essentially about God) (ibid., p. 72), and asserts that, 'even if all "religions" were to blow away like mist, the necessity of virtue and the reality of the good would remain' (ibid., p. 428). For mysticism, the spiritually proper attitude to morality, would not be destroyed – nor could it be.

Finding a way to reintegrate the spiritual in a believable form in the current context is for Murdoch a great challenge, and we must address 'what exactly religion is and where in the mass of religiosity and religious stuff it "really resides"' (ibid., p. 138). Murdoch's solution is of course a moral one; indeed, she contends that her whole argument (including her discussion about a godless religion) 'can be read as moral philosophy' (ibid., p. 481). Rediscovering 'religious modes of thought deep inside morals' (ibid., p. 304) is, Murdoch believes, the proper task of moral philosophy: just as moral recognition is a fundamental aspect of human experience, so too is spiritual experience. Such a redefinition of the religious is necessary if philosophy is to offer an accurate picture of the moral (human) world, which for her includes 'a mode of belief in the unique sovereign place of goodness or virtue in human life' (ibid., p. 426). Ultimately, Murdoch's concern, and this is the last thought in *Metaphysics as a Guide to Morals*, is that moral philosophy should accurately represent the breadth of human knowledge and experience and thus it must include 'those matters of "ultimate concern", our experience of the unconditioned and our continued sense of what is holy' (ibid., p. 512).

## Conclusion

Murdoch's basic concern as regards religion is to retain spirituality as an essential aspect of human experience, liberating it from its previous narrow preserve and connecting it explicitly to morality. Hence she has been accused of simply reducing religion to morality: Murdoch has 'given us her version of the long familiar position that reduces Christianity to morals' (Allen, 1993, p. 25). Without a doubt, Murdoch's discussion of religion is narrow; she addresses a very small area of Christianity and theology, as Gregory Jones points out: 'one has to wonder about the theological sophistication of a book on "metaphysics and morals" and on issues of "God" and "Good" which devotes more space to Don Cupitt than to Thomas Aquinas' (Jones, 1993, p. 689). Murdoch does not engage with the theological debates of the time – 'only a "demythologised" Christian theology is invited to the table' (ibid.) – and as a result 'her perspective seems rather arbitrary – and ultimately unsatisfying' (ibid.). Moreover, Murdoch's starting assumption that religion, particularly Christianity, is declining in the face of ever more prominent scientific ideologies is not borne out by the evidence. Her Enlightenment conception of the inevitable decline of religious belief as a consequence of

# Religion and the Moral Life

increasingly rational frameworks has proved false. As Diogenes Allen notes, 'for a time it was generally held that religious beliefs had been "thought away" by Hume and Kant. We have recently learnt that they did not succeed' (Allen, 1993, p. 25), and, consequently, her view that 'God is a dispensable notion, intellectually and morally, appears arbitrary' (ibid.). Therefore Jones is justified in commenting on the 'dubiousness of her claim that Christianity is fading' (Jones, 1993, p. 689). In addition, and perhaps more damaging to Murdoch's hypothesis, there is the fact that the type of religious belief that is currently growing is not the individual, intellectual, mystical religious path (which Murdoch deems similar to the point of identification with the moral quest), but rather the fundamentalist, more literal forms of religious belief. Apparently, Murdoch is wrong to claim that religious belief is impossible in the modern world. Likewise Murdoch's claims that many believers do not believe literally, and already use biblical images simply as images, again appear arbitrary. Even believers who do use images as spiritual guides may still retain more traditional belief than is allowed in the Murdochian system. Murdoch seems to equate a lack of literal belief in the historical Jesus, or the gospel stories, with a lack of belief in a personal God. Belief in a personal God prevails both inside and outside institutional religion and, for many, even sophisticated believers (in Murdoch's sense of regarding images as spiritual guides rather than truths) continue to believe in a personal God, and the possibility of a relationship with Him is at the heart of their religious belief. From the believer's perspective, as Hauerwas points out, 'Murdoch's world is too lonely for those of us called Christian, those who believe that we were created to be friends with God' (Hauerwas, 1996, p. 207). Far from believing the religious path to be delusional, such believers regard those who do not share their beliefs as deluded, and to assert the non-existence of God as the most deluded position. Once again, Hauerwas counters Murdoch's conclusions, stating that 'a people who know their salvation and have been secured through Jesus' cross and resurrection are accordingly required to live resisting the false consolations of the world' (ibid.).

Given this, it would seem that Murdoch's wish to update religion to fit a world in which it is no longer possible to believe in a literal belief system seems to be a personal, and indeed an arbitrary, position, and, moreover, one which ignores the reality of faith which continues to be the majority position of people on the planet. Furthermore, in her keenness to maintain some form of spirituality, she accepts that she treats the content of religious faith 'as if it did not matter that much' (Murdoch, 1992, p. 458), a treatment which is at odds with the position of most believers. However, even if we are unlikely to see the Murdochian 'godless religion' adopted in great numbers by believers, Murdoch's mystical morality may still be an option for those who, like Murdoch, find traditional belief impossible. Ann Loades states that Murdoch's vision is 'attractive to those able to dispense with divine transcendence, but who still hanker after some kind of ethical transcendence' (Loades, 1986, p. 147).

156 *The Moral Vision of Iris Murdoch*

Furthermore, even if one rejects Murdoch's wish to find a way to continue a non-literal form of Christianity, there may still be merit in Murdoch's assertion that the spiritual aspect of human experience should be included in any adequate picture of human being. At the heart of Murdoch's vision is the wish to present a holistic account of the human condition, which does justice to all aspects of human experience and defends these essential human capacities against what she regards as the reductionist philosophies of the age. Yet, if her wish is simply to assert the importance of spirituality and spiritual experience in pointing one towards the real, it is not clear why maintaining Christianity (especially in light of the criticisms of religion which she largely accepts) is so important to Murdoch. Just as her insistence that only 'great art', narrowly and controversially defined, can lead us towards the real seems to be an arbitrary position, and in part based on the prejudices of her own experience, so does her attachment to the stories of Christianity. If Murdoch's concern is that stories can be illustrative and useful in the moral life, there does not seem to be any reason (apart from her own upbringing which has given these stories a special status) why any story or practice which functions in this way cannot aid the moral life. Again, if Murdoch is concerned with the function of art and religion to aid the moral life, it seems strange to be attached to any particular type of art or religion for any reason other than how effective they prove to be in performing this task. This criticism is one which Murdoch seems to recognize (and more so with religion than she did with art) in her questioning of the possibility of any form of non-literal Christian transformation, and in her insistence that any story can inspire. Moreover, her conviction that even if all religion disappeared spiritual experiences would remain suggests that her wish to find a way for Christianity to continue is simply a practical move: that transforming the religion we have is likely to be easier and more truthful (because of the moral recognition already involved and because of the importance of continuity) than creating a new religion. Even if Murdoch's wish that Christianity should become a non-literal, non-dogmatic, 'godless religion' were successful it is still questionable whether this would really be a continuity of religion in any real sense. Murdoch's concept of religion is so broad that many of those who continue to be religious adherents would no doubt deny that Murdoch's proposed godless religion can be called religion in any meaningful sense: as Kerr notes, 'a thinker is religious in Murdoch's sense, when he finds there is no gap, ultimately, between the facts and our values' (Kerr, 1997, pp. 86–7).

Yet even if we are dissatisfied with her proposals for Christianity, which are not likely to be accepted by believers or non-believers who are (as Murdoch recognizes) ever more removed from religious imagery, Murdoch's wish to include the spiritual in any adequate picture of a human life is vital for present-day concepts of humanity. As always, Murdoch's concern is that human moral beings are pictured in the fullest manner possible and that spiritual experiences, even in a world without belief in God, should be respected and recognized. Therefore, even if one struggles with her proposals for religion (just as one

*Religion and the Moral Life* 157

could disagree with her definition of great art), one can still find merit in her inclusion in human experience of the spiritual.

## Notes

1   Although, as we shall see, Murdoch is also highly critical of religion and asserts that, although religion can encourage moral action, it can also be a great danger to morality and undermine the authority of moral values.

2   The humanist critique of religion states that religion is damaging to morality for two main reasons: first, by making morality dependent on religion, the authority and objectivity of religion is threatened; and second, the motivation of the moral agent is compromised by competing religious reasons. We shall discuss portions of the humanist critique of religion in this chapter as and when it influences Murdoch's thinking.

3   In the literature, the example of Abraham and Issac is always taken literally (Adams, 1981a; Quinn, 1978, 1981, 1990). However, critics (such as the Old Testament theologian Gerhard Von Rad), have suggested that the story should be read, not as concerned with Abraham's willingness to sacrifice Isaac, but rather as showing God's disapproval of child sacrifice, as sacrificing first-born children was commonplace in the culture of the time.

4   So called 'strong' divine command theories reject this reasoning and argue that to judge the commands of God according to human reason is both impudent and nonsensical; obedience, not understanding, is required. Brody and Geach are two examples of such theorists: Brody arguing that God, as the creator, has property rights over his creation and therefore 'if God the creator does wish us not to use the things of the world in certain ways, he will entail certain moral restrictions on property rights that might not be present otherwise' (Brody, 1981, p. 146); and Geach arguing that we should obey God simply because he is all-powerful, for 'defiance of an Almighty God is insane: it is like trying to cheat a man to whom your whole business is mortgaged and who you know is well aware of your attempts to cheat him' (Geach, 1981, p. 172).

5   Certain 'weak' divine command theorists argue that God's commands are in accord with that which is morally good. For example, Adams argues that God does not command immoral actions; because 'x is wrong' does not simply mean that 'x is contrary to the commands of God' but rather that 'x is contrary to the commands of a loving God' (Adams, 1981a, p. 86). Likewise Quinn asserts that 'the theist need only be committed to obeying God's commands because they are necessarily morally legitimate themselves; he need not be committed to obeying such commands simply because they are the decrees of a superior power' (Quinn, 1981, p. 55). However, such conclusions mitigate against morality being dependent on God, as what is being assumed is a human standard of morality according to which we judge whether the commands of God are justified, which suggests that it is morality not God which is absolute and unchangeable. As Westmoreland notes, 'justification in terms of God's reasons for his commands suggests that ultimately it is those reasons, and not the fact that it is God who invokes them, which give the commands normative force' (Westmoreland, 1996, p. 20). Therefore, if we need to use our moral judgment to determine whether God's commands are good, we must have a concept of morality which is not derived from the commands of God; thus 'our criteria must be at least logically independent of God' (Nielsen, 1982, p. 340).

6   Murdoch here is again drawing on the humanist critique. For example, Nowell-Smith echoes Murdoch's reasoning in his statement that, even if we believe we have been commanded to act in a certain way, 'it still makes *sense* . . . to ask whether or not I *ought*

158                    *The Moral Vision of Iris Murdoch*

to do it (Nowell-Smith, 1966, p. 97); similarly, Nielsen contends that 'we must quite unavoidably use our own moral insight to decide that God's acts are good' (Nielsen, 1982, p. 339).

7   As Conradi notes, it is important to recognize 'how contemporary a figure Plato is to her' (Conradi, 1989, p. 89). Murdoch regards fifth-century Athens as facing similar questions about the nature of the world and the human condition: new scientific paradigms were threatening the previous value systems, traditional beliefs in anthropomorphic gods were declining, as were the corresponding religious institutions and social norms. Therefore, in both contexts, traditional beliefs are disintegrating and 'the customary foundations of morality are shaken' (Mitchell, 1980, p. 86). Indeed, Murdoch goes as far as to equate the sophist response to the decline of morality to the response of the structuralists and postmodernists she criticizes so vehemently.

8   While Murdoch recognizes that religion can be morally efficacious, in encouraging the agent in good habits, it may also encourage non-moral conduct, and Murdoch states that 'traditional Christian superstition has been compatible with every sort of conduct from bad to good' (Murdoch, 1970a, p. 74).

9   Although, as we have seen, this is not necessarily the case, as religion may console and delude and engender immoral conduct.

10  Murdoch recognizes that some very immoral myths have been inspiring (Murdoch, 1992, p. 136).

11  Kerr asserts that, at least since 1966 and the publishing of *The Time of Angels*, 'Murdoch's fictions have explored what morality might mean in a world without God' (Kerr, 1997, p. 73).

12  Conradi reports that part of this fictional vision or dream was inspired by a dream Murdoch had in 1947 (Conradi, 2001, pp. 554–5).

Chapter 8

# The Future of Iris Murdoch's Moral Vision

Having looked at the component parts which make up Murdoch's moral vision, we are now in a position to evaluate her philosophy in its entirety and consider her legacy. In all the chapters, each of which examines one theme of Murdoch's thought, there are elements which provide insights and pointers for contemporary ethics. Before moving on to consider this legacy, we will first take some time to consider Murdoch's moral vision. It is only when it is all taken together that we can see why it has been suggested that Murdoch is a visionary rather than a philosopher in the more usual sense; Murdoch really does concern herself with the totality of human life and she has tried to address the question of 'How can I be good?'[1]

## Assessing Murdoch's Moral Vision

Only in the holistic telling do certain aspects of Murdoch's philosophy make sense. For example, we saw clearly in Chapter 4 that her arguments for 'the good' are open to criticism from all sides. Moreover, if the good is considered separately from views about experience and the moral life, her protestations that knowing the good is an ordinary part of human living seem unconvincing. In order to understand what Murdoch means by the reality of the good, one needs to understand that, for Murdoch, human beings are fundamentally moral beings and that human reality is moral reality. Moreover, her assertions that all human beings know in which direction the good lies seem over-optimistic and unrealistic, if they are taken apart from her picture of the human condition and the difficulty involved in escaping egoistic delusion. To give another example, her assertion that the moral life is spiritual, and that spirituality is a basic human capacity, can only be properly understood when one takes into account Murdoch's broad conception of religion and consciousness and her conviction that art too gives access to transcendence. Likewise her insistence on the primacy of the inner as the locus of moral change, illustrated by the example of the mother-in-law's change of heart, shows the ordinary everyday nature of moral activity and saves her picture of the moral life (a pilgrimage from illusion to reality) from appearing as arcane and esoteric Platonic mysticism.

159

160                    *The Moral Vision of Iris Murdoch*

Yet although these threads weave together to make Murdoch's vision complete, it is the completed vision itself which may cause the most criticism, as here Murdoch's prescriptivity comes forcibly to the fore. While many agree with Murdoch that present-day moral philosophy is narrow and reductionist, and that a broader conception of human being is necessary for philosophy to be relevant and accurate, it is another matter to adopt her version of moral realism, let alone endorse her programme for moral living. Consequently, while admiring her insight and agreeing with her critiques, many may find her constructive philosophy too much to swallow.

As we have noted throughout the book, there are problems with Murdoch's philosophy, not least in her style and manner of presentation, which is unsystematic and lacks clarity. Moreover, when her vision is looked at in its entirety, her prescriptivity is overwhelming, she is proclaiming a moral way of life that begins to look more like an alternative belief-system, rather than a moral philosophy. This in itself is not necessarily surprising, given Murdoch's assertion that philosophy *should* be prescriptive and should address questions of 'how can I be good?' Yet, even if one agrees with this premise, her vision may still feel stifling.

Murdoch's foundation and return point is the reality of individual experience, and it is precisely from this perspective that criticisms spring. Murdoch's premise that experience proves her vision can be countered by different experiences; critics may simply feel that 'it's just not like that!' Murdoch reports in her journal that she struggles to get 'a hard intellectual grip on certain problems which I only grasp imaginatively and emotionally. I am not sure whether I can really think philosophically at all' (Conradi, 2001, p. 254) and from a similar emotional perspective many reject her vision. For example, Simon Blackburn finds Murdoch's vision 'repellent' (Blackburn, 1992, p. 3): a picture of human being that he does not recognize in his own experience. In fact Blackburn deems her vision of life to be unbearably bleak, a picture he believes she puts forward simply 'to exalt the mystery of the necessary and unconditional Good by the debasing of the everyday' (ibid.). Moreover, he finds that instead of searching for the truth, she presents a picture which masks the truth (Murdoch's own criticism of the philosophies she opposes), one which engages in rhetoric and manipulation in order to seduce the reader into accepting her brand of Platonism.

Such responses to Murdoch's vision are difficult, if not impossible, for Murdoch to counter. She herself insists on the validity of experience, and the importance of temperament in the type of philosophical vision one is attracted to.[2] From her philosophical perspective, there is no way to counter the experiential difference: Blackburn sees and experiences a different vision of the human condition and the world. Murdoch's only defence would be to view his vision as wrong, misguided or deluded as, for Murdoch the realist, there are better and worse visions of the world, pictures which are more true or less true, and she could judge his to be less true. However, if he fails to see her vision, and recognize it in his own experience, her attempt ends. Her philosophy

The Future of Iris Murdoch's Moral Vision                    161

does not offer the kind of arguments that can tackle such criticisms. In fact, given the assertion of individual experience, she lays herself open for exactly this type of criticism. Perhaps it is as simple as this: either we recognize Murdoch's vision in our own experience or we do not. This, of course, is true for every philosophy and vision of the world to some extent, but Murdoch's style of argument and emphasis on experience makes the criticism all the more valid in her case, for it is to experience, from first to last, that Murdoch appeals.

Even those who do not find Murdoch's vision immediately repellent and do recognize at least certain aspects of life as portrayed in her vision may still struggle with the totality of her view. As noted at the end of Chapters 6 and 7, her definitions of 'good' art and even more so 'true' religion are problematic. In the divisions between that which she considers illusion-ridden and mediocre and that which she regards as true and real, Murdoch is at her most elitist. Yet it is not only here that Murdoch could be accused of presenting an elitist view. Murdoch, like Plato, can be accused of presenting a thoroughly elitist moral vision: escape from the Cave is the prerogative of the few; the path to the good is hard; higher qualities of consciousness are available to the few not the many, to whom higher qualities of consciousness are unrecognizable. According to Murdoch's description of the human condition, human beings are almost irredeemably sunk in illusion and the promise of salvation, while potentially available to all, in that we all feel the draw of the good and know the direction in which it lies, is an achievement that few, if any, will attain: the good is always beyond. Such a mystical vision, which draws so much from religion, is hard to support in the secular world.

Murdoch's elitism cannot be denied and is fundamental to her concept of moral improvement and, while Plato too is accused of elitism, his elitism is of a slightly different order. To begin with, the context of Plato's elitism is significantly different; while Plato lived in, supposedly, the first democracy, fifth-century Athens was nothing if not elitist. Hierarchy and elitism were a way of life; some people simply did count more than others, and certain classes of people, for example slaves and women, hardly counted at all (despite the passage in the *Meno*, which suggests that the slave too has access to the real). Indeed, both of Plato's own pictures of ideal government, found in the *Republic*, which is so enlivened by the passages about the good, and the bleaker and more cynical *Laws*, propose elitist systems of government, by the intellectual, moral elite, that have escaped from the Cave, the famous philosopher rulers. In addition, although Murdoch considers that Plato, like her, was focused on being good in this life, in many dialogues he has a view of the soul continuing (returning to this life or continuing in another form), a belief which reduces the charge of elitism, as there are subsequent possibilities of recognizing goodness. Likewise the religions which she draws upon, particularly Christianity and Buddhism, also have doctrines about the afterlife or subsequent lives and therefore are somewhat excused the charge of elitism. Murdoch is not in this tradition, but in the secular, liberal democratic tradition, of which

162         *The Moral Vision of Iris Murdoch*

she is critical, but which she nonetheless supports, in her assertion of the importance of every individual and her conviction that there is no afterlife. In this democratic tradition the charge of elitism is hard to counter.

Furthermore, not only is Murdoch open to the charge of elitism as regards the moral life, but she also invites, particularly in her discussion of art and religion, the charge of a culturally-specific elitism. As we discussed briefly at the end of Chapter 6, her definition of great art, which begins with Shakespeare and Greek tragedies and extends to very little else, appears to be supremely culturally conditioned. Uncomfortably, it suggests an English Oxbridge type of blue-stocking prejudice and superiority. Moreover, it goes against Murdoch's own suggestion that attention to any object potentially has moral worth in its ability to point the individual away from selfish preoccupation and towards the good; although admittedly she does claim that some objects are better objects of attention than others. However, if only some art objects lead to the real, while others confuse, seduce and lead to illusion, the possibility of broadening one's concept of art and beauty into one that is less culturally relative is a dangerous one. Yet if the place of art (and love as a similar starting-point for the moral life) is going to be advocated by philosophical and religious thinkers and have any place in the global context, such a broadening is necessary.

In a similar manner, Murdoch's discussion of true religion, which comes down to a kind of moral mysticism, also has arbitrary and apparently prejudiced premises. If Murdoch is really advocating a mystical morality, there is no reason why any form of religious or spiritual belief which helps the individual to move away from selfish obsession and focus on the reality of others should not be deemed to be spiritual. If this were the case then Murdoch would not only be arguing for a revival of Christianity along Buddhist or mystical lines, but she would also accept many of the types of spirituality which abound in society today; amongst these would be 'new age' spiritualities and, arguably, certain types of psychologies which, given Murdoch's broad understanding of religion, meet at least some of Murdoch's criteria. In fact, such individualist spiritualities might fit Murdoch's vision more easily as, unlike Christianity, they do not have the institutional and literal aspects of which Murdoch is so critical. Yet Murdoch does not allow this move; she is emphatically critical of psychotherapy and psycho-analysis, which is perhaps justifiable as, arguably, these frameworks do lead directly into self-knowledge and do not progress beyond this to knowledge beyond the self and to the real. However, it is hard to see why, on Murdoch's criteria, other forms of spirituality which do not exalt the self and lead the individual towards the real should not be acceptable to her. Murdoch's interest in maintaining Christianity, despite its history and beliefs, no matter how difficult such a transition, again, like her definition of great art, could be regarded as a personal commitment or prejudice to traditional religion. Granted that 'new age' religions may be more individualized and therefore potentially more likely to lead the individual towards self-illusion, this is no less true of traditional forms of mysticism, which are always individual

The Future of Iris Murdoch's Moral Vision 163

spiritual paths rather than community religion.[3] Perhaps this commitment to Christianity, like her commitment to Shakespeare, can be traced to a certain type of background. However, even if this is the case and her particular vision of a demythologized Christianity is open to question, her assertion that spirituality is a fundamental human capacity still has merit.

These criticisms of elitism, with regard to Murdoch's moral vision and to art and religion, which suggest historical and cultural commitments, raise the question of whether Murdoch's vision collapses into subjectivism and relativism. Murdoch's moral vision is individual; it is about individual progress inspired by those things which point the particular individual towards goodness. This sounds particularist, subjectivist and even relativist. However, as a realist, Murdoch can deny these charges by asserting the reality of moral values and of the good. An action or quality of consciousness is not good, or better, merely because one thinks that this is the case. An action is good if, and only if, it moves one towards the good. Likewise one moves towards reality or is drawn further into illusion. The good and the real are objective (or perhaps intersubjective), they are not subjective concepts; hence Murdoch's insistence on the authority of the good. Murdoch maintains that, if one truly attends, then one will know the better act, as 'the love which brings the right answer is an exercise of justice and realism and really *looking*' (Murdoch, 1970a, p. 91). However, this is not easy to judge as it is hard 'to keep the attention fixed upon the real situation and to prevent it returning surreptitiously to the self with consolations of self-pity, resentment, fantasy and despair' (ibid.). Given this difficulty the problem of interpretation remains; how can one be certain that one is moving towards the real rather than being deluded into something that is not real? The danger of delusion, as shown powerfully in Chapters 6 and 7, is not one that Murdoch denies; indeed, it is ever-present in the moral quest. Yet Murdoch does seem to believe that it is possible to know whether one is truly acting in a way which takes us towards the good. One suspects that it is this need to ensure that her philosophy does not collapse into an individualist subjectivism which led her to the arguments for the good, and not just to the argument for perfection but to the ontological argument, which, as we saw in Chapter 4, complicates rather than clarifies her position. Her use of the ontological argument prevents even those who hold generally realist views, and who therefore would be willing to grant her argument from perfection and human experience and who accept that moral experience is real, from accepting her realism.

## Murdoch and Modern Ethics

Even if one does not wish to endorse Murdoch's moral vision in its entirety and one struggles with her concept of the good and picture of the moral life, there are still aspects of her philosophy which are important and useful. While her moral vision as a whole may be a little overwhelming, the advantage in

164 *The Moral Vision of Iris Murdoch*

presenting such a holistic conception is that Murdoch does indeed encourage one to question the assumptions of current philosophy. In her rejection of what she deems to be false dichotomies, in particular those of fact and value, objectivity and subjectivity and immanence and transcendence, she succeeds in showing the fallacy of presuming that such divisions are absolute. There are other ways of conceptualizing reality; Murdoch offers one, but she also permits the space for others.

This can be seen in the impact she has had on current thinkers, for example the moral realists and virtue ethicists referred to in the first chapter. Indeed, both of these schools of thought, while having already been influenced by Murdoch's thinking, could potentially benefit from adopting some of Murdoch's more radical thought. For example, modern realists, in their attempt to have values included as part of the fabric of the world, have tended to accept the anti-realist premise that, for values to be real, they must be shown to have the characteristics of 'facts', and facts of the scientific kind.[4] By accepting this premise realists have continued to regard anything which cannot be established as 'fact' as being of dubious reality, and this has led to a similar reduction of inner experience and values as encountered in the philosophies of the anti-realists.[5] A more thorough rejection of the fact/value dichotomy such as that supplied by Murdoch not only reclaims values, but also acknowledges that knowledge, which is derived from experience, consists of more just than facts: knowledge arising from individual inner experience, which includes emotion and value. This recognition that values and emotion are no less important than the recognition of facts (in fact they are potentially more important, as they constitute the meaning of human being, our understanding of ourselves and our world) would be useful in the current realist/anti-realist debate. Likewise a rejection of such dichotomies would also assist the realist cause in the debate about moral motivation.

Currently, realists struggle to account for motivation because, again, as they did with the fact/value division, they have accepted the anti-realist premise that motivation has to be accounted for using the belief/desire model. For Murdoch, belief and desire are connected, because value and thought, emotion and belief, are all factors in knowledge. Knowledge comes from our whole experience of the world, therefore moral knowledge and emotional knowledge all form part of cognitive judgment and thus belief and desire are not separate. Rather one's knowledge is limited by how truthful one's response to the world is; emotional, moral and factual aspects are all part of the human response and influence each other. It is our whole vision that is important because the moral colour of the world, how we see the world, determines the facts that we can see. Consequently, moral judgment and judgment about the facts cannot be separated. Such recasting of vision is where Murdoch has most to offer this current debate, and even for those who reject her moral vision she shows the limitations of the current debate and opens up the possibility of alternative conceptions. One may not choose to adopt the Murdochian vision, yet one is at least led to see that the current picture of

*The Future of Iris Murdoch's Moral Vision* 165

human being, moral value and motivation is simply that: just one picture – a picture which is not proved but which competes with other pictures, both historically and in the global context where the liberal democratic vision, which Murdoch associates with the post-Kantian picture of man, is but one vision among many. This realization alone is important in the present philosophical climate where structural premises, such as the fact/value dichotomy, have become philosophical orthodoxy.

In the revival of virtue ethics, something of this different picture can be seen. Virtue ethics, which moves away from post-Enlightenment moral philosophy of right action and universal rules and towards concepts of the good life, is a movement in moral philosophy with which, had it existed at the time, Murdoch might have found herself more at home. It is only in the last decade or two that virtue ethics has become mainstream on the syllabuses of moral philosophy. The beginning of the revival of virtue ethics is often traced to an article by Elizabeth Anscombe, Murdoch's contemporary and friend, first published in 1958, entitled 'Modern Moral Philosophy'.[6] In this article Anscombe, like Murdoch, bemoans the state of the moral philosophy of her contemporaries. She criticizes both Utilitarianism and Kantianism, arguing that 'the concepts of obligation, and duty . . . and of what is *morally* right and wrong, and of the *moral* sense of "ought", ought to be jettisoned' (Anscombe, 1997, p. 26). Like Murdoch, she calls for moral philosophy to focus again on moral psychology and to consider human flourishing. These calls are echoed in Murdoch's work, which continues and extends Anscombe's call for a working moral psychology and a robust conception of the individual. It is no surprise that Murdoch's final and largest philosophical work, *Metaphysics as a Guide to Morals*, is dedicated to Elizabeth Anscombe. Although Murdoch and Anscombe are very different philosophers, both proclaim the inadequacy of the moral theories of their contemporaries and call for renewed philosophical interest in the moral individual. Murdoch's work, particularly in *The Sovereignty of Good*, and also in *Metaphysics as a Guide to Morals*, has foreshadowed and inspired much of the current revival of virtue ethics, including the work of Alasdair MacIntyre and Charles Taylor (as mentioned in Chapter 1), although neither of them would follow Murdoch's vision.[7]

If Murdoch was working in the present-day climate, she might find herself less alone than she did amongst the analytical philosophers who were so predominant in the Oxford of her day. This broadening of ethics is in part a result of Murdoch's own contribution, something which is not an insubstantial legacy in itself. However, even though philosophy is now more open to a broader conception of ethics, and the narrowness of the visions of Murdoch's opponents is being recognized, few philosophers have Murdoch's breadth of interest. Perhaps this is due to Murdoch's dual role as author and novelist, which has led her to suffer criticisms for being too philosophical a novelist and too rhetorical a philosopher. Thus, even in the present context, it may be the case that Murdoch 'being half-artist and half-intellectual' (Conradi, 2001, p. 268) would still be 'entirely at home nowhere' (ibid.).

## Murdoch's Vision and the Future of Ethics

The world of ethics has changed since Murdoch's writing of philosophy, and particularly since she stopped teaching at Oxford in 1963, and left the world of the professional philosopher. Questions of ethics and values have moved ever more to the fore, not just in philosophy, but in the wider academic world and also in the public consciousness, a move which would have no doubt pleased Murdoch greatly. Once again ethics is being conceived of in its broadest Platonic sense as being 'no ordinary matter . . . but the right conduct of life' (*Republic*, 352d, Plato, 1989, p. 603).

This ancient Platonic description fits well the current revival of ethics, as we find ethical terminology used across the public sphere, from regulating the workplace and professions to questions of international relations. Indeed, imagining public debates which ignore ethical factors is almost inconceivable at the present time. Think of the recent (ethical) debate over the war in Iraq and the British Prime Minister, Tony Blair's use of the term 'moral imperative' to justify his case, and the oft-cited 'ethical foreign policy' (whatever one feels about the implementation, or lack of it). Such language and the supporting ideology indicate the central (and presumably vote-winning) nature of ethics (or at least the appearance of ethics) in modern political debate.[8]

In academia the revival of ethics can be seen in the gradual return to the field of moral philosophy by philosophers, as well as a broadening of what constitutes ethics, signified, for example, by the renewed interest in virtue ethics. Moral philosophers are again becoming involved in multidisciplinary work, practical issues and ethics in its broader public aspect (although, in philosophical circles, the term 'applied ethics' is still too often considered the poor relation of 'proper' philosophy).[9] In addition to philosophers, many others are entering the fields of ethics, for instance medical ethics, business ethics, environmental ethics and now global ethics.[10] Medical ethics, the longest-established of these applied ethical disciplines, is a clear example of the gradual increase in the importance of ethics over the last century and it is now a compulsory part of medical curricula in the UK (GMC, 1993). Bioethics has become a prominent discipline in response to new technologies and its practitioners are looked to for advice in the regulation of issues of public concern and controversy. This can be seen in the area of genetics: for example, in public fears about genetic manipulation, such as the possibility of cloning and parents creating so-called 'designer babies'. The 'genetic revolution' raises questions about the way identifying information is to be processed and to whom it belongs,[11] as well as deeper questions about meaning and identity.[12] Parallel comments can be made about other young ethical disciplines; for example, environmental ethics as a response to the environmental crisis, business ethics (or issues of corporate responsibility) to the globalization of business and organizations beyond the traditional boundaries of the nation state, and global ethics to encompass all aspects of the theory and practice of ethics.

## The Future of Iris Murdoch's Moral Vision

167

Why ethics appears to be the discipline of choice to address these issues is an area of controversy in the current literature. There is much talk in liberal democracies, both in academia and in the public sphere, of a 'moral crisis', and discussions about 'demoralization' and MacIntyre's definition that 'we have – very largely, if not entirely – lost our comprehension, both theoretically and practically, of morality' (MacIntyre, 1991, p. 2) has been much quoted.[13] Often, in not dissimilar arguments to those presented by Murdoch, moral uncertainty has been traced back to the decline of Christianity as a shared source of moral authority in the West. Murdoch prefigures MacIntyre, as in 1958 she declared that 'a religious and moral vocabulary is the possession now of a few; and most people lack the word with which to say just [why] what is felt to be wrong is wrong' (Murdoch, 1997 [1962], p. 182).[14] The modern uncertainty about moral values Murdoch captures well, stating that the absence of a shared understanding of values as, for instance, provided by Christianity, 'may be felt as the senselessness of everything, the loss of any discrimination and sense of value, a giddy feeling of total relativism, even a cynical hatred of virtue and the virtuous: a total absence of love' (Murdoch, 1992, p. 503). In addition, the concerns of much applied ethics, particularly those of bioethics, for instance, worries about genetics and biological determinism, echo many of the concerns expressed in Murdoch's philosophy. Her fears of determinism, both philosophical and scientific, were forcibly expressed in her critique of structuralism and her wider fear was that our picture of human being is increasingly seduced and limited by an overwhelming scientific worldview. Thus she argues that 'what perhaps we *should*, however, in our great technological era and on our smaller and more vulnerable planet, be *afraid of* might be described as a sort of plausible amoralistic determinism, something which lies at a deeper level than our social problems' (ibid., p. 198).

However, whether ethics in its current form is fulfilling Murdoch's wish for a philosophy which, like existentialism, could be a 'philosophy that one could live by' (Murdoch, 1970a, p. 47) and so fill the current 'philosophical void' (ibid.) remains to be seen. The revival of ethics indicates public and academic concern with these moral issues, but whether it provides any substantial conception of value or is simply a language to discuss the issues in liberal democracies is not yet clear. Murdoch's belief that moral philosophy should be prescriptive may yet prove to be a conviction embraced by contemporary ethics. Certainly, given the pressure on ethicists to engage with practical moral issues (from bioethics to international relations), the luxury of neutrality, adopted by Murdoch's contemporaries, is not possible. Yet, although ethics is reviving in a manner which Murdoch would welcome, it is not clear how much of her own vision can be utilized by present-day ethicists. Murdoch's moral vision, as we have clearly seen, is predominantly, indeed fundamentally, individual, making it difficult to transfer the insights of her moral philosophy to the wider global issues of modern ethics. This is a difficulty which besets all virtue ethicists to some extent, in that they focus on the good life rather than good action and therefore tend to eschew rules and the universalization

168     *The Moral Vision of Iris Murdoch*

of rules as a proper understanding of morality.[15] Murdoch, likewise, while recognizing that rules are a useful part of morality, is, to say the least, sceptical of moralities of rules and she argues that 'there are kinds of moral outlook which it seems pointless to crush at all costs into the universal rules formula' (Murdoch, 1997 [1956], p. 87).[16] However, rules at certain levels are necessary in public morality, as it is laws, guidelines and codes which are used to regulate public behaviour. Therefore, even if one holds that morality is properly concerned with being good, rules are still necessary at a public level, at least in order to engender the conditions which enable individuals to be good.

It is not that Murdoch is not concerned with the public and political: in her fear of structuralism and her concern to create an intellectual and moral environment in which a full picture of the individual is possible, her fear of the wider political and social context is palpable. Murdoch fears that determinism may best capture the mood of the age: a time in which 'religious beliefs fade, and seem to be *inevitably* superseded by scientific and technological modes and conceptions of human existence' (Murdoch, 1992, p. 426). Determinism threatens not only the individual, but also society. It is a social and communal problem as well as an individual problem: 'the fragmentation of morality menaces this individual, as it menaces the society in which he flourishes' (ibid., pp. 426–7). She believes that the prevalence of deterministic views affects both society and the individual and, when referring to structuralism, argues that 'the severance of meaning from truth, and languages from the world, can be seen, not only as philosophically baseless and morally intolerable, but as politically suicidal' (ibid., p. 214). For Murdoch, public and private morality are connected, and just as we need to fight to retain non-deterministic concepts of human being, without which she believes that the reductionism of philosophy will become reality, we also need to fight for broad political and social concepts: 'in morals and politics we have stripped ourselves of concepts' (Murdoch, 1997 [1961], p. 295).

Thus the essential fight, for Murdoch, is one for concepts, for pictures, for non-reductionist understandings of human beings, and 'everyone, every moral being, is involved in this fight, it is not reserved for philosophers, artists and scientists' (Murdoch, 1992, p. 216). Reductionism affects, not just the individual, but also the society, which determines the framework and accordingly the possible pictures of human being. Given this, perhaps Murdoch would argue for a robust restating of non-reductionist pictures of community in a parallel manner to that of the individual.[17] It is possible that Murdoch would call for a prescriptive political philosophy, one which, unlike liberal democratic ideology, asserts concepts and structures which support the good life; a prescriptive social philosophy to match her prescriptive personal philosophy.[18] However, this is merely speculative and we cannot know how Murdoch would have translated her philosophy to the public sphere, as unfortunately she never wrote her promised lecture on 'the uses of the good in politics and the marketplace' (Conradi, 2001, p. 566), which was intended to be part of her 1982 Gifford lectures, upon which *Metaphysics as a Guide to Morals* is based.

*The Future of Iris Murdoch's Moral Vision* 169

Even though Murdoch did not write specifically political philosophy, she was concerned with public morality, as is shown in her recognition that some may ask 'why waste time on private morality? There are dreadful human fates, even in "sheltered" lives there is black misery, bereavement, remorse, frustrated talent, loneliness, humiliation, depression, secret woe' (Murdoch, 1992, pp. 498–9). Her vision was shaped by the horror of the war, which one suspects fed into her question, 'when so many suffer is it not an impertinence to try to think of individual shattered lives?' Murdoch, it seems, would answer such questions negatively and insist that indeed it is here at the level of the individual that we must focus. She does not allow her picture of the good to blind one to the needs of individuals. Indeed, recognizing the needs of others is a fundamental part of becoming good: 'goodness is needful, one has to be good, for nothing, for immediate and obvious reasons, because somebody is hungry and somebody is crying' (Murdoch, 1997 [1970], p. 233).[19] It is the individual that is paramount; the individual, not the society, is the fundamental locus of morality, the place where morality resides. Murdoch was deeply concerned about the types of social structure and the extent to which they allow and encourage human flourishing; her experience of the refugee camps and of the totalitarian, dehumanizing regimes that created them remained with her. As Conradi notes, 'fear gave her vision edge' (Conradi, 2001, p. 561), and perhaps this accounts for her passionate criticisms of determinism and her dedication, for over 40 years, to the protection of the individual and to providing a picture which places the individual's experience to the fore. This balance, between the individual and the good, could perhaps be regarded as the most enlightening aspect of Murdoch's philosophy. She succeeds in providing a realist vision of the good, which transcends the individual, while still maintaining a place for the individual which celebrates unique individual experience.

Others may continue to go further in this attempt to apply Murdoch's ethics in the broader social–political context, seeking to explore what kind of society could enable the good life. As for Murdoch's legacy, perhaps it is enough that she has encouraged us to think about the relationship between the individual, society and goodness in a secular context. Murdoch has led the way in her criticisms of reductionist philosophies, and the revival of ethics may well represent the return of philosophy to the public sphere where it may once again wrestle with the perennial question of 'how can I be good?' as well as the broader political questions of 'how can we be good?'[20] Murdoch claims that 'the sketch which I have offered, a footnote in a great and familiar philosophical tradition, must be judged by its power to connect, to illuminate, to explain, and to make new and fruitful places for reflection' (Murdoch, 1970a, p. 45). Whether or not one is captured by her moral vision, this at least we can grant she has done: she has engendered different philosophical paths, connecting with and illuminating many. If, at times, her explanations are not all that we would wish, this is of little importance when compared with the vision that she sets before us. This is a vision which is both very ancient and

170  *The Moral Vision of Iris Murdoch*

also before its time, and one which could yet prove vital in the task of negotiating ethics in our contemporary, pluralistic world.

## Notes

1 This could be regarded as a comment on the state of modern ethics, as we have many past examples of philosophical visionaries, not least Plato and Sartre.

2 In *Sovereignty of Good*, Murdoch muses that 'perhaps it is a matter of temperament whether or not one is convinced that all is one' (Murdoch, 1970a, p. 50).

3 Buddhist and Christian mystics are also in danger of falling into illusion, as they too are on individual spiritual paths. Yet, arguably, because these individuals are in communities, they are less likely to be deluded as the community will play a part in regulating revelation; some religious denominations have elaborate verification procedures.

4 Some moral realists have argued that there are moral facts, equivalent to scientific facts. For further information, see the works of Richard Boyd, David Brink, Gilbert Harman and Nicholas Sturgeon, (Boyd, 1988; Brink, 1989; Harman, 1989; Sturgeon, 1986).

5 John McDowell has not attempted to make moral values directly equivalent to scientific facts in order to escape some of the criticisms of this position. However, he has remained within the scientific paradigm by drawing an analogy between moral values and secondary qualities, such as colour (McDowell, 1985).

6 Anscombe was a student of Wittgenstein, and a philosopher that Murdoch immensely admired, despite their different perspectives, and Murdoch referred to her as my 'old friend–foe' (Conradi, 2001, p. 285).

7 Indeed, a recent very welcome book on virtue ethics happily includes Murdoch's essay, 'The Sovereignty of Good over Other Concepts', taken from *The Sovereignty of Good*. Murdoch's work is described as an 'attempt to combine aspects of ancient virtue ethics with a certain scepticism about objective accounts of the good' (Crisp and Slote, 1997, p. 10) and as 'characteristic of much contemporary work on the virtues' (ibid.). This in itself shows the changes in contemporary philosophy: Murdoch is no longer alone.

8 This is a new trend in the way that liberal democracies respond to global problems, as Booth, Dunne and Cox note: 'a point of view emphasising the unity of politics and ethics would have struck many students and practitioners of international relations over the years as misconceived' (Booth et al., 2001, p. 2).

9 Academics from many disciplines are playing a wider role in the public sphere, as evidenced by the role Murdoch's friend Baroness Warnock played as chair of the inquiry that led to the HFE Act (Human Fertilisation and Embryology Act) and the setting up of the HEFA (Human Embryology and Fertilisation Authority).

10 'Global ethics' is a new term which has come into use in the last few decades. In this short time it has appeared in very different disciplines, for example in theology (Küng, 1990, 1993, 1998), philosophy (Dower, 1998) and international relations and political theory (Booth et al., 2001). This interest is further signified by the establishment of the Centre for Global Ethics at the University of Birmingham, a multidisciplinary centre with the remit of addressing ethical issues that cannot be resolved in one area of governance or in one nation state.

11 Genetic information is different in kind from other medical data, as it provides information not just about the individual, but about consanguineous relations and the wider ethnic group; it also continues to provide identifying information for current and future generations.

## The Future of Iris Murdoch's Moral Vision 171

This leads to fears of its misuse, for example, by insurance companies, employers and those with discriminating political and racial agendas, now or at any time in the future.

12   Exactly how genetics will affect our concepts of human being is unclear. However, there are two identifiable, and somewhat contradictory, strands of thinking about genetics evident in the public arena. On the one hand, there is the fear that the mapping of the human genome will allow for individual genetic blueprints and comprehensive testing, providing information about each individual's future health and lifespan. Such assumptions lead to theories of genetic determinism and reductionism, which threaten notions of human dignity and individual identity (Nelkin and Lindee, 1995). In addition, such information would lead to discrimination and a genetic underclass could be created, so limiting individuals' opportunities according to the capabilities indicated by their genetic blueprint (Rothstein, 1997; Shickle, 1997). On the other hand, genetics is portrayed as the answer to all human ills, allowing humans to manipulate and design life and explain the previously inexplicable (for example, behaviour, emotion, sexuality). This train of thought is manifest in the language surrounding genetics, for example referring to the genome as 'the book of life', and genetically treated/chosen babies as 'designer babies' (Harris, 1998).

13   Evidenced, for example, by Ralph Ferve's book on the topic of demythologization (published in 2002) and the conference organized on the same theme and sponsored by the Institute for Public Policy Research.

14   An earlier paper addresses this issue in more detail: 'Religion as a Moral Source: Can Religion Function as a Shared Source of Moral Authority and Values in a Liberal Democracy?', *Heythrop Journal*, 2004.

15   Some modern virtue ethicists are taking up this challenge and applying virtue ethics to practical ethical and political issues. For an example, see Rosalind Hursthouse's paper on 'Virtue Theory and Abortion'.

16   Murdoch does recognize the importance of duty, but believes it should only be a part of morality, as briefly discussed in Chapter 5. She states that 'the concept of duty is . . . of the greatest importance as a formulation of our sense of the absolute nature of moral obligation. It represents a kind of *certainty*' (Murdoch, 1992, p. 348). Rules and duty are also useful to check oneself against, as a part of duty 'consists of the ability to act against our own natural inclinations' (ibid.). However, although duty is a useful tool, it is not morality at its highest, as the truly good man would not need to rely on duty at all: 'Duty (practical reason, the categorical imperative) does not constitute the whole of the moral life. But the concept of duty remains a steady moral force' (ibid., p. 494).

17   Perhaps it is these possibilities, latent in Murdoch's philosophy, which have so inspired Hauerwas and his communitarian theology.

18   The liberal democratic ideology, upon which liberal democracies are based, supposedly endorses no single conception of the good life, nor a set of substantive values (although happily this assumption is now being questioned); rather, liberal democracies endorse 'thin' procedural values (Dworkin, 1978). What is expected of citizens is compliance with minimal laws which mediate between individuals and groups.

19   Murdoch was concerned with balancing the individual and the authority of the good, thus she comments, 'I begin to suspect that freedom and virtue are concepts which ought to be pinned into place by some more fundamental thinking about the proper quality of human life, which *begins* at the food and shelter level' (Murdoch, 1997 [1970], p. 231).

20   More usual terminology for goodness in the public sphere would be that of justice and equity.

# Bibliography

Adams, R. (1981a), 'A Modified Divine Command Theory of Ethical Wrongness', in Paul Helm (ed.), *Divine Commands and Morality*, Oxford: Oxford University Press, pp. 83–108.

Adams, R. (1981b), 'Divine Command Metaethics as Necessary A Posteriori', in Paul Helm (ed.), *Divine Commands and Morality*, Oxford: Oxford University Press, pp. 109–19.

Allen, Diogenes (1993), 'Review of *Metaphysics as a Guide to Morals* by Iris Murdoch', *Commonweal*, April, 24–5.

Annas, Julia (1981), *An Introduction to Plato's Republic*, Oxford: Clarendon Press.

Anscombe G.E.M. (1997), 'Modern Moral Philosophy', in Roger Crisp and Michael Slote (eds), *Virtue Ethics*, Oxford: Oxford University Press, pp. 26–44.

Anselm (1968a), 'St Anselm's Ontological Argument', in Alvin Plantinga (ed.), *The Ontological Argument*, London: Macmillan Press, pp. 3–6.

Anselm (1968b), 'St Anselm's Reply to Gaunilo', in Alvin Plantinga (ed.), *The Ontological Argument*, London: Macmillan Press, pp. 6–13.

Antonaccio, Maria (1996) 'Form and contingency in Iris Murdoch's ethics', in Maria Antonaccio and William Schwiker (eds), *Iris Murdoch and the Search for Human Goodness*, London: University of Chicago Press, pp. 223–42.

Antonaccio, Maria (2000), *Picturing the Human: The Moral Thought of Iris Murdoch*, Oxford: Oxford University Press.

Ayer, A.J. (1988), 'Critiques of Ethics and Theology', in Geoffrey Sayre-McCord (ed.), *Essays on Moral Realism*, New York: Cornell University Press, pp. 27–40.

Baldanza, Frank (1974), *Iris Murdoch*, New York: Twain Publishers.

Baron, Marcia W. (1995), *Kantian Ethics Almost Without Apology*, London: Cornell University Press.

Baron, Marcia W., Philip Pettit and Michael Slote (1997), *Three Methods of Ethics*, Oxford: Blackwell Publishers.

Bayley, John (1999), *Iris: A memoir of Iris Murdoch*, London: HarperCollins.

BBC (1989), *Iris Murdoch: A Certain Lady*, interview with Iris Murdoch, 29 December.

Blackburn, Simon (1992), 'The Good and the Great: Knowledge Virtue and Uplift in a Benighted World. A Review of *Metaphysics as a Guide to Morals*', *The Times Literary Supplement*, October, 23–4.

174 *The Moral Vision of Iris Murdoch*

Booth, Ken, Tim Dunne and Michael Cox (2001), *How Might we Live? Global Ethics in the New Century*, Cambridge: Cambridge University Press.

Boyd, Richard N. (1988), 'How to be a Moral Realist', in Geoffrey Sayre-McCord (ed.), *Essays on Moral Realism*, New York: Cornell University Press, pp. 181–228.

Brink, D.O. (1989), *Moral Realism and the Foundation of Ethics*, Cambridge: Cambridge University Press.

Brody, B. (1981), 'Morality and Religion Reconsidered', in Paul Helm (ed.), *Divine Commands and Morality*, Oxford: Oxford University Press, pp. 141–53.

Burns, Elizabeth (1997), 'Iris Murdoch and the nature of good', *Religious Studies*, **33**, pp. 301–13.

Byatt, A.S. (1970), *Degrees of Freedom: The Novels of Iris Murdoch*, London: Chatto & Windus.

Conradi, Peter (1989), *Iris Murdoch: The Saint and the Artist*, London: Macmillan Press.

Conradi, Peter (1997), 'Editor's Preface', *Existentialists and Mystics: Iris Murdoch's Writings on Philosophy and Literature*, ed. P. Conradi, London: Chatto & Windus, pp. xix–xxx.

Conradi, Peter J. (2001), *Iris Murdoch: A Life*, London: HarperCollins.

Crisp, Roger and Michael Slote (eds) (1997), *Virtue Ethics*, Oxford: Oxford University Press.

Cross P.C. and Woozley A.D. (1966), *Plato's Republic: A Philosophical Commentary*, London: Macmillan Press.

Dancy, Jonathan (1993), *Moral Reasons*, Oxford: Blackwell Press.

Diamond, Cora (1996), '"We are Perpetually Moralists": Iris Murdoch, Fact and Value', in Maria Antonaccio and William Schwiker (eds), *Iris Murdoch and the Search for Human Goodness*, London: University of Chicago Press, pp. 79–109.

Dipple, Elizabeth (1982), *Iris Murdoch: Work for the Spirit*, London: Methuen and Co.

Dipple, Elizabeth (1996), 'The Green Knight and Other Vagaries of the Spirit; or, Tricks and Images for the Human Soul; or Uses of Imaginative Literature', in Maria Antonaccio and William Schwiker (eds), *Iris Murdoch and the Search for Human Goodness*, London: University of Chicago Press, pp. 138–68.

Dower, Nigel (1998), *World Ethics: The new agenda*, Edinburgh: Edinburgh University Press.

Dunbar, Scott (1978), 'On Art, Morals and Religion: Some Reflections on the Work of Iris Murdoch', *Religious Studies*, **14**, 515–24.

Dworkin, Ronald (1978), 'Liberalism', in Stuart Hampshire (ed.), *Public and Private Morality*, Cambridge: Cambridge University Press.

Findlay, J.N. (1968), 'Can God's existence be disproved?', in Alvin Plantinga (ed.), *The Ontological Argument*, London: Macmillan Press, pp. 111–22.

Gamwell, Franklin I. (1996), 'On the loss of Theism', in Maria Antonaccio and William Schwiker (eds), *Iris Murdoch and the Search for Human Goodness*, London: University of Chicago Press, pp. 171–89.

# Bibliography

Gaunilo of Marmoutiers (1968), 'In behalf of the fool', in Alvin Plantinga (ed.), *The Ontological Argument*, London: Macmillan Press, pp. 13–27.

Geach, P. (1981), 'The moral law and the law of God', in Paul Helm (ed.), *Divine Commands and Morality*, Oxford: Oxford University Press, pp. 165–74.

GMC (1993), *Tomorrow's Doctors: Recommendations on undergraduate medical education* (http://www.gmc-uk.org/med_ed/tomdoc.htm).

Hague, Angela (1984), *Iris Murdoch's Comic Vision*, London: Associated University Presses.

Hampshire, Stuart (1959), *Thought and Action*, London: Chatto & Windus.

Harman, Gilbert (1989), 'Ethics and Observation', in James P. Sterba (ed.), *Contemporary Ethics: Selected Readings*, Englewood Cliffs, NJ: Prentice-Hall, pp. 289–93.

Harris, John (1998), *Clones, Genes and Immortality*, Oxford: Oxford University Press.

Hartshorne, Charles (1968), 'The necessarily existent', in Alvin Plantinga (ed.), *The Ontological Argument*, London: Macmillan Press, pp. 123–35.

Hauerwas, Stanley (1996), 'Murdochian Muddles: Can we get through them if God does not exist?', in Maria Antonaccio and William Schwiker (eds), *Iris Murdoch and the Search for Human Goodness*, London: University of Chicago Press, pp. 190–208.

Hepburn, R.W. (1978), 'Review of *The Fire and the Sun: Why Plato banished the artists* by Iris Murdoch', *Philosophical Quarterly*, **28**, 269–70.

Hume (1975 [1777]), *Enquiries: Concerning human understanding and Concerning the principles of morals*, ed. L.A. Selby-Bigge, Oxford: Clarendon Press.

Hurtshouse, Rosalind (1997), 'Virtue Theory and Abortion', in Roger Crisp and Michael Slote (eds), *Virtue Ethics*, Oxford: Oxford University Press, pp. 217–38.

Jasper, David (1986), 'And after art ... nothing: Iris Murdoch and the possibility of metaphysic', *Culture Education and Society*, **40**, 137–46.

Johnson, Deborah (1987), *Iris Murdoch*, Brighton: Harvester Press.

Jones, Gregory (1993), 'Review of *Metaphysics as a Guide to Morals* by Iris Murdoch', *The Thomist*, **57**, 687–9.

Kaalikoski, Katri (1997), 'Replacing God: Reflections on Iris Murdoch's metaphysics', *Journal of Speculative Philosophy*, **11**, 143–60.

Kerr, Fergus (1997), *Immoral Longings: Versions of transcending humanity*, London: SPCK.

Kleinig, John (1971), 'Review of *The Sovereignty of Good* by Iris Murdoch', *Australian Journal of Philosophy*, **49**, 112–13.

Küng, Hans (1990), *Global Responsibility: In Search of a New World Ethic*, London: SCM Press.

Küng, Hans (1993), *A Global Ethic: The Declaration of the Parliament of the World's Religions*, London: SCM Press.

Küng, Hans (1998), *A Global Ethic for Global Politics and Economics*, Oxford: Oxford University Press.

176 *The Moral Vision of Iris Murdoch*

Lloyd, Genevieve (1982), 'Iris Murdoch on the ethical significance of Truth', *Philosophy and Literature*, **6**, 62–75.

Loads, Ann (1986), 'Iris Murdoch: The vision of the Good and the *Via Negativa*', *Culture, Education and Society*, **40**, 147–55.

MacIntyre, Alasdair (1991), *After Virtue: A Study in Moral Theory*, London: Gerald Duckworth & Co.

MacIntyre, Alistair (1982), 'Good for Nothing: Review of *Iris Murdoch: Work for the Spirit* by Elizabeth Dipple', *London Review of Books*, **4** (10), June, 15–16.

Mackie, J.L. (1977), *Ethics: Inventing Right and Wrong*, London: Penguin Books.

Mackie J.L. (1980), *Hume's moral theory*, London: Routledge & Kegan Paul.

Malcolm, Norman (1968), 'Malcolm's statement of Anselm's Ontological Arguments', in Alvin Plantinga (ed.), *The Ontological Argument*, London: Macmillan Press, pp. 136–59.

Maritain, Jacques (1974), *Creative Intuition in Art and Poetry*, New York: Meridian Books.

McDowell, John (1978), 'Are Moral Requirements Hypothetical Imperatives?', *Proceedings of the Aristotelian Society*, **52**, 13–42.

McDowell, John (1983), 'Aesthetic Value, Objectivity and the Fabric of the World', in Eva Schaper (ed.), *Pleasure, Preference and Value: Studies in Philosophical Aesthetics*, Cambridge: Cambridge University Press, pp. 1–16.

McDowell, John (1985), 'Values and Secondary Qualities', in Ted Honderich (ed.), *Morality and Objectivity: A Tribute to J.L. Mackie*, London: Routledge & Kegan Paul, pp. 110–29.

McNaughton, D. (1988), *Moral Vision: An Introduction to Ethics*, Oxford: Blackwell Books.

Mitchell, Basil (1980), *Morality Religious and Secular*, Oxford: Clarendon Press.

Mounce, H.O. (1972), 'Review of *The Sovereignty of Good* by Iris Murdoch', *Philosophy*, **47**, 178–80.

Moravcsik, Julius (1992), *Plato and Platonism: Plato's Conception of Appearance and Religion in Ontology, Epistemology and Ethics, and its Modern Echoes*, Oxford: Blackwell Publishers.

Murdoch, Iris (1953), *Sartre: Romantic Rationalist*, Cambridge: Bowes and Bowes.

Murdoch, Iris (1954), *Under the Net*, London: Chatto & Windus.

Murdoch, Iris (1956), *The Flight from the Enchanter*, London: Chatto & Windus.

Murdoch, Iris (1958), *The Bell*, London: Chatto & Windus.

Murdoch, Iris (1963), *The Unicorn*, London: Chatto & Windus.

Murdoch, Iris (1965), *The Red and the Green*, London: Chatto & Windus.

Murdoch, Iris (1966), *The Time of Angels*, London: Chatto & Windus.

Murdoch, Iris (1968), *The Nice and the Good*, London: Chatto & Windus.

## Bibliography

Murdoch, Iris (1970a), *The Sovereignty of Good*, London: Routledge & Kegan Paul.

Murdoch, Iris (1970b), *A Fairly Honourable Defeat*, London: Chatto & Windus.

Murdoch, Iris (1973), *The Black Prince*, London: Chatto & Windus.

Murdoch, Iris (1974), *Sacred and Profane Love Machine*, London: Chatto & Windus.

Murdoch, Iris (1976), *Henry and Cato*, London: Chatto & Windus.

Murdoch, Iris (1978), *The Sea, The Sea*, London: Chatto & Windus.

Murdoch, Iris (1981 [1980]), *Nuns and Soldiers*, London: Penguin Books.

Murdoch, Iris (1983), *The Philosopher's Pupil*, London: Chatto & Windus.

Murdoch, Iris (1987), *Acastos: Two Platonic Dialogues*, London: Penguin Books.

Murdoch, Iris (1992), *Metaphysics as a Guide to Morals*, London: Chatto & Windus.

Murdoch, Iris (1997 [1950a]), 'The novelist as metaphysician', *Existentialists and Mystics: Iris Murdoch's writings on Philosophy and Literature*, ed. P. Conradi, London: Chatto & Windus, pp. 101–7.

Murdoch, Iris (1997 [1950b]), 'Sartre's *The Emotions: Outline of a theory'*, *Existentialists and Mystics: Iris Murdoch's writings on Philosophy and Literature*, ed. P. Conradi, London: Chatto & Windus, pp. 116–21.

Murdoch, Iris (1997 [1951]), 'Thinking and Language', *Existentialists and Mystics: Iris Murdoch's writings on Philosophy and Literature*, ed. P. Conradi, London: Chatto & Windus, pp. 33–42.

Murdoch, Iris (1997 [1952]), 'The existentialist political myth', *Existentialists and Mystics: Iris Murdoch's writings on Philosophy and Literature*, ed. P. Conradi, London: Chatto & Windus, pp. 130–45.

Murdoch, Iris (1997 [1953]), 'Nostalgia for the particular', *Existentialists and Mystics: Iris Murdoch's writings on Philosophy and Literature*, ed. P. Conradi, London: Chatto & Windus, pp. 43–58.

Murdoch, Iris (1997 [1956]), 'Vision and choice in morality', *Existentialists and Mystics: Iris Murdoch's writings on Philosophy and Literature*, ed. P. Conradi, London: Chatto & Windus, pp.76–98.

Murdoch, Iris (1997 [1957a]), 'Metaphysics and ethics', *Existentialists and Mystics: Iris Murdoch's writings on Philosophy and Literature*, ed. P. Conradi, London: Chatto & Windus, pp. 59–75.

Murdoch, Iris (1997 [1957b]), 'Hegel in modern dress', *Existentialists and Mystics: Iris Murdoch's writings on Philosophy and Literature*, ed. P. Conradi, London: Chatto & Windus, pp. 146–50.

Murdoch, Iris (1997 [1959a]), 'The sublime and the good', *Existentialists and Mystics: Iris Murdoch's writings on Philosophy and Literature*, ed. P. Conradi, London: Chatto & Windus, pp. 205–20.

Murdoch, Iris (1997 [1959b]), 'The sublime and the beautiful revisited', *Existentialists and Mystics: Iris Murdoch's writings on Philosophy and Literature*, ed. P. Conradi, London: Chatto & Windus, pp. 261–86.

178      *The Moral Vision of Iris Murdoch*

Murdoch, Iris (1997 [1961]), 'Against dryness', *Existentialists and Mystics: Iris Murdoch's writings on Philosophy and Literature*, ed. P. Conradi, London: Chatto & Windus, pp. 287–95.

Murdoch, Iris (1997 [1962]), 'House of Theory', *Existentialists and Mystics: Iris Murdoch's writings on Philosophy and Literature*, ed. P. Conradi, London: Chatto & Windus, pp. 171–86.

Murdoch, Iris (1997 [1966]), 'The darkness of practical reason', *Existentialists and Mystics: Iris Murdoch's writings on Philosophy and Literature*, ed. P. Conradi, London: Chatto & Windus, pp. 193–202.

Murdoch, Iris (1997 [1970]), 'Existentialists and mystics', *Existentialists and Mystics: Iris Murdoch's writings on Philosophy and Literature*, ed. P. Conradi, London: Chatto & Windus, pp. 221–34.

Murdoch, Iris (1997 [1972]), 'Art is the imitation of nature', *Existentialists and Mystics: Iris Murdoch's writings on Philosophy and Literature*, ed. P. Conradi, London: Chatto & Windus, pp. 243–57.

Murdoch, Iris (1997 [1976]), 'The Fire and the Sun: Why Plato banished the artists', *Existentialists and Mystics: Iris Murdoch's writings on Philosophy and Literature*, ed. P. Conradi, London, Chatto & Windus, pp. 386–463.

Murdoch, Iris (1997 [1978]), 'Literature and Philosophy: A Conversation with Bryan Magee', *Existentialists and Mystics: Iris Murdoch's writings on Philosophy and Literature*, ed. P. Conradi, London: Chatto & Windus, pp. 3–30.

Nelkin, D. and S. Lindee (1995), *The DNA mystique: The gene as a cultural icon*. New York: W.H. Freeman & Co.

Nielsen, Kai (1966), 'Some Remarks on the Independence of Morality from Religion', in Ian Ramsey (ed.), *Christian Ethics and Contemporary Philosophy*, London: SCM, pp. 140–51.

Nielsen, Kai (1982), 'God and the Basis of Morality', *Journal of Religious Ethics*, **10**, 335–50.

Nowell-Smith, P. (1966), 'Morality: Religious and Secular', in Ian Ramsey (ed.), *Christian Ethics and Contemporary Philosophy*, London: SCM, pp. 95–112.

Nussbaum, Martha (1978), 'Review of *The Fire and the Sun: Why Plato banished the artists* by Iris Murdoch', in *Philosophy and Literature*, **2**, 125–6.

Nussbaum, Martha (1996), 'Love and Vision: Iris Murdoch on Eros and the Individual', in Maria Antonaccio and William Schwiker (eds), *Iris Murdoch and the Search for Human Goodness*, London: University of Chicago Press, pp. 29–53.

Ostenfeld, Erik Nis (1982), *Forms, Matter and Mind: Three Strands in Plato's Metaphysics*, The Hague: Martinus Nijoff Publishers.

Parekh, Bhikhu (2000), *Rethinking Multiculturalism: Cultural Diversity and Political Theory*, Basingstoke: Palgrave.

Plato (1989), 'Laws', in Edith Hamilton and Cairns Huntington (eds), *Plato: The Collected Dialogues*, trans. A.E. Taylor, Princeton: Princeton University Press, pp. 1225–1513.

Bibliography 179

Plato (1989), 'Phaedrus', in Edith Hamilton and Cairns Huntington (eds), *Plato: The Collected Dialogues*, trans. R. Hackforth, Princeton: Princeton University Press, pp. 475–525.

Plato (1989), 'Symposium', in Edith Hamilton and Cairns Huntington (eds), *Plato: The Collected Dialogues*, trans. Michael Joyce, Princeton: Princeton University Press, pp. 526–74.

Plato (1989), 'Republic', in Edith Hamilton and Cairns Huntington (eds), *Plato: The Collected Dialogues*, trans. Paul Shorey, Princeton: Princeton University Press, pp. 575–844.

Plato (1989), 'Timaeus', in Edith Hamilton and Cairns Huntington (eds), *Plato: The Collected Dialogues*, trans. Benjamin Jowett, Princeton: Princeton University Press, pp. 1151–1211.

Quinn, Philip L. (1978), *Divine Commands and Moral Requirements*, Oxford: Clarendon Press.

Quinn, Philip L. (1981), 'Religious Obedience and Moral Autonomy', in Paul Helm (ed.), *Divine Commands and Morality*, Oxford: Oxford University Press.

Quinn, Philip L. (1990), 'The Recent Revival of Divine Command Ethics', *Philosophy and Phenomenological Research*, **L Supplement**, 345–63.

Ramanathan, Suganda (1990), *Iris Murdoch: Figures of the Good*, London: Macmillan.

Rothstein, M.A. (1997), *Genetic secrets: Protecting privacy and confidentiality in the genetic era*, London: Yale University Press.

Sayre-McCord, Geoffrey (1988), 'Moral Theory and Explanatory Impotence', in Geoffrey Sayre-McCord (ed.), *Essays on Moral Realism*, New York: Cornell University Press, pp. 256–81.

Shickle, D. (1997), 'Do "all men desire to know"? A right of society to choose not to know about the genetics of personality traits', in Ruth Chadwick et al. (eds), *The Right to Know and the Right not to Know*, Aldershot: Ashgate.

Smith, Michael (1991), 'Realism', in Peter Singer (ed.), *A Companion to Ethics*, Oxford: Blackwell Publishers, pp. 399–410.

Spear, Hilda D. (1985), *Iris Murdoch*, London: Macmillan Press.

Stocker, Michael (1997), 'The Schizophrenia of Modern Ethical Theories', in Roger Crisp and Michael Slote (eds), *Virtue Ethics*, Oxford: Oxford University Press, pp. 66–78.

Sturgeon, Nicholas (1986), 'What Difference does it make if Moral Realism is True?', *The Southern Journal of Philosophy (Supplement)*, **24**, 115–42.

Taylor, Charles (1994), *Multiculturalism*, ed. Amy Gutmann, Chichester: Princeton University Press.

Taylor, Charles (1996), 'Iris Murdoch and Moral Philosophy', in Maria Antonaccio and William Schwiker (eds), *Iris Murdoch and the Search for Human Goodness*, London: University of Chicago Press, pp. 3–28.

Taylor, Charles (1999 [1982]) 'The Diversity of Goods', in *Utilitarianism and Beyond* ed. Amartya Sen and Bernard Williams, Cambridge: Cambridge University Press, pp. 129–44.

180                    *The Moral Vision of Iris Murdoch*

*The Times*, (1964), 'Speaking of writing XII: Iris Murdoch', interview with Iris Murdoch, 13 February, p. 15.

Tracy, David (1996), 'Iris Murdoch and the Many Faces of Platonism', in Maria Antonaccio and William Schwiker (eds), *Iris Murdoch and the Search for Human Goodness*, London: University of Chicago Press, pp. 54–75.

Wallace, Douglas (1970), 'Review of *The Sovereignty of Good* by Iris Murdoch', *Dialogue*, **8**, 726–7.

Westmoreland, Robert (1996), 'Two Recent Metaphysical Divine Command Theories of Ethics', *International Journal for Philosophy of Religion*, **39**, 15–31.

Widdows, Heather (2004), 'Religion as a Source of Moral Authority', *Heythrop Journal*, **XLV**, April, 197–208.

Wilson, A.N. (2003), *Iris Murdoch: As I knew her*, London: Hutchinson.

# Index

Action 8, 13, 25, 27, 29, 30, 33, 39, 40, 45, 46–8, 56, 61, 66, 72, 75, 76, 90, 91, 98, 105, 107–10, 118, 129, 141

Anselm 78–81, 85

Art 7, 8, 10, 14, 15, 64, 65, 71, 73, 76, 89, 93, 94, 101, 107, 111, 117–36, 140, 143, 144–9, 156, 157, 159, 161–3

Attention 14, 40, 81, 85, 89, 105–13, 117, 122, 126, 129, 136, 139, 144, 149, 152, 162, 163

Ayer 29, 30, 46

Bayley, John 1, 3, 5, 6

Beauty 89, 107, 111–13, 117–23, 125–7, 131, 162

Behaviourism 27, 29, 31, 33, 49

Buber 142, 153

Buddhism 90, 92, 98, 100, 139, 147, 150, 151, 153, 161, 162

Cartesian *see* Descartes

Cave, The 9, 74, 89–92, 95–101, 103, 105, 107, 120–3, 134, 136, 148, 161

Choice 25, 27–9, 31, 33, 39, 40, 63, 85, 103, 104, 109, 131

Christianity 15, 79, 80, 83, 98, 105, 139–56, 161–3, 167

Consciousness 13, 21–41, 48, 56, 61, 62, 64, 66, 102, 104, 105, 108, 111, 112, 131, 143, 153, 159, 161, 163, 166

Cupitt, Don 150, 154

Deconstruction *see* Structuralism

Demythologisation 15, 80, 102, 150, 151, 154, 163

Derrida 10, 13, 14, 26, 31, 32, 46, 51–4, 109

Descartes 21, 23, 24 30, 32, 33, 35

Determinism 32, 56, 167–9

Divine command 74, 140–42

Duty 64, 65, 93, 110, 165

Ego 90, 98–102, 105–10, 112, 122–8, 133, 134, 139, 145–7

Egotistical 7, 14, 28, 65, 91, 98–102, 105, 106 , 110, 113, 120–24, 130, 134, 141, 145, 159

Empiricism 13, 23, 26, 29–32, 55, 62, 66

Ethics 3, 12, 13, 15, 23, 44, 46, 50, 91, 163–70; *see also* Virtue Ethics

Evil 5, 6, 40, 64, 65, 72, 92, 100, 141

Existentialism 13, 23, 26–33, 167

Fact/value dichotomy 11, 14, 45–66, 71, 75, 82, 90, 103, 113, 164, 165

Foot, Philippa, 4–6

Friendship 1–4, 6

God 22, 74, 78–86, 105, 106, 135, 139–56

Good 3, 5–10, 13–15, 40, 41, 47, 49, 62, 64–6, 71–86, 89–96, 98–133, 117–23, 125, 126, 131, 134–6, 141, 146, 147, 149, 150, 152–4, 159–64, 168, 169

Hampshire, Stuart 26, 27, 29, 30

Hauerwas, Stanley 8, 155

Hume 14, 23–6, 34, 46–9, 155

Illusion 7, 14, 22, 65, 89, 92, 96, 98–106, 108–10, 113, 120–26, 129, 130, 132, 134, 136, 139, 144–9, 159, 161–3

Images 65, 74, 89, 91, 92, 94, 102–5, 107–9, 112, 121, 126, 127, 145, 147–50, 153, 155

Imagination 8, 40, 62, 107, 108, 112, 121, 129–33, 135

Individual 2, 3, 7, 8, 10, 13–15, 21–41, 45, 49, 52, 53, 56–8, 60–62, 64, 66, 77, 82, 84, 85, 99, 102, 103, 113, 118, 119, 123, 129, 131, 133, 136, 139, 141, 142, 146, 147, 150, 152, 155, 160–65, 168, 169

Inner life 10, 13–15, 21–41, 45, 99, 102, 103, 113, 143, 149, 159, 164

Intellectual discipline 14, 72, 81, 89, 94, 107, 111, 112, 129

Kant 10, 14, 23–7, 29, 31, 33, 46, 48–51, 62, 64, 79, 90–93, 118, 132, 155

181

182    *The Moral Vision of Iris Murdoch*

Language 31, 32, 46, 51–7, 64, 65, 91, 128, 144

Literature 35, 37, 38, 54, 117, 121, 127, 128, 131, 132, 135; *see also* Novels

Love 1, 3–6, 14, 37, 38, 54, 55, 64, 76, 78, 85, 89, 93–5, 101, 107, 111–13, 122, 126, 129, 135, 136, 146–8, 162, 163, 167

MacIntyre, Alasdair 7, 8, 10, 165, 167

Marx 9, 46, 49

Meaning 8, 27, 30, 31, 32, 49, 51–6, 58–60, 75, 79, 80, 125, 144, 164, 166, 168

Metaphor 9, 52, 58, 62, 80, 82, 86, 89, 93, 97, 103, 104, 107, 108, 109, 121, 127, 148

Moore 46, 49

Moral realism *see* Realism

Murdoch, Iris
  Life 1–6
  Novelist *see* Novelist
Mystical *see* Mysticism
Mysticism 5, 15, 64, 83, 95, 97, 99, 101, 106, 140, 142, 150–55, 159, 161, 162
Mystics *see* Mysticism

Novelist 1, 7, 127, 128, 131–5, 165

Novels 1–7, 11, 23, 37, 38, 123, 127, 128, 131–5, 151, 152; *see also* Literature

Ontological argument 14, 75, 78–86, 134, 135, 163

Pilgrimage 65, 89–96, 98, 102–5, 107, 109, 110, 113, 119–21, 127, 129, 130, 132, 134, 136, 139, 144, 146–8, 150, 159; *see also* Quest

Plato 9, 10, 14, 62, 65, 74, 77, 82, 84, 89–98, 100–105, 111, 112, 117–23, 125, 126, 131, 136, 142, 147, 148, 150, 161

Platonist 9, 13, 65, 83, 85, 86, 91, 104, 117–23, 125, 142, 150, 159, 160, 166

Post-structuralism *see* Structuralism

Prayer 105, 106, 139, 144, 149

Pseudoscientific *see* Scientific

Psychology 10, 25, 28, 29, 35, 76, 90, 98, 100, 101, 162, 165

Quest 14, 65, 83–5, 89–95, 97, 100, 103, 104, 106–8, 110–13, 117–19, 125, 126,

129, 131, 148, 149, 154, 155, 163, 167, 168; *see also* Pilgrimage

Realism 8, 9, 14, 33, 45–7, 61–3, 65, 66, 71–3, 76–8, 82, 84, 86, 141, 160, 163, 164

Realist *see* Realism

Reductionism 8, 11, 32, 27, 28, 33, 41, 45, 49, 50, 56, 58, 59, 66, 91, 124, 156, 160, 164, 168, 169

Religion 5–8, 10, 14, 15, 22, 71, 79, 80, 83, 84, 89–92, 95, 97, 98, 101, 103, 106, 113, 118, 131, 139–57, 159, 161–3

Sartre 7, 11, 26–31, 46, 132, 133

Science 8, 26, 29, 32, 50, 51, 55, 56, 59, 60, 65, 111, 131, 144

Scientific 8, 23, 29, 46, 49–60, 62, 73, 139, 142–4, 154, 164

Self 10, 11, 13, 21–41, 45, 71, 90, 91, 99–101, 105, 110–13, 125, 126, 130, 132, 134, 136, 143, 147

Shakespeare 10, 123, 124, 127, 128, 133, 162, 163

Spiritual 8, 14, 23, 31, 33, 49, 58, 89–97, 102, 111–13, 122, 126, 128, 129, 131, 132, 135, 140, 143, 144, 148–57, 159, 162, 163

Spirituality *see* Spiritual

Structuralism 13, 14, 22, 26, 31–3, 46, 49, 51–8, 66

Taylor, Charles 8–10, 12, 165, 166

Transcendence 12, 14, 48, 53, 64, 72–7, 80, 81, 84, 86, 90, 92, 94, 113, 117, 120, 123, 131, 136, 151, 155, 159, 164

Transcendent *see* Transcendence

Truth 14, 29, 32–4, 45–8, 51–66, 74, 85, 90, 92, 93–5, 99–102, 106, 110, 112, 119, 121, 122, 124–9, 131, 136, 143, 145, 147, 150, 153, 155, 160, 168

Truth-seeking *see* Truth

Unselfing 109, 112, 113

Virtue Ethics 8, 165

Will 22, 25–33, 40, 41, 47, 48, 61, 62, 109, 144, 163, 165, 167

Wittgenstein 10, 14, 29, 30–32, 46, 48, 50, 51, 132